William Bright

Notes on the canons of the first four general councils

William Bright

Notes on the canons of the first four general councils

ISBN/EAN: 9783743351714

Manufactured in Europe, USA, Canada, Australia, Japa

Cover: Foto ©Lupo / pixelio.de

Manufactured and distributed by brebook publishing software (www.brebook.com)

William Bright

Notes on the canons of the first four general councils

NOTES ON THE CANONS

OF THE

FIRST FOUR GENERAL COUNCILS

BRIGHT

London

HENRY FROWDE

OXFORD UNIVERSITY PRESS WAREHOUSE

7 PATERNOSTER ROW

NOTES ON THE CANONS

OF THE

FIRST FOUR GENERAL COUNCILS

BY

WILLIAM BRIGHT, D.D.

CANON OF CHRIST CHURCH
REGIUS PROFESSOR OF ECCLESIASTICAL HISTORY

𝔒𝔵𝔣𝔬𝔯𝔡
AT THE CLARENDON PRESS
1882

[All rights reserved]

PREFACE.

THE following Notes, which are an expansion of lectures delivered to my Class, are intended for the younger students of ancient Ecclesiastical History.

The reader is supposed to have the Greek text of the Canons[1] before him, and the ordinary books of reference within reach. He will do well to consult the ancient translations,—that of Dionysius Exiguus and the Isidorian[2] given in Mansi's Concilia, the Prisca and the Vetus, which are given by the Ballerini in their appendix to St. Leo, with two versions of the Nicene canons, the untrustworthy 'Antiquissima' as the Ballerini call it, and the very interesting version made by Philo and Evarestus (incorrectly called 'Teilo' and 'Tharistus'), and sent from Constantinople in 419 to the African bishops,—which is appended to 'the sixth Council of Carthage' in the fourth volume of Mansi. To these should be added the modern version by Hervetus, also in Mansi. The Latin notes to the canons in Routh's 'Scriptorum Opuscula,' and the comments in Beveridge's 'Pandectæ Canonum,' might also be consulted. It cannot be necessary to do more than men-

---

[1] Oxford: Clarendon Press, 1877, or in Routh's 'Script. Opusc.'

[2] Ascribed to 'Isidore Mercator,' but (see Robertson, Hist. ch. iii. 318) the person intended is Isidore bishop of Seville (600-636), and 'mercator' seems a copyist's error for 'peccator,' a term assumed by bishops out of humility. The Ballerini regard this version as long prior to the time of Isidore, and as older even than the Prisca, to which Dionysius, in the sixth century, is supposed to refer (De Ant. Collect. Can. ii. c. 2. § 2, 3).

tion Bishop Hefele's great work on the Councils. The Nicene and Constantinopolitan Councils are treated of in the first and second volumes of the English translation by Mr. Clark and Mr. H. N. Oxenham.

Other histories of the period may be referred to, along with Hefele's work, for an account of the several Councils. Here it is enough to remind the reader that—

(1) The Council of Nicæa was assembled by Constantine in the summer of A.D. 325, principally in order to settle the Arian controversy, and subordinately to deal with the Meletian schism in Egypt, and with the question as to the calculation of Easter.

(2) The Council of Constantinople met in May, 381, at the summons of Theodosius I., in order, says Hefele, 'to secure the triumph of the Nicene faith over Arianism' and Macedonianism, to check the progress of Apollinarianism, and 'to arrange the affairs of the Church' in Constantinople. It was purely an Eastern Council.

(3) The Council of Ephesus, convoked by Theodosius II. in order to decide the doctrinal question raised by Nestorius, was opened on the 22nd of June, 431, and held sittings until the end of July.

(4) The Council of Chalcedon, convoked by the Emperor Marcian in order to undo the mischiefs caused by the triumph of the Eutychian party at the so-called 'Latrocinium' or Robbers' Meeting of Ephesus in 449, sat from the 8th of October to the 1st of November in 451.

W. B.

CHRIST CHURCH,
January 14, 1882.

CONTENTS.

	PAGE
NOTES ON THE CANONS OF NICÆA	1
NOTES ON THE CANONS OF CONSTANTINOPLE	79
NOTES ON THE CANONS OF EPHESUS	109
NOTES ON THE CANONS OF CHALCEDON	123
INDEX	213

NOTES ON THE CANONS OF NICÆA.

Canon I.

This canon is best explained by a reference to Eusebius, H. E. vi. 8. The act by which Origen, in his youthful enthusiasm, carried out a literalist interpretation of the third clause of Matthew xix. 12, was viewed by Demetrius his bishop (of whose motives, however, Eusebius is no unbiassed judge) as canonically disqualifying him for ordination, although it had been no bar to his continuance in the office of catechist. The rule on which this judgment was based may have been, at least in part, called forth by the fanaticism of the Valesian heretics, of whom Epiphanius says, εἰσὶ δὲ πάντες ἀπόκοποι (Hær. 58. 1). The Council, by this canon, perpetuates it (probably with a view to the conduct of Leontius, afterwards an Arianizing bishop of Antioch, see Athanasius, Apol. de Fuga, 26), but carefully exempts from its scope cases in which the mutilation was performed for medical reasons, or inflicted by barbarian captors or slave-owners (compare Sozomen, viii. 24). The 'rule,' it is declared, allows such persons, if proved in other respects worthy, to be ordained. It is a question whether the canon alludes to the so-called Apostolic canons 21, 22, 23 (al. 20, 21, 22), or whether they were suggested by it. They do not notice the contingency of 'disease:' but they mention what the Council omits, the contingency of 'persecution,' and the case referred to in the first clause of Matt. xix. 12; compare Euseb. v. 28 (quoting, probably, from Hippolytus) on Melito, and vii. 32 on Dorotheus, a presbyter of Antioch.

With regard to the phraseology of the canon; ἐξετάζεσθαι, which recurs in Nic. Can. 13, 16, 17, 19, means the being numbered or 'registered' among the clergy. Hervetus' rendering, 'examinatum,' is a mistake. Κλῆρος is used by Clement of Alexandria for the body of Christian ministers, in the story of St. John and the young robber (Euseb. iii. 23): the idea of the term being a 'portion' of work or office assigned to the person ordained. It is so used for a field of episcopal labour in Athanasius' Apology against the Arians, c. 6. Κανών, as an ecclesiastical term, has a very interesting history. See Westcott's account of it, On the New Testament Canon, p. 498 ff. The original sense, 'a straight rod' or 'line,' determines all its religious applications, which begin with St. Paul's use of it for a prescribed sphere of apostolic work (2 Cor. x. 13, 15) or a regulative principle of Christian life (Gal. vi. 16). It represents the element of definiteness in Christianity and in the order of the Christian Church. Clement of Rome uses it for the measure of Christian attainment (Ep. Cor. 7). Irenæus calls the baptismal creed 'the canon of truth' (i. 9. 4); Polycrates (Euseb. v. 24) and probably Hippolytus (ib. v. 28) call it 'the canon of faith;' the Council of Antioch in A.D. 269, referring to the same standard of orthodox belief, speaks with significant absoluteness of 'the canon' (ib. vii. 30). Eusebius himself mentions 'the canon of truth' in iv. 23, and 'the canon of the preaching' in iii. 32; and so Basil speaks of 'the transmitted canon of true religion' (Epist. 204. 6). Such language, like Tertullian's 'regula fidei,' amounted to saying, 'We Christians know what we believe: it is not a vague "idea" without substance or outline: it can be put into form, and by it we "test the spirits whether they be of God."' Thus it was natural for Socrates to call the Nicene Creed itself a 'canon,' ii. 27. Clement of Alexandria uses the phrase 'canon of truth' for a standard of mystic interpretation, but proceeds to call the harmony between the two Testaments 'a canon for the Church,' Strom. vi. 15. 124, 125. Eusebius speaks of 'the ecclesiastical canon' which recognised no other Gospels than the four (vi. 25). The use of the term and its cognates in reference to the Scriptures is explained by Westcott in a passive sense, so that 'canonized' books, as

Athanasius calls them (Fest. Ep. 39), are books expressly recognised by the Church as portions of Holy Scripture. Again, as to matters of observance, Clement of Alexandria wrote a book against Judaizers, called 'The Church's Canon' (Euseb. vi. 13); and Cornelius of Rome, in his letter to Fabius, speaks of the 'canon' as to what we call confirmation (Euseb. vi. 43), and Dionysius of the 'canon' as to reception of converts from heresy (ib. vii. 7). The Nicene Council in this canon refers to a standing 'canon' of discipline (comp. Nic. 2, 5, 6, 9, 10, 15, 16, 18), but it does not apply the term to its own enactments, which are so described in the 2nd canon of Constantinople (see below) and of which Socrates says that it passed what 'are usually called "canons"' (i. 13), as Julius of Rome calls a decree of this Council a 'canon' (Athan. Apol. c. Ari. 25); so Athanasius applies the term generally to Church laws (Encycl. 2; cp. Apol. c. Ari. 69). The use of κανών for the clerical body (Nic. 16, 17, 19; Chalc. 2) is explained by Westcott with reference to the rule of clerical life, but Bingham traces it to the roll or official list on which the names of clerics were enrolled (i. 5. 10); and this appears to be the more natural derivation, see 'the holy canon' in the 1st canon of the Council of Antioch, and compare Socrates (i. 17), 'the virgins enumerated ἐν τῷ τῶν ἐκκλησιῶν κανόνι,' and (ib. v. 19) on the addition of a penitentiary 'to the canon of the church;' see also George of Laodicea in Soz. iv. 13. Hence any cleric might be called κανονικός, see Cyril of Jerusalem, Procatech. 4; so we read of 'canonical singers,' Laodic. can. 15. The same notion of definiteness appears in the ritual use of the word for a series of nine 'odes' in the Eastern Church service (Neale, Introd. East. Ch. ii. 832), for the central and unvarying element in the Liturgy, beginning after the Tersanctus (Hammond, Liturgies East. and West. p. 377), or for any Church office (Ducange in v.): also in its application to a table for the calculation of Easter (Euseb. vi. 22; vii. 32), to a scheme for exhibiting the common and peculiar parts of the several Gospels (as the 'Eusebian canons'), and to a prescribed or ordinary payment to a church, a use which grew out of one found in Athanasius' Apol. c. Ari. 60.

CANON II.

This canon is directed against premature baptism, followed by premature ordination or consecration. It recites that a practice had grown up (on the part of bishops, although this is not expressed) 'of bringing at once to the spiritual laver persons who had but lately come over from heathen life to the faith, and had been but a short time under catechetical training, and of then promoting them, immediately after their baptism, to the office of bishop or of presbyter.' This had been done on the ground of 'necessity, or otherwise of some urgency on the part of men,' i. e. of persons who had set their hearts on the ordination or consecration of some particular convert to Christianity. The Council prohibits any such proceeding in future, as being 'contrary to the rule of the Church,' and to that religious common sense, as we may call it, which demands both an adequate 'time' for ante-baptismal instruction, and a yet 'longer' period for 'probation' of character with a view to high office in the Church, and which was embodied in St. Paul's prohibition to ordain a neophyte, lest the sudden elevation should foster pride, and 'bring him into judgment and the snare of the devil' (1 Tim. iii. 6). The practice in question had thus involved a double transgression of rules not technical but moral. (1) It was a fundamental maxim with the early Christians, that Gospel gifts were not to be lightly imparted, lest they should be unworthily received. For the due appreciation of the blessings, and the due acceptance of the responsibilities, of Baptism, here called 'the spiritual laver' or bath in allusion to Tit. iii. 7 (compare Justin Martyr, Apol. i. 61, and see Pusey, Script. Views of Holy Baptism, p. 59; and compare also 'spiritual table' in the Liturgy of St. James); there was needed a time of serious preparation, and of elaborate instruction in matters of faith and duty. The convert must 'count the cost' of adherence to his new Master, and be 'catechized,' or orally instructed (see Luke i. 4, Acts xviii. 25, 1 Cor. xiv. 19, Gal. vi. 6) point by point, as to what he would have to believe and to do. The great Catechetical School of Alexandria 'was a pattern to other churches in its diligent and systematic preparation' of persons looking forward to 'full discipleship' (Newman's Arians, p. 42). When it was possible, this process extended over two or three years: compare the Council of Elvira, c. 42, and Apost. Const. viii. 32; in urgent cases it might be greatly abridged,—compare the cases mentioned by Socrates (vii. 4, 30): but some process of preparatory instruction and moral training (cp. Euseb. iii. 23) was absolutely indispensable; and Ven. Bede, in his language to this effect (ii. 14, iii. 1, iv. 16), is but the exponent of a primeval tradition. If one who was going through this course suffered martyrdom, it was esteemed a 'baptism of blood,' or of 'fire' (Euseb. vi. 4). The postulant had to be made a catechumen by a special rite (comp. Euseb. Vit. Con. iv. 61, Augustine, Confess. i. 11, De Catech. Rud. 14, Sulpicius Severus, Dial. ii. 4). He spent most of his preparation-time in the lower class of catechumens, which the Nicene Council calls that of Hearers (Nic. 14); so Cyprian in Epist. 18 and 29. When he had passed through this stage, and therein received that preliminary teaching which, according to Tertullian, was dispensed with among heretics ('ante sunt catechumeni perfecti quam edocti,' Præscr. Hær. 41), he entered the higher class, that of 'Catechumens' proper in the language of the Council, but afterwards called the class of φωτιζόμενοι, as about to receive baptismal 'illumination' (Cyril, Procatechesis, 6) or of 'competentes,' as candidates for baptism at the ensuing Easter, or other solemn time of administration of that sacrament (cf. Ambrose, Epist. 20. 4, Augustine de Fide et Operibus, 6)— the name 'catechumens' being then restricted to the lower class (Cyril, l.c.; Ambrose, l.c.); although the 'Clementine' Liturgy distinguishes the 'Hearers' from the Catechumens as well as these from the φωτιζόμενοι (Hammond, Liturgies,

p. 3); it apparently uses 'Hearers' in a non-technical sense (see Cotelerius' note); and generally speaking, only two classes of Catechumens appear to have been recognised (so Beveridge, after Aristenus). Both classes were stationed in the 'narthex,' outside the 'naos' or nave; and were dismissed at different stages of the 'Missa Catechumenorum.' The 'Traditio Symboli,' or formal communication and exposition of the Creed to members of the higher class on different days in Lent, according to the usage of different churches (Neale's Essays in Liturgiology, p. 146), is indicated in Laodic. can. 46. Thus was the Church to discharge her duty as to the preparation of converts for baptism: and by the practice here censured individual prelates had left this duty unperformed. (2) The precept to 'lay hands suddenly on no man' (1 Tim. v. 22), has usually been referred, as our Prayer Book refers it, to ordination or consecration; and at any rate, the idea involved in that interpretation was rooted in the mind of the early Church. It is one of the main points of Cornelius' case as against Novatian that he was not suddenly raised to the episcopate, but, as Cyprian words it, 'per omnia ecclesiastica officia promotus, et in divinis administrationibus Dominum sæpe promeritus, ad sacerdotii sublime fastigium cunctis religionis gradibus ascendit' (Epist. 55. 6). The 80th Apostolic canon is probably an imitation of the Nicene; it urges that 'it is not right that one who has given no proof of his own fitness should be a teacher of others;' but it provides for exceptional cases indicated by 'divine grace.' The Nicene rule was followed up also by the 10th Sardican canon, declaring that no one ought to be 'prompte ac facile' appointed bishop, presbyter, or deacon; by the 3rd Laodicene, 'it is not right that those who have been but recently illuminated should be promoted to sacred orders;' and by various directions of Roman bishops, as Innocent I., forbidding any one to be made reader, acolyth, deacon, or priest 'cito' (Epist. 4. 5),—Celestine I., referring to rules which provided for a gradual ascent to the episcopate, 'ut minoribus initiati officiis ad majora firmentur' (Epist. 2. 3), and Leo the Great, urging that persons fresh from baptism, or lately converted from 'secular' life, cannot have given 'experimentum sui probabile' (Epist. 12. 4). But the rule admitted of exceptions: Cyprian himself, as his biographer Pontius tells us, was ordained very soon after his baptism, but this irregularity was gloriously justified by the result. The most famous instance of a departure from rule, both as to catechetical training before, and probation after baptism, is that of St. Ambrose. Bingham, indeed, is not accurate in saying that he was consecrated bishop at once (ii. 10. 7), if we may rely on what his biographer Paulinus mentions as a report, that 'after his baptism he fulfilled all the ecclesiastical offices, and on the eighth day was consecrated bishop' (Vit. S. Ambr. 9). But this rapid passing through the inferior offices was, as in the long subsequent case of Photius, merely a formal compliance with one requirement: and we know that Ambrose had not gone through the exercises of a catechumen when he was baptized, and that he begged that hi 'ordination' might be deferred, but in vain, for 'popular urgency' prevailed over 'præscriptio' (Epist. 63. 65), and thus he was 'raptus de tribunalibus' (from his civil magistracy) 'ad sacerdotium' (de Offic. Ministr. i. 1. 4). The demand of the Milanese people was attributed to a divine inspiration overruling ordinary forms,—in the language of the Apostolic canon, to 'divine grace.' In other instances the rule was broken with less felicitous results. Eusebius, the predecessor of St. Basil in the archbishopric of Cæsarea, had been tumultuously elected while yet a catechumen (Greg. Naz. Orat. 18. 33), and difficulties arose which hampered his work (ib. 43. 28). Gregory describes such inconsiderate promotions as too common in his time: bishops came, he says, to their office from the army or navy, from the plough or from the forge, and spiritual pride soon indicated their unfitness: without having gone through any due probation, they were deemed at once fit for sees (Carm. de Episcopis, 155-174, 380). He himself, as bishop of Constantinople, had for his successor an elderly ex-senator, unbaptized when Theodosius, according to the story, marked him out for the vacant office, and consecrated while still wearing the white vesture of a neophyte (Soz. vii. 8) : and the consequence of this strange choice was a relaxed state of clerical discipline, which entailed much trouble on St. Chrysostom. Jerome, who complacently records the fact that Nepotian was ordained presbyter 'per solitos gradus' (Epist. 60. 9), complained, about A.D. 397, that no one observed the precept of 1 Tim. iii. 6, and that one who was yesterday a catechumen became a 'pontifex' to-day (Epist. 69. 9). One can understand the temptation to commit an influential person to the cause of the Church by entrusting him at once with pastoral functions, and to call this precipitancy a venture of generous faith.

The concluding sentence of the canon points specially to the prematurely ordained, but is understood by Hefele to apply also to any cleric. It is supposed that the person contemplated may, after his ordination, be convicted of a ψυχικὸν ἁμάρτημα, a phrase which has been variously understood as a 'sensual sin,' in a specific sense (comp. James iii. 13, Jude 19, where ψυχικός is equivalent to unspiritual), and as 'a sin seriously affecting the life of the soul.' In that case he is to cease from ministration ; and neglect of this ruling is to entail forfeiture of the clerical state, as the penalty for daring to 'resist the great Council' (a name which the Council claims for itself in can. 6, 8, 14, 17, 18, and which Julius of Rome gives to it in Athan. Apol. c. Ari. 22).

Canon III.

Paul of Samosata, the heretical bishop of Antioch in the middle of the third century (see on can. 19), had been wont to retain female inmates in his house: some of his clergy had followed his example, and the Council of Antioch which deposed him asserted that some had been then betrayed into sin, that others had at least incurred suspicion, and that his conduct, if not sinful, was scandalous (Euseb. vii. 30). To these women the Antiochese people gave the name of συνείσακτοι, 'introduced as companions,' in a sense conveying some reproach. This kind of intimacy had obviously grown up 'side by side with the practice of celibacy' (Stephens, Life of St. Chrysostom, p. 219), and a very offensive form of it had been previously condemned by Cyprian, who quotes the text, 'Do not give place to the devil' (Epist. 4). The Spanish Council of Elvira, early in the fourth century, had forbidden any cleric to entertain as an inmate any 'extraneous woman,' i. e. any woman save a sister, or a virgin daughter dedicated to God (can. 27); and that of Ancyra in 314 had forbidden unmarried women to live as sisters with men, i.e. under the name of 'spiritual sisters' (can. 19). The present canon, adopting the word συνείσακτον (for that this, and not the various reading ἐπείσακτον, is genuine, may be inferred from Basil, Epist. 55), disallows of any female inmate (Ruffinus renders 'extraneis,' Isidore Mercator 'extraneam,' while Philo and Evarestus and Dionysius Exiguus give the more literal rendering 'subintroductam') 'except a mother, a sister, an aunt, or any other persons who are above all suspicion.' That a wife was not regarded as συνείσακτος may appear from the story of Paphnutius' speech and the consequent resolution of the Council (Soc. i. 11). The restriction was often disregarded: Epiphanius says that the women in question were called 'agapetæ' (Hær. 43. 2), and Jerome complains of the 'agapetarum pestis' (Epist. 22. 14); while Basil has to remind a priest named Paregorius that in enforcing the prohibition he is but carrying out this law of 'our holy fathers in the Nicene Council' (Epist. 55), and Chrysostom wrote one discourse 'against persons ἔχοντας παρθένους συνεισάκτους,' exhorting them to give up a connection which was at once discreditable and morally dangerous, and another urging the 'canonicæ' or dedicated virgins not to live with men. Compare his remarks in De Sacerdotio, iii. 16. On the whole subject, see Bingham, vi. 2. 13.

Canon IV.

The immediate subject of this canon is the right way of filling up vacant sees. But in order to estimate the directions given in regard to it, we must observe the organization of provincial churches at this period. Naturally, and in conformity with circumstances, the Church had adopted the civil divisions of the Empire: the bishops in each province had drawn together, and he whose see was in the 'metropolis' had become chief bishop of the province, i. e. 'metropolitan,' just as the bishop of a city which was the capital of a 'diocese' or aggregate of provinces had a presidency over all its provincial churches. (Comp. Euseb. v. 23; Apost. Can. 35.) When a new bishop has to be appointed, the Council rules that, if possible, all the comprovincial bishops shall concur. But a question at once arises: What of the elective rights of the clergy and laity? The Council did not mean to ignore them: its letter in Soc. i. 9 recognises 'the choice of the people' as a condition of every appointment. It confines itself in this passage to a later stage of the process: supposing that the people have expressed their wishes, and the clergy have given their testimony (compare Cyprian, Epist. 55. 7 and 67. 5; Euseb. vi. 11. 29; and much later, Peter II. of Alexandria in Theodoret, iv. 22); how are the bishops to act? Their action is expressed by καθίστασθαι, the appointing of the new bishop (compare Irenæus, iii. 3. 3, as to the appointment of Xystus, and κατέστη in Euseb. vii. 32), when taken in connection with τὴν χειροτονίαν ποιεῖσθαι, as in the Synodical letter (Soc. i. 9) τοὺς ὑπ' αὐτοῦ κατασταθέντας is equivalent to τῶν ὑπ' αὐτοῦ χειροτονηθέντων. What then is χειροτονία? Originally, a voting by show or stretching-out of hands,—then generally, a voting: but as χειροτονέω, properly to vote in this way, or generally to elect (comp. 2 Cor. viii. 19) came also to mean appoint or designate, without any notion of election (Acts xiv. 23, cp. Sclater's Orig. Draught of Prim. Church, p. 119; and Soc. i. 38), and, in ecclesiastical Greek, to appoint with the ceremony of laying on hands or stretching out hands on the ordained, so it is with χειροτονία. As in the 19th Antiochene and 5th Laodicene canons χειροτονεῖσθαι and χειροτονίας should be interpreted of ordination, not, as Zonaras and Balsamon say, of election (comp. Antioch. can. 18, where χειροτονηθείς is clearly 'when ordained'): so here too, the Greek canonists are certainly in error when they interpret χειροτονία of election. The canon is akin to the 1st Apostolic canon, which, as the canonists admit, must refer to the consecration of a new bishop: and it was cited in that sense at the Council of Chalcedon, sess. 13 (Mansi, vii. 307). We must follow Rufinus and the old Latin translators, who speak of 'ordinari,' 'ordinatio,' and 'manus impositionem,' in accordance with Jerome's explanation of χειροτονία, 'id est, ordinationem' by imposition of hands (on Isaiah, c. 58, C. 16). Philo and Evarestus, indeed, render χειροτονίαν here by 'manus impositionem;' and Renaudot gives this as the ordinary though not quite invariable sense of χειροτονία (Lit. Orient. i. 380, cp. Bingham iv. 6. 11). Compare χειροθετουμένους in can. 8, and χειρεπιθεσία used of Novatian's consecration in Euseb. vi. 43; and see too Cypr. Ep. 67. 5, 'manus ei imponeretur . . . ordinationem;' and Basil, Epist. 240. 3, 251. 3, treating the manual act as a matter of course in consecrations. For this rite, then,—the canon means,—it were well that all the bishops should assemble: but if this is not feasible, 'owing to some urgent necessity or to distance, then three at least must come for the purpose, with the written consent of their brethren' (comp. Antioch. can. 19). This was intended to prevent such irregular consecrations as had given rise in Egypt to the Meletian schism. There were to be in future no clandestine or partisan appointments. The 'three' are not mentioned as an absolute minimum for conferring the episcopal character: consecration by two bishops, or even by one, was not regarded as invalid (see e.g. Athanasius' recognition of Siderius' consecration, as referred to by Bingham, ii. 11. 5): strictly speaking, the Apostolic canon would allow of 'two' consecrators as well as of three; and the first Council of Arles requires three beside the metropolitan, if seven cannot be had (c. 20). Innocent I. compresses the case into a few words: 'Nec unus episcopus ordinare præsumat episcopum, ne *furtivum* beneficium præstitum videatur' (Epist. 2. 2), not as if consecration by one conveyed no 'beneficium' whatever. Provision is thus made for the right of the comprovincials to take real part in the filling up of a vacant see (comp. Euseb. vi. 11 on the appointment of Alexander of Jerusalem, and Cyprian, Epist. 67. 4, and Laodic. can. 12). On the other hand, the metropolitan is to have τὸ κῦρος, i. e. he may give or withhold his sanction from the proceedings (comp. Athan. Hist. Ari. 52, that no judgment of the Church received τὸ κῦρος from the Emperor; and see below, can. 15, 16). As he had to summon his brethren to the provincial synod, preside over them when assembled, visit their dioceses, give them letters of commendation when they were going abroad, and administer dioceses while vacant (Bingham, ii. 16. 12 ff.), so here the appointment of a new bishop is to be confirmed or disallowed by him (compare Antioch. can. 9, 16, and see too Chalc. 25 below): and the second Council of Arles, referring to 'the great Council,' rules that any one consecrated without the metropolitan's knowledge ought to be treated as no bishop, i. e. as not canonically in possession (Mansi, vii. 879).

CANON V.

This canon treats of (1) the status of persons excommunicated by their bishop; and (2) as suggested by this, the regular holding of provincial synods.

The word ἀκοινώνητος is here applied (as in Const. 6, Chalc. 23, etc.) to clerics and laymen who have been put out of communion by their respective bishops. Such sentences are 'to hold good, according to the rule which prescribes that persons excommunicated by some bishops are not to be received into communion by others,' until a higher authority has reversed the sentence. This 'rule' (see Bingham, xvi. 2. 10) was involved in the principle of the unity of the episcopate, asserted with such earnestness by Cyprian (de Unit. Eccl. 5; Epist. 55. 20, 68. 3), from which it followed that so long as any one bishop kept within his duty, his acts of disciplinary government were respected by all his brethren. So Cornelius of Rome had refused to admit to communion Felicissimus, who had been excommunicated in Africa (Cypr. Epist. 59. 1). So the 53rd canon of Elvira had declared that any bishop who received an excommunicate without consent of his excommunicator 'would have to answer it before his brethren, and risk removal from his office.' More briefly the Council of Arles in 314, can. 16: 'where a person has been excommunicated, there he must obtain communion.' See too Apost. can. 33, Antioch. 6. The 'rule' was acted on in three memorable post-Nicene cases: (1) when St. Athanasius excommunicated a wicked governor of Libya, and St. Basil wrote to acknowledge the notification of his sentence, and assured him that the church of Cæsarea would regard the offender as ἀποτρόπαιος (Epist. 61; see also the last words of Basil, Ep. 55): (2) when St. Chrysostom refrained from giving communion to the 'Tall Brothers' excommunicated by Theophilus; and (3) when Synesius, bishop of Ptolemais, informed all bishops by a circular that he had excommunicated the savage tyrant Andronicus, governor of Pentapolis, and protested that any one who, despising the church of Ptolemais 'as belonging to a small city, should receive those whom she had put under ban, would incur the same sentence' (Epist. 58). On the other hand, the rule was broken by Dioscorus of Alexandria, when he ignored the excommunication of Eutyches by Flavian of Constantinople (see Newman's note to Transl. of Fleury, vol. iii. p. 357, 'It belonged to the very essence of Catholic unity that he who was excommunicate in one church should be held excommunicate in all churches').

But there was the obvious possibility that the excommunicating bishop might have acted without judicial impartiality, and 'in a spirit of petty animosity or contentiousness, or some unkindliness of that sort.' Μικροψυχία is used here, as thrice in Julius' letter in Athan. Apol. c. Ari. 21, 34, 35, for pique or petty jealousy; and similarly Socrates uses μικροψυχήσαντες for 'having got into a petty quarrel' (v. 23) Ἀηδία corresponds to our popular use of 'unpleasantness.' Ἀποσυνάγωγοι, as a synonym for ἀκοινώνητοι, is taken from John ix. 22. Observe the frank way in which this great episcopal assembly recognises the liability of bishops to ignoble faults in their administration of Church law. So the saintly Bishop Wilson, tenacious as he was of his own church discipline, observes that 'the Holy Ghost ... never makes Himself the minister of the passions of men' (Sacra Privata, p. 220). Was a man to be perpetually outlawed from Church fellowship, because he had thus suffered from a misuse of sacred authority? By no means. 'In order that' such cases 'may undergo due examination,' let 'synods be held twice a year in every province, that when all the bishops of the province have met together, such questions may be examined.' This wording of itself shows, what we infer from notices in Eusebius (e.g. v. 16), that these assemblies, which are traced to the latter part of the second century, but were not established as a regular institution until the third, were properly composed of bishops alone. As in the General Councils, of which the Nicene was the first, so in the provincial, clerics and laymen might be present, and might by permission speak, but were not constituent members, and had no 'votum decisivum.' (See Hefele, Councils, Introd. s. 4.) Shortly before the Nicene Council, Licinius had forbidden the bishops in his dominions to hold synods, although, says Eusebius, 'it was impossible to manage important matters by any other means' (Vit. Const. i. 51). The present canon directs that at these provincial synods complaints as to excommunication shall be heard (as by a court of appeal), so that those who, on inquiry, shall be found to have 'undeniably given offence to their own bishop,' and thus incurred Church censure, shall be 'with good reason regarded by all' the comprovincials 'as excommunicate, until it shall please the general body of bishops to pronounce a more indulgent decision in their behalf.' Here ψῆφος is used not for a vote or expression of desire, but for a decisive resolution, as in Nic. 6, Eph. 8, Chalc. 28; and φιλανθρωποτέραν is illustrated by φιλανθρωπότερόν τι in Nic. 12, φιλανθρωπίας in Nic. 11, and Chalc. 16, and φιλάνθρωπον in Chalc. 30: compare the Ancyrene canons 16, 21, and Neocæsarean 2, where the noun and its cognates refer to a merciful interpretation of a case, dispensing with the strict application of law. It is observable that Gelasius of Cyzicus reads, after τῷ κοινῷ, not τῶν ἐπισκόπων, but ἢ τῷ ἐπισκόπῳ (Hist. Conc. Nic. ii. 31), as Philo and Evarestus had rendered, 'in commune aut episcopo;' and the Prisca alters it still more, 'quamdiu episcopo.' Compare with this passage Constant. 2, Chalc. 19.

The time of these two annual provincial synods is fixed by the last sentence of the canon. 'One is to be held before Lent, that all petty animosity being laid aside, the "gift" may be offered in purity to God: the other about the time of the late autumn.' Although τεσσαρακοστή was a phrase then established, there was not an uniform observance of forty days' fasting before Easter. The difficult passage of Irenæus, cited by Eusebius in v. 24, implies that in his day the ante-paschal fasting was confined to the latter part of Holy Week. Dionysius of Alexandria, in the third century, says that all do not observe alike 'the six days of fasting,' the week days of Holy Week (Routh, Rell. Sac. iii. 229): and in the post-Nicene period, although Cyril of Jerusalem (Procatech. 4), Chrysostom (c. Judæos, iii. 4), and Augustine (Epist. 55. s. 32) speak of 'forty days' as if fixed by Church custom, yet Socrates mentions three varieties of ante-paschal fasting time, only one of which extends over six weeks; and wonders that all agree in calling the fast 'tessaracoste' (v. 22): while Sozomen mentions five such varieties (vii. 19). The Arabic paraphrase of the Nicene canons explains 'before Lent' by 'after the feast of Lights' or Epiphany. The object of this provision was that all the bishops might enjoy an Easter Communion undisturbed by any soreness or ill-will. The 'gift' (δῶρον, rendered 'munus' by Latin translators) is a phrase borrowed from Matthew v. 23, the adjective καθαρόν being taken from the θυσία καθαρά of Mal. i. 11. There was no need to say what this 'gift' was, any more than to explain the phrase προσφορά or προσφέρω in canons 11 and 18. The Eucharist was universally regarded as the Christian sacrifice (Justin Mart. Dial. 70, 117; Irenæus, iv. 17. 5 etc.), the solemn oblation of the bread and cup was the second stage in the threefold process of their consecration: and the phrase 'gifts' is applied liturgically to them, as in the 'Clementine' Liturgy, where it is explained by 'this sacrifice,' and in those called after SS. James and Basil; see Hammond's Liturgies Eastern and Western, pp. 18, 20, 43, 46, 114, 118, 122. (It is probable that a Eucharistic sense should be admitted where Clement of Rome speaks of δῶρα in Ep. Cor. 44.) So also the Syrian Ordo Communis speaks of 'this Corban' (see Howard's Christians of St. Thomas, p. 222), so the Ethiopic Liturgy (see Renaudot, Lit. Orient. ii. 497); and the Roman canon of the Mass unites 'dona' and 'munera' with 'sacrificia.' It was not forgotten that all things given to God must first have been given by Him: compare the phrase in St. Mark's Liturgy, 'We have set before Thee Thine own gifts out of Thine own;' and in a deeper sense 'doni tui,' in the Liturgy of Adæus and Maris. This provision may be illustrated by Chrysostom's request to another bishop 'to present the gifts for him,' when he himself was 'disturbed in mind' (Palladius, Dial. p. 51).

The 38th Apostolic canon (probably later than the Nicene) places the first annual synod in the fourth week of Eastertide, and the second on the 10th day of Hyperberetæus, i.e. October 15; and the 20th canon of the Dedication-Council of Antioch, in 341, specifies the third week after Easter (so that the synod might end in the fourth) and the 15th of October. Later Western synods, following the Council of Hippo in its provision for the national synods of Africa (Mansi, iii. 919), allowed the provincial synod to meet only once annually, two meetings being found inconvenient (2nd Orleans, 3rd and 4th Toledo); and so the English Council of Hertford fixed the 1st of August as the annual day of meeting (Bede, iv. 5). It is significant that at the Council of Reims in 991, the bishop of Orleans observed that this canon, while providing for two annual synods, did *not* direct them to refer to the authority of the Roman bishop (Mansi, xix. 136).

Canon VI.

This canon is, in a historical sense, the most important in the Nicene series.

It begins by stating a principle, with a particular application. 'Let the ancient customs prevail.' This is in harmony with the conservative tone of the whole code, exhibited in its frequent references to 'rule,' 'usage,' 'tradition.' And what customs were specially intended? Those which gave to the bishop of Alexandria a certain fulness of jurisdiction throughout Egypt, Libya, and Pentapolis, or, as Epiphanius describes it, over 'Egypt, Thebais, Mareotes, Libya, Ammoniaca, Mareotis (qy. Marmorica?), Pentapolis' (Hær. 68. 1), i.e. the six provinces of Upper and Lower Libya, Thebais, Egypt proper, Arcadia, Augustamnica, which were politically under the 'Augustal Prefect' (see Bingham, ix. 1. 3, 6; 2. 6). One question as to the nature of this jurisdiction is, whether the bishop of Alexandria, called in that age specifically the Pope (see Athan. Apol. c. Ari. 69; de Synod. 16), was in 325 the sole metropolitan throughout the territory described. Beveridge in his annotations, Le Quien (Oriens Christ. ii. 353), and Neale (Introd. East. Ch. i. 111) answer in the affirmative. Valesius (Observat. in Soc. et Soz. lib. 3) and Hefele hold that there were metropolitans subordinate to the Alexandrian see, because e. g. Ptolemais was, according to Synesius (Epist. 67), a metropolitical see under Athanasius. Bingham speaks rather inconsistently (ii. 16. 23; 17. 8): but in the second passage inclines to the latter opinion. Among these writers, Beveridge alone holds that he who confessedly was supreme over six provinces was 'a mere metropolitan.' Rather, he was a metropolitan and much more: the 'throne of St. Mark' had even at this time a very ample authority, which after the Nicene Council grew, and deserved to grow, while entrusted to one who was not less confessor than patriarch, but proved itself excessive in less truly royal hands, amid the sunshine of 'external prosperity.' (See Cardinal Newman's Historical Sketches, iii. 339.) The height which it had attained in the middle of the fifth century will appear from what is called the 30th canon of Chalcedon. In the canon before us, it is clearly intended to protect this authority against such assaults as it had sustained from the schismatical conduct of Meletius of Lycopolis; and the Council, abhorring all breaches of Church unity, and venerating in Alexander of Alexandria an active upholder of the true faith, resolves to guarantee to him and his successors their traditional authority. So far all is clear. But we have now to consider the reason given: 'since this also is customary for the bishop in Rome.' Here the case of the Roman see is cited as a precedent, or as a parallel case to that of the Alexandrian; the claims of the latter, on the ground of custom, to a certain authority within its own domain, are supported by the fact that the former, by like usage, holds a like power. What, then, was the jurisdiction referred to as possessed by the Roman bishop? Rufinus, in his free version of the canons, (1) makes the canon ordain that 'the old custom' shall prevail in Alexandria 'and' in Rome—not, as in Rome; (2) describes the authority which, according to this rendering, is to be retained by the Roman bishops, as 'the care of the suburbicarian churches.' Now the suburbicarian churches were, most probably, (not those of the territory within 100 miles of Rome, governed civilly by the 'Præfectus Urbis,' but) those of the ten provinces governed by the 'Vicarius Urbis,' i.e. Picenum suburbicarium, Campania, Tuscia and Umbria, Apulia and Calabria, Bruttii and Lucania, Valeria, Sicily, Sardinia, and Corsica—as distinct from the seven provinces of North Italy, dependent ecclesiastically on the see of Milan (see Bingham, ix. 1. 6, 9; Fleury, b. 27. c. 11; Palmer, On the Church, ii. 417). Tillemont, after citing Zonaras' opinion that the Roman see had then by custom authority over the whole West, says that 'Rufinus had better means of information,' and that 'if one means to treat the question ingenuously, there is great reason to think that this region comprised Italy except Cisalpine Gaul, and also the three islands.' (Mem. vi. 670.) Hefele argues that the 'suburbicarian' region was the narrower territory of the Præfectus, but that, besides, the Roman bishop's authority extended over all the West:—which is more than Rufinus even hints at. He might, perhaps, have used 'suburbicariarum' inaccurately, but could not have meant by it only the churches of the district near Rome, nor, on the other hand, would he have so strained it as to take in all the West. As far as appears, then, he did *not* suppose that in A.D. 325 the Roman bishops had patriarchal authority over the whole West, or, in other words, that the whole West was in that relation towards Rome in which the Egyptian provinces stood towards Alexandria. And to suggest that it was so, on the ground of Augustine's indefinite language as to Pope Innocent's 'presiding over the Western Church,' in the early part of the next century (c. Julian. i. 5. 13), or of Jerome's words implying that Damasus might represent the West as Peter represented Egypt (Epist. 17), is to ignore the difference between pre-eminence and that supreme authority which, in the famous case of Apiarius, the African church denied the Roman to have over her, and for the establishment of which over Gaul Leo the Great, in 445, procured from Valentinian III. an edict affecting the Western empire. Indeed, the resolution of the Council of Sardica, some nineteen years after the Nicene, to entrust the bishop of Rome with a certain limited power of receiving appeals—a resolution which seems to have been but little known to Western churches—is proof enough that previously the Roman see was not for the West generally what the Alexandrian was for the churches of the six provinces of Egypt. The phrase of the ante-Nicene Council of Arles, in an address to Sylvester of Rome, 'te qui majores diœceses tenes,' is best explained according to the context by understanding 'diœceses' as meaning provinces, not those aggregates of provinces to which technically the word was applied in the Constantinian division of the empire. (See on Constant. 2.)

It appears, then, that the authority which the Council contemplated as customarily belonging to the Roman bishop, and as analogous to that which was to be retained by the Alexandrian, extended over the churches of Central and Southern Italy and the three adjacent islands; and there is reason to think that within this territory, with the exception of Caliaris for Sardinia, and perhaps of Capua for Campania, the Roman was the only metropolitical church. Nothing is said about that 'primacy of honour' which the Roman church confessedly held in regard to all other churches. It was doubtless taken for granted; there was no occasion to mention it, because it was not connected with jurisdiction, and the matter in hand was jurisdiction of a certain kind. Even in the spurious Latin version of this canon, beginning, 'Quod Ecclesia Romana semper habuit primatum,' which was produced by the Roman delegate Paschasinus at the Council of Chalcedon, and instantly confronted with the Greek original (Mansi, vii. 443), the context shows that 'primatus' meant, so to speak, patriarchal authority, such as the Alexandrian see by rights had over Egypt; and the same may be said of a like version in the Codex Canonum, where, however, a hasty Roman hand has added as a title, 'De primatu ecclesiæ Romanæ,' as if 'primatus' meant primacy over the whole church. The 'Prisca Versio' tries to blend the original with the Roman gloss, 'Antiqui moris est ut urbis Romæ episcopus habeat principatum;' whereas the Isidorian translation is fair, 'Mos antiquus perduret in Ægypto,' and so the Dionysian, 'Antiqua consuetudo servetur per Ægyptum,' and the Vetus Interpretatio (discovered at Verona) to the same effect; and the earlier version of Philo and Evarestus (Mansi, iv. 410) is accurate, 'Antiqui mores obtineant,' as is the Coptic Fragment in Spicil. Solesm. i. 528, 'Mores antiqui stabiles permaneant.' The Arabic paraphrase of this canon, and the Arabic 'canon 8,' are also true to the sense of the original; while Paschasinus' reading is embodied in the rough and inaccurate version called 'Antiquissima.'

But while it would have been irrelevant to mention the 'honorary primacy,' we cannot but see that if the Nicene fathers had recognised what is called the 'Papal supremacy,' they could not but have noticed it in this canon. For they were considering the subject of authority, and of such authority as was held, in different areas, by Rome and Alexandria alike. But if they had believed Sylvester of Rome (represented in their assembly by two of his own priests, but not, according to good evidence, by Hosius of Cordova, who is thought to have acted as president) to be the divinely appointed ruler of the whole Church, the one universal overseer and the fountain of all episcopal jurisdiction, they could not have been content to say that the bishop of Alexandria ought, according to custom, to have power in one region, because the bishop of Rome had similar power in another. It would have been impossible to use his patriarchal status as a precedent, without a saving clause acknowledging his unique and sovereign position as the one Vicar of the Church's Divine Head. The omission is a proof, if proof were wanted, that the First Œcumenical Council knew nothing of the doctrine of Papal supremacy.

To proceed with the canon. It goes on to secure to the church of Antioch, and to all other churches 'in the provinces,' all their rightful privileges. The word πρεσβεῖα here, as in Chalc. 28, implies prerogatives, not being limited, as in Constant. 3, by τιμῆς. The prerogatives of Antioch were smaller than those of Alexandria, for they did not include the consecration of all provincial bishops: but, such as they were, they were upheld, doubtless not without special regard for the then bishop Eustathius, who took a leading part in the Council; so that this illustrious see was still, as Le Quien says (Or. Christ. ii. 67), to 'rank as the third,' and to rule the provincial churches of the great region called 'Oriens,' including Syria, Phœnicia, Arabia, Euphratensis, Osrhoene, Mesopotamia, Cilicia, and Isauria (see Neale, Introd. East. Ch. i. 125). Jerome (in c. Joan. Jerosolym. 37) and Innocent I. (Epist. 18. 1) refer to this canon in favour of the rights of Antioch (see below, on Eph. 8). Beveridge, indeed, infers from the words, 'With regard to Antioch, and in the other provinces,' that the bishop of Antioch at this time had only one provincial church under him: but this is to strain the text, and confound the two prepositions, both of which Beveridge renders by 'in.' We may say, then, that this decree recognises as existing three virtual patriarchates, while it further includes in its scope all existing rights of metropolitan churches (as Philo and Evarestus take it), but with special reference to the great primatial sees of Ephesus, Cæsarea in Cappadocia, and Heraclea in Thrace.

In the second sentence of the canon, the provision of can. 4, that the metropolitan is to have the right of disallowing an episcopal election, is made more stringent: 'it is quite obvious that if any one is made a bishop without the consent of the metropolitan, the great Council determines that he ought not to be bishop,' i.e. he ought to be deposed. The last sentence speaks for itself: 'if in a provincial synod, two or three, out of their own contentiousness, contradict the general resolution of all' (i.e. of the great majority), 'when it is reasonable and accordant with Church rule, let that resolution prevail,' their opposition being treated as frivolous.

CANON VII.

On the ground of 'custom and ancient tradition' (compare Nic. 6. Const. 2. Eph. 8), it is ruled that the bishop who is in Ælia, i.e. Jerusalem, should 'have τὴν ἀκολουθίαν τῆς τιμῆς, the honour due to him in consequence of, or in accordance with, such tradition, reserving however to the metropolis (Cæsarea) its proper dignity. This, rather than the 'second place after Cæsarea' (Beveridge), appears to be conveyed by the phrase. Ælia was the city which Hadrian had begun to build on the ruins of the ancient Jerusalem before the revolt of Barchochab (as to the time, we must correct Euseb. iv. 6 by Dion Cassius, lxix. 12: cp. Milman, Hist. Jews, ii. 425). Its name, derived from one of the names of the imperial founder, had superseded that of Jerusalem, in popular speech, at the time of the Great Persecution (see the striking story of the Egyptian martyr in Euseb. Mart. Pal. 11). The church of 'Ælia' was purely Gentile, although it boasted of possessing the chair used by St. James the Just, first bishop of Jerusalem (Euseb. vii. 19). Cæsarea was the undoubted metropolis of Palestine: and its bishop Theophilus had, in the latter part of the second century, presided over a synod of Palestinian bishops (Euseb. v. 23). All its metropolitan rights are saved by the present canon, which must have been very gratifying to Eusebius: at the same time 'Ælia' is equally secured in its precedency among the suffragan churches (see Neale, Introd. East. Ch. i. 158). The alleged discovery of the Holy Sepulchre soon after the Council naturally tended to invest the see of Ælia with the sacred associations of the mother church of Christendom; and while one of its bishops, Macarius, is said to have consecrated a bishop for Lydda (Soz. ii. 20) the quarrel between Cyril and the metropolitan Acacius is described by Theodoret (ii. 26) as a contest about 'precedency,' as if Cyril had asserted the dignity of his see against that of Cæsarea (cp. Tillemont, viii. 431). Relying on the canon, Acacius deposed Cyril, who thereupon set the example of appealing to a higher court (Soc. ii. 40). John, the next bishop of Jerusalem, took no direct steps towards independence, but Jerome blamed him for invoking the see of Alexandria in Palestinian church affairs, referred him to the Nicene Council as having 'decreed that Cæsarea should be the metropolis of Palestine, and Antioch of all the East,' and upbraided him with not 'rendering due honour to his metropolitan' (c. Joan. Jeros. 37). Fifteen years later, John obeyed the summons of Eulogius of Cæsarea to a provincial synod (Aug. de Gest. Pelag. s. 9, 37). Praylius, who succeeded John, consecrated Domninus to the metropolitan see of Cæsarea (Theodoret, Epist. 110); and Juvenal, who succeeded Praylius, went so far as to assert, in the fourth session of the Council of Ephesus, that the bishop of Antioch himself (with whom the Council was then at feud) ought to be subject to the 'apostolic see of Jerusalem' (Mansi, iv. 1312). Cyril of Alexandria said nothing at the time, but afterwards wrote to Leo, before he became bishop of Rome, against this pretension (Leo, Epist. 119. 4). 'After a long contention with Maximus of Antioch, the matter was compromised' (Neale, i. 159) in the seventh session of Chalcedon by an arrangement which left the Phœnicias and Arabia subject to 'the throne of St. Peter' at Antioch, and established the patriarchate of Jerusalem—or, as Juvenal called it, of 'the Holy Resurrection of Christ,'—as including 'the three Palestines.' The rights of Cæsarea in regard to Ælia, guaranteed by the First Council, were thus extinguished by the Fourth (Mansi, vii. 180). It may be added that Arabia was transferred from the patriarchate of Antioch to that of Jerusalem at the Fifth General Council (Neale, i. 127).

Canon VIII.

This is an important canon on the treatment of converts from the Novatians or self-styled 'Cathari.' Novatian (wrongly called Novatus by Eusebius and other Greek writers, although Eusebius preserves a passage in which Dionysius of Alexandria writes the name correctly, vii. 8) was a Roman presbyter of learning and high character, who, after being passed over in the election of the Roman see, made a schism in A.D. 251, and procured for himself a clandestine and irregular consecration. His plea was that the Church had fallen into laxity on a cardinal point of discipline. Persons who had lapsed under persecution and professed repentance, ought not, he maintained, under any circumstances, to regain their forfeited Christian privileges. They were not, indeed, to despair of Divine forgiveness: but they were not to be assured of it through the Church's instrumentality. God might forgive, but His ministers might not absolve them (Soc. i. 10: iv. 28). This was Novatian's principle: and those who adopted it called themselves 'the Pure,' as being content to make great sacrifices for the sake of maintaining Christian strictness. The assumption of this title naturally provoked the Catholics to denounce them as self-righteous (cp. Euseb. vi. 43; Augustine, Hær. 58; cp. Tillemont, iii. 482) and as on that ground *im*pure (Epiphan. Hær. 59. 6). But in an age when devout minds sincerely dreaded the influence of the world over the Church, the standard of 'purity' and 'discipline' attracted many adherents: the Novatians were led by consistency to apply their maxim to the two other chief sins, murder and adultery: they copied the Montanists in the prohibition of second marriages; they extended their sect, by the foundation of rival episcopates, through various countries, and particularly in Phrygia and Paphlagonia, where the grave temperament of the people (Soc. iv. 28) would predispose them to welcome an austere type of religion. Constantine is said to have invited to the Nicene Council a Novatian bishop named Acesius, and when the Creed was settled and the Easter question determined, to have asked him whether he agreed with these decisions. 'Yes,' he answered; 'they are in accordance with what I have been taught.' 'Why then do you stand aloof from the Church's communion?' Acesius stated the Novatian principle, whereupon the emperor, with humorous impatience, bade him 'set up a ladder, and climb up into heaven by himself' (Soc. i. 10). But there were Novatian clerics who, unlike this prelate, were minded to conform to the Church—which is for the first time called in this canon, and in the anathema at the end of the original Nicene Creed, 'Catholic and Apostolic.' The Council resolved ὥστε χειροθετουμένους τούτους μένειν οὕτως ἐν τῷ κλήρῳ. Here is a difficulty: what is the force of this participle? (1) It seems that, whatever the χειροθεσία was, the canon points to it as connected with the future treatment of the persons in question. Although the Greek commentators, and the compilers of the Arabic canons, followed by Beveridge, understand it as meaning, 'supposing they have previously received χειροθεσία,' i.e. in their former sect, 'they may then (οὕτως) continue in the clerical body,' or in their clerical position, yet the use of a present rather than an aorist participle supports the Latin translators, e.g. 'ut impositionem manus accipientes' (Dionysius), 'ut per manus impositionem' (Prisca, Antiquissima), 'ut manus eis impositio fiat' (Vetus.), that is, 'they are to remain in the clergy on condition of receiving χειροθεσία.' (Compare a like use of οὕτως in Basil, Epist. 188. 1.) So Pope Innocent I. understood it, 'ut accepta manus impositione, sic maneant in clero' (Epist. 22. 5). And so Hefele takes it. But then (2) what sort of χειροθεσία? The Apostolic Constitutions (ii. 41) mention a χειροθεσία which accompanied the absolution of penitents, and which is referred to in the dictum, 'A presbyter χειροθετεῖ, οὐ χειροτονεῖ' (ib. viii. 28); and so Augustine says, 'manus hæreticis correctis imponitur' (de Bapt. v. s. 33); and so it has been supposed that the canon requires the ex-Novatians to receive a benedictory imposition of hands, which would seal their reconciliation to the Church, and give them 'mission' to officiate within its pale (see Tillemont, iii. 477, and Hefele). On this view the Council would recognise Novatian ordinations as valid, though irregular; and the next paragraph of the canon may seem to favour such an interpretation. Against this it is urged that χειροθεσία would here more naturally mean ordination (compare Neocæs. 9, Antioch. 10, Chalc. 6, and χειρεπιθεσία in Euseb. vi. 43, and the use of χειροθετεῖν for 'to ordain,' in the Council's letter, Soc. i. 9; that Theophilus of Alexandria, in a 'canonical' answer, explains χειροθετουμένους in this passage by saying, 'The great Council ordered that the self-styled Cathari, on joining the Church, χειροτονεῖσθαι' (Mansi, iii. 1257), which naturally means 'should be ordained:' that the Council settled the less serious case of the Meletian schismatics by ordering that, on their return to the Church, those who had been 'appointed bishops by him should be confirmed μυστικωτέρᾳ χειροτονίᾳ,' which naturally means 'a more sacred ordination,' (see Valesius and Routh, Scr. Opusc. i. 416, and compare χειροτονηθέντων a few lines above, evidently meaning those who were ordained by Meletius), although Tillemont (vi. 814), Neale (Hist. Alex. i. 146), and Hefele would explain χειροτονίᾳ also in that passage as a mere benedictory imposition of hands, which should give licence to officiate:—and that Basil probably represents the general Eastern view when he says that Novatians, as schismatics, have no power to ordain (Epist. 188. c. 1). This interpretation of χειροθετουμένους is emphasized by the Isidorian rendering, 'ut ordinentur,' and that of Philo and Evarestus, 'eos ordinatos;' and yet more by Rufinus, 'sed ordinatione data,'—words which Beveridge seems to overlook (Annot. p. 67). Besides receiving this 'laying on of hands,' the ex-Novatians are before all things to give written promise that they will adhere to all the decrees (δόγμασι, used as in Acts xvi. 4) 'of the Catholic Church' on all points; two being expressly specified. (1) Those who have married twice are not to be treated as sinners unfit for Church fellowship. 'Digamy' on the part of a lay Christian was indeed regarded as a weakness (cp. Clem. Alex. Strom. iii. s. 82), mainly from the consideration indicated in 1 Cor. vii. 39, 40 (cp. Routh, Rell. Sac. iv. 195) and enforced by a dread of the coarse and self-indulgent tone of mind so commonly associated with marriage before the Christian principle, investing it with a mysterious sanctity, had had time to 'leaven the whole lump.' An individual Church writer, like Athenagoras, might go further and call it 'a specious adultery' (Legat. 33), thereby approximating to the Montanist position (cp. Tertull. de Monogam. 9), afterwards adopted by the Novatians, but given up by most of them in the fifth century (Soc. v. 22). But when Gibbon ascribed this view to the Catholic Church of early ages (ii. 187) he ignored the context of a passage of Justin Martyr (Apol. i. 15) which refers to the case of a man putting away his lawful wife and then marrying another; and he forgot that Tertullian bears witness that Churchmen, or as he calls them 'the psychics' (or unspiritual), treated the Montanist view as heretical (de Monog. 2). It must however be owned that the Neocæsarean Council of 314 had gone so far as to impose a slight penance on digamists (can. 7; cp. Basil, Epist. 188. 4). The question was afterwards raised whether the apostle's words, μιᾶς γυναικὸς ἄνδρα (1 Tim. iii. 2), which were understood to make digamy, i.e. successive second marriage, a disqualification for the presbyterate, applied to one who had lost his first wife before his own baptism: and Jerome argued that such a man might be ordained (Epist. 692). The 17th Apostolic canon had explained the disqualification as pertaining to him who had been involved in two marriages after his baptism.' (2) The Council requires the ex-Novatian to communicate with those who had lapsed in the persecution. The term παραπεπτωκόσιν, thus used, reminds us of Heb. vi. 5: it is also similarly used by Dionysius of Alexandria (ap. Euseb. vi. 42). The lapsed were to do penance for a prescribed period (compare Cyprian, Epist. 55. 4, etc. and the canons of Peter of Alexandria, who had suffered martyrdom fourteen years before the Council, Routh, Rell. Sac. iv. 26).

The Council then orders that 'wherever in cities or villages no other persons are found to have been ordained (πάντες should apparently be corrected to πάντῃ, anywhere) ex-Novatians who are thus found in the clerical order shall continue in the same rank as that which they held in their former communion. Σχήματι means external position or status (see on c. 19). On the second of the two views stated above, reordination must be presumed (see the Isidorian and the Antiquissima). 'But if in the place where they come over to the Church there is a Catholic bishop or presbyter' (Hefele suggests that perhaps we should read που for τοῦ), 'it is clear that the bishop of the Church must hold the dignity of *the* bishop, while he who was styled a bishop among the so-called Cathari must have the rank of a presbyter, unless the bishop shall think good to allow him the honorary title (of bishop). If the bishop is not pleased to do so, he must find him a position as chorepiscopus or as presbyter, in order that he may appear to have a real clerical status. This provision is to prevent the anomaly of there being two bishops in one city.'

The 'honorary rank of bishop,' implying the episcopal character without episcopal jurisdiction, was conceded by this

Council to Meletius (Soc. i. 9) and by the Council of Ephesus to an ex-metropolitan named Eustathius, who had weakly resigned his see (Mansi, iv. 1476).

This concluding passage of the canon raises the question of the functions of the Chorepiscopi or 'rural bishops.' It is probable that at this period the name was given to men who had really received the episcopal character, but who were by the terms of their appointment obliged to act under restrictions, and as deputies, in the rural districts, of the bishops of cities. This view, which is that of Beveridge (Annotat. p. 176), Bingham (ii. 14. 2), Routh (Rell. Sac. iv. 156, 204), Newman (note in Transl. Fleury, vol. i. p. 59), and Bishop Wordsworth (Church Hist. p. 46), is not seriously affected by the comparison drawn in the 13th Neocæsarean canon between Chorepiscopi and the seventy disciples of Luke x. 1; it is supported by the apparent meaning of 'bishops of neighbouring country districts' as distinct from 'bishops of cities' in the synodal letter of the first Council of Antioch (Euseb. vii. 30, see Valesius), and more distinctly by the 10th canon of the second or Dedication Council of Antioch, which forbids chorepiscopi, 'although they have received episcopal χειροθεσίαν' (see Zonaras), to ordain deacons or priests without leave from the actual bishop of the city (while the 13th Ancyrene canon seems to mean that chorepiscopi ought not even in the country to ordain priests and deacons, 'and at any rate not to ordain priests for the city without the leave of the bishop in each diocese,' reading ἑκάστῃ for ἑτέρᾳ); by Athanasius' statement that the district of Mareotis had never had either 'bishop or chorepiscopus, but only presbyters in charge of its villages' (Apol. c. Ari. 85); by the curious passage in which Gregory Nazianzen complains that Basil, although, after that division of the province of Cappadocia which took away from the metropolitan see of Cæsarea most of its suffragan bishoprics, he still retained fifty chorepiscopi, 'yet, as if these were too few for him,' had erected a new suffragan see at Sasima, and constrained him, Gregory, to accept it (Carm. de Vita sua, 447); and by one of Basil's own letters to these same chorepiscopi, in which, although he restrains the discretion allowed to their class in the Antiochene canon by requiring them to consult him before admitting men even to minor orders, he clearly distinguishes them from presbyters (Epist. 54). It is observable that fifteen chorepiscopi, of whom five were from Cappadocia, signed the Nicene decrees. The 57th canon of the Laodicene Council (held some time in the middle of the fourth century) ordering that 'in villages and country districts no bishops shall thereafter be appointed, but only visitors (περιοδευταί), and that the bishops already appointed shall not act without consent of the bishops of the city, even as the priests may not act without it,'—has been interpreted in different ways. Suicer, who considers chorepiscopi to have been merely presbyters deputed to act for the bishop, thinks that it was resolved to prevent them from being confounded with bishops, and therefore to change their name. But the canon does not say that they are to be called visitors, any more than that no 'other class of bishops' than visitors are to be appointed in villages (Hatch's Bamp. Lect. p. 194), but simply that visitors are to be substituted for them. It certainly appears to regard them as really bishops, although restricted in their action by the terms of their appointment: and its motive, so to speak, is akin to that of the 6th Sardican canon, which forbids the appointment of a bishop 'in vico aliquo, aut in modica civitate,' where a single presbyter is sufficient, lest the episcopal title and dignity should be cheapened. The Laodicene decree was not universally observed even in Asia Minor: we hear of Timotheus, a Cappadocian chorepiscopus, in the beginning of the fifth century, who ordained Elpidius as priest for a monastery (Palladius, Hist. Lausiac. 106); and Cæsarius, 'chorepiscopus of the city of Arca,' appears among the bishops who signed the deposition of Nestorius (Mansi, iv. 1217). But generally the title became a designation of priests who were somewhat analogous to our rural deans, or the 'vicarii foranei' of the diocese of Milan; for Gregory Nazianzen in 382 speaks of the chorepiscopus Eulalius as his fellow-presbyter (Epist. 152). Theodoret, in 449, employs as his messenger to Leo the Great two presbyters whom he calls chorepiscopi (Epist. 113); in the Arabic canons translated by Turrianus, the chorepiscopus, while competent to ordain young clerics, takes rank below the archdeacon (whereas in Echellensis' version he is to 'appoint priests,' not, as in the former, to 'procure' their ordination, Mansi, ii. 970, 999); and the chorepiscopi whom the 2nd Nicene Council describes as having the duty of ordaining readers with the bishop's permission (c. 24) were probably not bishops (Robertson, Hist. Ch. ii. 429). Towards the close of the twelfth century, Balsamon thus curtly ends his note on the 13th Ancyrene canon: 'I had thought of writing something on this; but since the order of chorepiscopi has long become utterly obsolete, I have no mind to lose my labour.' In the West the first genuine mention of chorepiscopi is in the 3rd canon of the Gallican Council of Riez (A.D. 439), which, expressly referring to this Nicene canon, allows the deposed bishop Armentarius to have the bare name of a chorepiscopus, but without the right to ordain even the lowest cleric, nor to offer the Eucharist in the city even in the bishop's absence (contrast Neocæsarean canon 14). The Western chorepiscopi appear to have acted without due subordination to their diocesans, and thus aroused, a strong feeling of hostility' (see Dict. Chr. Antiq. i. 354); we find the reality of their episcopal character denied, apparently, by Gallican synods of the ninth century, but admitted virtually by Isidore of Seville (de Eccl. Off. ii. 6), and explicitly by Nicolas I. (Append. i. Epist. 19. 1). The statement that Leo IV., when consulted by Charles the Great, declared that they were not bishops, and ought to be condemned and exiled,—which Baluze included in his edition of the Capitularies, and assigned to 803,—is rejected as spurious by Pertz (Mon. Germ. Hist. Legum, ii. app. p. 118, cp. ib. p. 128). But the order gradually died out: according to Gervase (Act. Pontif. Cantuar. in Hist. Angl. Scriptores Decem, 1650) a line of bishops of St. Martin's at Canterbury, who were 'as chorepiscopi to the archbishops, came to an end after Lanfranc's accession;'

but here, obviously, the name is used for 'episcoporum urbicorum vicarii' rather than 'episcopi rurales' (Routh, Rell. Sac. iv. 156); while in some continental dioceses it became attached to archdeacons or cathedral dignitaries.

This arrangement as to an ex-Novatian bishop is recommended as preventing an anomaly: 'that there may not be two bishops in one city,' (words which Rufinus places by themselves, as if they formed a distinct canon). The theory of the episcopate implied that each diocesan church should have one and only one chief pastor, representing within its area the One invisible and Supreme Bishop. Cornelius of Rome had sarcastically described 'the rigorist disciplinarian Novatian as not aware that there ought to be but one bishop in a Catholic Church' (Euseb. vi. 43); and so Cyprian writes to him that schisms arise from forgetting 'that there is one bishop (sacerdos) at a time in a church' (Epist. 59. 7; cp. ib. 61. 2; 66. 5). The principle is not so much enforced as assumed by the Council. The most vivid expression of it was the reply of the Roman Church people, in 357, to Constantius' proposal of a joint episcopate: 'One God, one Christ, one bishop!' (Theodoret, ii. 17). Sometimes, for peace' sake, proposals were made which involved a temporary departure from it, as when Meletius is said to have suggested to his rival Paulinus that they should place the Gospels on the throne, and sit on each side of it as joint-pastors of an united flock (Theod. v. 3; and again in the 'Conference of Carthage,' Collat. Carthag. c. 16, Mansi, iv. 62; see Bingham, ii. 13. 2). But on the whole the maxim was treated as fundamental: it was urged by Chrysostom against the Novatian bishop Sisinnius (Soc. vi. 22); and Augustine was so fearful of infringing it, that he regarded this Nicene canon as a bar to the appointment of an episcopal coadjutor (Epist. 213). This scruple, indeed, was needless; for by 'two bishops' the Council clearly meant two diocesans (see Bingham, ii. 13. 4). The bishop of London at present has, indeed, no coadjutor, but a 'suffragan' bishop, and an archdeacon who is a 'vacant' bishop. This does not violate the ancient principle: for he remains sole bishop 'of' his church.

Canon IX.

This canon brings us back to one of the topics of Canon 2. It supposes (1) the case of persons who 'have been promoted to the presbyterate' without that due 'scrutiny' of their conduct which is required implicitly by 1 Tim. v. 22 (assuming that text to refer to ordination), expressly by ib. iii. 2 and Tit. i. 7, and was always insisted on by the ancient Church. 'Præsident probati quique seniores,' says Tertullian (Apol. 39); and not very long after his time the custom was so much a matter of notoriety that Alexander Severus avowedly imitated it by causing the names of men designated for high provincial office to be published, and 'exhorting the people ut *si quis* quid haberet criminis, probaret manifestis rebus,' Lamprid. 45 (compare the bishop's addresses to the people in our Ordinal). Cyprian, somewhat later, tells his clergy and laity that it is his custom before holding an ordination 'to consult them, et mores et merita singulorum communi consilio ponderare' (Ep. 38. 1), and again that men ought to be 'selected ad sacerdotium Dei plena diligentia et exploratione sincera' (Ep. 67. 2). Similarly the Council of Elvira (c. 24) orders that persons baptized abroad be not ordained 'in another province, because their lives can be but little known.' The 61st Apostolic canon directs that no Christian shall be ordained against whom a charge of 'fornication or adultery, or any other forbidden action,' has been made good. So, after the Nicene times, the Sardican Council observes, as a recommendation of a graduated promotion to the episcopate, that by means of it 'potest probari qua fide sit, quave modestia (the Greek has ἡ τῶν τρόπων καλοκἀγαθία), gravitate, et verecundia' (can. 10). Basil rebukes his chorepiscopi for neglecting due inquiry before admitting to the subdiaconate (Ep. 54); Chrysostom says, 'the ordainer must first πολλὴν ποιεῖσθαι τὴν ἔρευναν' (de Sacerd. iv. 2), and more fully in his comment on 1 Tim. v. 22, ' "Not quickly" means, not after one, or two, or even three testings, but after frequent investigation and strict examination, for the matter is not without risk.' Theophilus of Alexandria directs that the bishop before ordaining a man shall ask whether the people can bear witness in his favour (Mansi, iii. 1257), and the Council of Hippo decrees that no one be ordained unless he is approved 'by the bishop's examination or the people's testimony' (ib. iii. 922). Such testimony was given (as in the case of bishops, Euseb. vi. 29, etc.) by an acclamation, 'He is worthy,' which in the Eastern Ordinal is still uttered by the choir.

(2) The second case supposed by this canon is that of candidates who, when thus examined as to their conduct, 'confess sins' which ought to disqualify them, and yet are ordained by too indulgent bishops, who, 'being induced to act contrary to rule,' i.e. moved by their entreaty or by the urgency of friends, 'lay hands upon them.' Among the sins alluded to, those of unchastity would doubtless be prominent: (compare the 9th and 10th canons of Neocæsarea); but the Arabic paraphrase strangely omits them, and mentions the marrying of two or of three wives or of a divorced woman,—together with acts of idolatry or divination (Mansi, ii. 714).

It is in reference to both of these cases that the canon says, 'Such persons the rule does not admit of' (Philo and Evarestus add, 'but rejects'), 'for it is only irreproachable characters (on τὸ ἀνεπίληπτον compare c. 19, and see 1 Tim. iii. 2, v. 7) that the Catholic Church vindicates,' and will uphold in her ministry. The person thus proved to be not irreproachable 'is deposed,' says Balsamon, a phrase which, of course, can only apply properly to the second case, but may be applied popularly to the first, as in c. 19.

CANON X.

This is the first of five canons relating to the penitential discipline.

It was a rule that 'lapsed' persons were not to be ordained: as Cyprian expressed it, 'although admitted to penance, they must be kept out of all clerical ordination and all sacerdotal dignity' (Epist. 67. 6), just as clerics who 'for fear of man' denied Christ were not only deposed but excommunicated (Apost. can. 62, with Balsamon's note). 'How,' asks Zonaras, 'can he be a priest, who is not thought worthy of the sacraments throughout life, until he is dying?' Even the Arians could not venture to ordain the 'sophist' Asterius, because he had 'sacrificed' during a persecution (Athan. de Synod. 18). So here the Council contemplates the case of such persons having been promoted to orders. Here προχειρίζομαι, which in the Council's letter (Soc. i. 9) apparently means 'to propose for ordination,' is used as in Mansi, vii. 345, and in the Eastern ordination formula, 'The Divine grace . . . promotes N. to this or that order.' The Council proceeds, 'Whether the ordainer acted in ignorance or with full knowledge of what he was about to do, this cannot prejudice the Church's rule: for such persons, when their disqualification is made known, are deposed.' This 'rule' cannot be Apost. can. 62, which deals with the case of a person lapsing after ordination. On this use of καθαιρεῖσθαι see c. 17 and Eph. 4, 5, 7: it occurs in thirty-seven of the Apostolic canons, and is equivalent to the phrases ' being made to cease from belonging to the clergy,' or 'from ministration' (Nic. 2, 18), and 'falling from their degree' (Eph. 2, 6: Chalc. 2, 10, 12, 18, 27). Bingham describes καθαίρεσις as a 'total and perpetual suspension of the power and authority committed to a clergyman at his ordination' (xvii. 1. 6). It is thus clearly distinguished from what is called the nullifying of an ordination (Nic. 16).

CANON XI.

The Council now passes to a kindred point. How are those persons to be treated who fell away (the word παραβάντων is illustrated by Athanasius' use of παραβάτης for a renegade, Encycl. 3) without that excuse which, as Cyprian so fully admits in a most vivid passage (de Lapsis, 13, compare St. Peter of Alexandria's 1st canon), the infliction of torture might be deemed to supply? For under the mild persecution of Licinius, who did not go so far as to proscribe Christianity (Mason's Persec. of Dioclet. p. 307), some Christians had consented to abjure their religion while they were in no 'peril' of life or limb, and had not undergone such confiscation of goods as had been resorted to in some cases by the 'extortioner,' who, as Eusebius puts it, 'seized upon any one's property as a windfall' (Vit. Const. i. 52). These men had, in short, suffered no 'pressure' of any kind: they were simply scared by the prospect, or probably, like the persons contemplated in the 6th canon of Ancyra, by the threat, of exile, of penal servitude, of loss of promotion in the civil or military service. To them, therefore, Cyprian's equitable judgment was inapplicable: they 'did not deserve indulgent treatment' (see on can. 5); yet 'the Council resolved to deal kindly' with them, on the supposition that they were 'genuinely sorry' (μεταμελεῖσθαι is here equivalent to μετανοεῖν, as in Chalc. 7) for weakness which had brought them so exceptionally low; compare St. Peter of Alexandria on those who 'deserted without having suffered anything, but now are come to repentance' (Routh, Rell. Sac. iv. 25). The contrition, says Zonaras, must be 'real, not affected,—fervent, thoroughly earnest.' And now we have before us the classification of penitents, as it had by that time established itself in the Church (see Bingham, xviii. 1. 4–6). We shall best understand it by placing ourselves, in imagination, within the precincts of a Christian basilica of the period. (1) In front of the 'proaulion,' propylæon, or vestibule, we see on each side of the gateway disconsolate 'Mourners' or 'weepers,' προσκλαίοντες, 'lugentes,' who were rather 'candidates for penance,' as Beveridge strikingly expresses it, than penitents in the technical sense, and so are not mentioned in this canon. St. Basil describes them as weeping beside the church gate (Epist. 199. 22; cp. ib. 217. 56, a passage briefly describing the various classes, and ib. 217. 75) and entreating those who passed in to pray for them, that they might be allowed to enter the church as penitents; and Socrates helps us to associate them with the story of the miserable time-serving sophist Ecebolius (iii. 13) who, having apostatized under Julian, repented under Jovian, and prostrated himself at the gate of the cathedral of Constantinople, crying out, 'Tread me underfoot! I am the salt that has lost its savour.' But the custom was as old as the time of Tertullian (de Pœnit. 9), and Zephyrinus (Euseb. v. 28). (2) We go on into the 'narthex' or pronaos (see Neale, Introd. Hist. East. Ch. i. 207); and passing by the two classes of catechumens, and the 'possessed' or energumens, who, according to Beveridge, were the persons called χειμαζόμενοι, we come to the first class of penitents proper, who, like the lower class of catechumens at this time, were called Hearers, ἀκροώμενοι (Ancyr. 4, etc.; Basil. Epist. 99. 4, 217. 75, etc.). (Possibly the change of the junior catechumens' designation, referred to above, was designed to prevent this verbal confusion.) (3) Passing through the 'royal gates' (cf. Neale, Introd. East. Ch. i. 196) into the 'naos,' regarded by Greek commentators as the church proper (so Beveridge in his 'Ichnographia'), we observe the second class of penitents called Kneelers, γονυκλίνοντες (a term also applied in Neocæs. 5 to the higher class of catechumens), ὑποπίπτοντες, '*succumbentes, substrati*.' Their status is described, in several Ancyran canons, and by St. Basil, as ὑπόπτωσις, and he once calls it specifically μετάνοια (Epist. 199. 22). It had been alluded to in 258 by St. Gregory of Neocæsarea, can. 8 (Routh, Rell. Sac. iii. 263). While they thus knelt with bowed heads, or prostrated themselves, the bishop was accustomed to offer a solemn prayer over them (see, e. g. the 'Clementine' form, in Hammond's Liturgies, p. 7), after which they were dismissed, and the 'Liturgy of the faithful' began. (4) Yet further on, and near the ambon or readers' desk, we should see those who, having completed the exercises of 'public confession' (ἐξομολόγησις, see Bingham, xviii. 3. 1) in the class of Kneelers, had ascended to the highest grade of penance, and were called συνιστάμενοι, or 'Consistentes,' as being allowed to 'stand with' the faithful (see below, on c. 20) throughout the Eucharistic service, but not to take part with them either in the presentation of offerings, principally bread and wine, which the celebrant used as, or from which he selected, the elements (Neale, i. 339: Hammond, p. xxxii: see St. Cyprian de Opere et Eleem. 15, Elviran can. 28, and the Liturgy of St. James, Hammond, p. 44, and ib. p. 308 on the existing Milanese use), or in the subsequent reception of the Eucharist. As Basil says, they were to 'refrain from participation of the Good Thing' (Epist. 188. 4; comp. ib. 217. 75; in 217. 57 he says 'the holy things'), attendance without communicating being thus the badge of a position below that of the faithful, as in the celebrated case of the 'Tall Brothers,' who, after withdrawing from Egypt, were treated by Chrysostom at Constantinople as temporarily under a cloud, in consequence of the displeasure of their own bishop Theophilus; and therefore, while permitted to 'join in the prayers,' that is, in all the prayers of the Liturgy, were debarred from 'communion in the mysteries' (Soc. vi. 9). These prayers (compare Apost. can. 10, τῇ προσευχῇ) were largely intercessory (see Hammond, p. 18, etc.). The absolute use of προσφορά (like δῶρον above, c. 5) for the Eucharistic offering is found in Apost. can. 9, Ancyr. 5–9, 16, Laodic. 58, Basil, Epist. 217. 56, etc.; see Julius in Athanasius, Apol. c. Ari. 28, 'How could προσφορὰν προκεῖσθαι when catechumens were present?' and compare Tertullian, 'quod confirmat oblatio' (ad Ux. ii. 9). See the kindred term θυσία in Apost. can. 3, 46.

The Nicene Council had some recent precedents for a graduated scale of penances, imposed as a test no less than as a penalty. The Council of Ancyra, for instance, had ordered those who had sacrificed to idols under pressure, but had afterwards 'looked cheerful' at the idol-feast,—to be Hearers one year, Kneelers three, and 'Consistentes' two, and then to come to 'the perfection' of Christian privilege in Holy

Communion; whereas those who had 'wept during the feast,' yet had eaten, were to be Kneelers three years,—if they had *not* eaten, two,—and then for another year, to communicate in prayers only;—and those who had brought and eaten their own victuals only 'were to be Kneelers two years,' and then admitted 'with or without the oblation,' according to the bishop's estimate of their general conduct. Those who had repeatedly sacrificed, though 'under force,' were to be Kneelers four years, and Consistentes two. Those who had actually forced, or been the occasion of forcing, their brethren to apostatize, were to be Hearers three years, Kneelers six, Consistentes one: 'their whole conduct' was also to be scrutinized. To come nearer the present point, those who had yielded to threats of exile or loss of property, and had not until recently given token of repentance, were to be Hearers until the next Easter, Kneelers three years, Consistentes two. With somewhat greater severity, the Nicene fathers direct the 'lapsed,' being baptized laymen or 'faithful,' whose case was before them, to stand among the Hearers for three years, to be Kneelers for seven, and then for two years to 'take part' (lit. communicate) 'with the people in the prayers' (of the Eucharistic service, but) 'apart from oblation,' as the Prisca says, 'sine Eucharistia' (compare Basil, 'without communion,' Epist. 217. 58). For οἱ πιστοί Beveridge reads ὡς πιστοί, which spoils the sense. The Vetus has 'baptizati.' On τρία ἔτη ποιήσουσιν see Acts xx. 3.

Canon XII.

This canon, which in the Prisca and the Isidorian version stands as part of canon 11, deals, like it, with cases which had arisen under the Eastern reign of Licinius, who having resolved to 'purge his army of all ardent Christians' (Mason, Persec. of Diocl. p. 308), ordered his Christian officers to sacrifice to the gods on pain of being cashiered (compare Euseb. H. E. x. 8; Vit. Con. i. 54). It is to be observed here that military life as such was not deemed unchristian. The case of Cornelius was borne in mind. 'We serve in your armies,' says Tertullian, Apol. 42 (although later, as a Montanist, he took a rigorist and fanatical view, de Cor. 11), and compare the fact which underlies the tale of the 'Thundering Legion,'—the presence of Christians in the army of Marcus Aurelius. It was the heathenish adjuncts to their calling which often brought Christian soldiers to a stand (see Routh, Scr. Opusc. i. 410), as when Marinus' succession to a centurionship was challenged on the ground that he could not sacrifice to the gods (Euseb. vii. 15). Sometimes, indeed, individual Christians thought like Maximilian in the Martyrology, who absolutely refused to enlist, and, on being told by the proconsul that there were Christian soldiers in the imperial service, answered, 'Ipsi sciunt quod ipsis expediat' (Ruinart, Act. Sinc. p. 341). But, says Bingham (xi. 5. 10), 'the ancient canons did not condemn the military life as a vocation simply unlawful . . . . I believe there is no instance of any man being refused baptism merely because he was a soldier, unless some unlawful circumstance, such as idolatry, or the like, made the vocation sinful.' After the victory of Constantine in the West, the Council of Arles excommunicated those who in time of peace 'threw away their arms' (can. 2). In the case before us, some Christian officers had at first stood firm under the trial imposed on them by Licinius. They had been 'called by grace' to an act of self-sacrifice (the phrase is one which St. Augustine might have used); and had shown 'their eagerness at the outset' ('primum suum ardorem,' Dionysius; Philo and Evarestus more laxly, 'primordia bona;' compare τὴν ἀγάπην σου τὴν πρώτην, Rev. ii. 4). Observe here how beautifully the ideas of grace and free will are harmonized. These men had responded to a Divine impulse: it might seem that they had committed themselves to a noble course: they had cast aside the 'belts' which were their badge of office (compare the cases of Valentinian and Valens, Soc. iii. 13, and of Benevolus throwing down his belt at the feet of Justina, Soz. vii. 13). They had done, in fact, just what Auxentius, one of Licinius' notaries, had done, when, according to the graphic anecdote of Philostorgius (Fragm. 5), his master bade him place a bunch of grapes before a statue of Bacchus in the palace-court; but their zeal, unlike his, proved to be too impulsive,—they reconsidered their position, and illustrated the maxim that in morals second thoughts are *not* best (Butler, Serm. 7), by making unworthy attempts,—in some cases by bribery,—to recover what they had worthily resigned. (Observe the Grecised Latinism βενεφικίοις, and compare the Latinisms of St. Mark, and others in Euseb. iii. 20, vi. 40, x. 5.) This the Council describes in proverbial language, probably borrowed from 2 Pet. ii. 22, but, it is needless to say, without intending to censure enlistment as such. (We may note, in passing, the absurd way in which the Arabic paraphrast of the canon drags in the monastic idea,—'whoever has ... sought to lead a monastic life, but afterwards, abandoning the service of God, has returned to the world, as a dog to its vomit,' Mansi, ii. 715. John Scholasticus takes a similar view. Even in the Vetus the title adopted is rather misleading, ' et iterum *ad sæculum* sunt conversi.') They now desired to be received to penance: accordingly, they were ordered to spend three years as Hearers, during which time 'their purpose, and the nature (εἶδος) of their repentance' were to be carefully 'examined.' Again we see the earnest resolution of the Council to make discipline a moral reality, and to prevent it from being turned into a formal routine; to secure, as Rufinus' abridgment expresses it, a repentance 'fructuosam et attentam.' If the penitents were found to have 'manifested their conversion by deeds, and not in outward show (σχήματι), by awe, and tears, and patience, and good works' (such, for instance, Zonaras comments, as almsgiving according to ability), 'it would be then reasonable to admit them to a participation in the prayers,' to the position of Consistentes, 'with permission also to the bishop to come to a yet more indulgent resolution concerning them,' by admitting them to full communion. This discretionary power of the bishop to dispense with part of a penance-time is recognised in the 5th canon of Ancyra and the 16th of Chalcedon, and mentioned by Basil, Epist. 217. c. 74. It was the basis of 'indulgences' in their original form (Bingham, xviii. 4. 9). But it was too possible that some at least of these 'lapsi' might take the whole affair lightly, 'with indifference,' ἀδιαφόρως—not seriously enough, as Hervetus renders,—just as if, in common parlance, it did not signify: the 4th Ancyrene canon speaks of lapsi who partook of the idol-feast ἀδιαφόρως, as if it involved them in no sin (see below on Eph. 5, Chalc. 4). It was possible that they might 'deem' the outward form of 'entering the church' to stand in the narthex among the Hearers (here, as in c. 8, 19, σχῆμα denotes an external visible fact) sufficient to entitle them to the character of converted penitents, while their conduct out of church was utterly lacking in seriousness and self-humiliation. In that case there could be no question of shortening their penance-time, for they were not in a state to benefit by indulgence; it would be, as the Roman presbyters wrote to Cyprian, and as he himself wrote to his own church, a 'mere covering over of the wound' (Epist. 30. 3), 'an injury' rather than 'a kindness' (de Lapsis, 16); they must therefore 'by all means' go through ten years as Kneelers, before they can become Consistentes. The reading here followed, τὸ σχῆμα τοῦ εἰσιέναι, is on all accounts preferable. It was the one known to Philo and Evarestus, who render, 'et ingressum sibi sufficere arbitrati sunt,'—to Gelasius of Cyzicus, to Dionysius, who renders, 'aditum introeundi.' to the authors of other Latin versions—the Isidorian version, the Prisca, and the Vetus—to the author of the Arabic version, 'et simulationem ingrediendi,' and to Zonaras, who describes the careless offender as content with being allowed to come into the church at all, and 'not grieved that he is stationed below the ambon, and goes out with the catechumens.' The reading which inserts μή before εἰσιέναι puts an obvious strain on the phrase 'entering into the church,' as if it meant, 'deemed it enough to observe the prohibition of attending the Liturgy.' It seems to have puzzled the writer of the 'Antiquissima Interpretatio,' who tries to make sense of it by taking μή as = 'seldom,'—'vel negligentius se tractaverint, *raro* apparentes in domo Dei.'

Canon XIII.

This is a deeply interesting canon: it answers the question, What is to be the treatment of persons who, before completing their penance, are attacked by mortal illness? 'Concerning those who are departing' (lit. going forth out of this life, ἐξοδευόντων,—the phrase, perhaps, was suggested by 2 Peter i. 15), 'the old and regular law shall still as heretofore be observed, to the effect that if any one is departing, he should not be deprived of the last and most necessary provision for his journey.' Here the 'any one' must be construed in connection with the preceding canons relating to cases of penance. It is to 'any one' of such persons that the canon directly refers. Suppose that such a penitent's life is despaired of; that he is, to all appearance, dying before he has gone through the prescribed period of discipline which would regularly entitle him to the full privileges of the faithful; what is to be done for him? The answer clearly means, 'let him have a final Communion;' as Rufinus says with significant terseness, '*Vacuum* nullum debere dimitti; si quis sane, accepta communione, supervixerit;' or as Gregory of Nyssa, with solemn pathos, 'The benevolence of the fathers ordained that a person in such circumstances should not be sent forth on that last long journey devoid of provision for the way, but after he had received the consecrated things' (Ep. canon. ad Letoium, Op. ii. p. 121). Such a comment, the pith of which Balsamon gives in his phrase, 'the excellent viaticum of the holy reception,' and which agrees with the rendering of Philo and Evarestus, 'novissimo juvamine . . . . communione sumpta,' and that of the Vetus, 'si quis . . communionem quaesierit, non eum tali viatico debere fraudari,' may suffice to dispose of the paradox that the 'viaticum' in question was absolution without the Eucharist. See too Elviran, c. 32. The word ἐφόδιον, which here responds, as it were, to ἐξοδεύοι, is used in LXX. Deut. xv.

14 for the supplies to be given to a Hebrew bondman set free in the year of release, and similarly in a temporal sense by Clement of Rome (Ep. Cor. 2) and Socrates (vii. 21, in the beautiful story of the charity of Acacius); but is also applied spiritually, (1) to means of salvation in general (Phileas in Euseb. viii. 10, and compare Basil, de Spir. Sanct. s. 66, Theodoret, H. E. iv. 5), includes good counsel (Athan. Vit. Anton. 3, ὥσπερ ἐφόδιόν τι, Basil, Epist. 57, ἐφόδια), or prayer (ib. Epist. 174), or the study of Scripture (Isidore of Pelusium, Epist. ii. 73), or a benediction (Theodoret, Hist. Relig. 12), and (2) to the sacraments in particular, as (1) baptism, which Basil describes as τὰ ἐφόδια (Hom. 13. 5), as Gregory Nazianzen uses ἐφοδιάζω for baptizing a dying person (Orat. 40. 11), and (2) more emphatically, as in this passage (perhaps with some reference to a spiritual application of 1 Kings xix. 8) to the Eucharist as received in the near prospect of death. So Paulinus, inaugurating, as it were, the Latin Church's technical use of the phrase for a last Communion, says that Ambrose, 'after receiving the Lord's Body, gave up the ghost, bonum viaticum secum ferens,' Vit. Ambr. 47. Gaudentius of Brescia, indeed, had already applied 'viaticum' to any Communion received amid the 'journey of life' (Serm. 2, addressed to the newly baptized, Collect. Patr. Brix. Eccl. p. 243): just as the Eastern Liturgy of St. Basil (Hammond, Liturgies, p. 126) and St. Mark's, enlarged from it (ib. p. 191), speak of devout communicants at an ordinary celebration as receiving the Eucharist εἰς ἐφόδιον ζωῆς αἰωνίου, as in the hymn of Thomas Aquinas—

> 'Ecce panis angelorum,
> Factus cibus viatorum.'

'But,' the canon proceeds, if the person in question, 'after having been despaired of, and received Communion (πάλιν in this clause seems a proleptic error of the copyist), should recover,' and 'again be found numbered among the living (on ἐξετασθῇ, cp. can. 1), let him rank with those who communicate in prayer only,' i.e. with the Consistentes, until he has completed his time. The text hardly bears out Balsamon's opinion that this refers only to those who had been co-standers before their illness: and Zonaras makes no such distinction. Rufinus alters the rule by saying, 'debere eum statuta tempora complere:' as Gregory of Nyssa (l. c.) says that he must 'await the appointed time' in his former 'rank,' and as Synesius, writing in 411 to Theophilus, says of such a case, 'Let him again be under the same penalty' (Epist. 67). On the other hand, Dionysius of Alexandria had ruled against 'binding' such a person 'again' (Ep. ad Basilidem, Routh, Rell. Sac. iii. 230); so that the Nicene canon represents a transitional view. The first Council of Orange, in 441, refers to this canon, saying that for penitents in these circumstances Communion suffices 'sine reconciliatoria manus impositione,' i.e. without formal absolution, 'according to the definitions of the fathers, who appropriately called such a Communion a viaticum: but if the persons should survive, they ought to stand in the rank of penitents, and, after exhibiting necessary fruits of repentance, to receive Communion in the regular way (legitimam), with imposition of the hand' (Mansi, vi. 436).

But the last clause of the canon, which Rufinus omits, covers a wider ground. 'But generally also, in the case of every person whatsoever at the point of death, who asks to receive the Eucharist, let the bishop, after testing his fitness to receive it, impart the oblation.' It is no longer a question of persons who have gone through part of their penance before they were stricken down. The Council takes pains to include 'every dying person whatsoever,' who asks for Communion in a right spirit, within the scope of this direction; ('generaliter autem homini morituro,' Philo and Evarestus; 'omnino autem cuilibet morituro,' Prisca; and similarly Dionysius). It opens wide the gate, so to speak, not only to those who, like the aged Serapion at Alexandria, had often since their fall expressed desire to do penance (Euseb. vi. 44), but to those who before their mortal illness had given no sign of contrition. Herein it seems to be enlarging the bounds of indulgence: this last clause does not appeal to any ancient law. Dionysius of

Alexandria, indeed, had anticipated it when he gave orders that all dying persons 'who asked for remission' (including Communion, Beveridge, Annot. p. 79), 'and especially if they had begged for it before' (he does not say 'provided that' they had done so) should receive it (Euseb. l. c.), and so the Roman presbyters in 250 had said that any lapsi 'who began to be ill, and showed penitence, and desired Communion, ought certainly to be succoured' (Cypr. Epist. 8. 3): but in some churches it seems that, as Innocent I. said, probably with this canon in his mind, the 'earlier usage,' in times of persecution, had refused Communion, even 'in extremis,' to Christians who had led profligate lives, and never asked for penance or Communion until they were dying: whereas later custom, originating in the cessation of persecution, and suggested by anti-Novatian feeling, granted Communion 'as a viaticum' to such persons when 'setting forth on their journey,' in the hope that they were 'vel in supremis suis pœnitentes' (Epist. 3. 2). Cyprian held that apostates who had never shown repentance during health were not to receive Communion in their last moments, because their request for it might be ascribed to fear rather than to contrition (Epist. 55. 19). The rigorous Council of Elvira had put nineteen cases under this same ban, in such phrases as 'nec in finem habere communionem.' The Council of Ancyra, referring to one of these cases, treated it 'somewhat more 'indulgently' (c. 21). The Council of Arles has two canons on the subject: false accusers, not only, as the 75th Elviran canon had said, of clergymen, but of their 'brethren,' are not to communicate 'usque ad exitum' (c. 14), and apostates such as Cyprian had described are not to communicate unless they recover and show real repentance (c. 22). Beveridge would understand the phrase 'usque ad exitum' as allowing communion *at* the last hour (Annotat. p. 79); but this is to strain it, and we must add that the severity of Arles in c. 22 gives greater significance to the tenderness of Nicæa. Observe that the Eucharist as imparted is here called 'the oblation;' so in the 16th Ancyrene canon, 'Let them obtain τῆς προσφορᾶς' is equivalent to 'Let them obtain τῆς κοινωνίας,' and St. Basil, 'He shall not partake προσφορᾶς ... He shall be debarred τῆς κοινωνίας' (Epist. 217. 56, 61). Philo and Evarestus, it may be added, paraphrase κοινωνίας τυχών above, by adding 'et oblatione percepta.' The Liturgies similarly regard the elements as retaining after consecration their oblatory character, as the 'Clementine' says, with significant simplicity, 'Let the bishop give' (i.e. administer) 'the oblation,' and in this Liturgy and those of SS. James and Chrysostom a verbal oblation is repeated after the invocation of the Holy Spirit (Hammond, pp. 18, 43, 113); see also the Armenian (ib. p. 157), and Ethiopic (ib. p. 259), and Cyril's Catechetical Lectures, 23. 6.

Canon XIV.

This is the last of the penitential canons of the Council. It provides that lapsed Catechumens of the higher class, here called Catechumens distinctively, whereas afterwards they were called φωτιζόμενοι or Competentes, the distinctive use of Catechumens being appropriated to the lower class, shall go back for three years into that lower class, now called 'Hearers,' and then be again allowed to 'pray with the Catechumens,'—to hear the prayer said over them to the effect that He 'who had appointed the spiritual regeneration through Christ would look upon them, and prepare them to become worthy of the true adoption.' (Prayer for φωτιζόμενοι in 'Clementine' Liturgy, Apost. Constit. viii. 8: see Hammond's Liturgies, p. 6: compare the briefer preceding prayer in this Liturgy for the lower class called 'Catechumens.') See above on can. 2.

Canon XV.

We now come to a series of canons dealing with practical abuses among ecclesiastics; and first to one which aims at correcting the disorders caused by the removal of bishops and clerics from one city to another, especially by the 'translation' of bishops. It is evident that the sunshine of the new Constantinian era had produced a crop of secularity within the Church. Many of its ministers had become 'conformed to this world:' the sees in great towns had become lures to ecclesiastical ambition: a restless and self-seeking temper had impelled bishops and even priests, conscious of popular talents and eager for a wider sphere of influence—in the interest, as they would say, of the faith and of the Church—to make themselves centres of partisan activity. Episcopal vacancies were too often occasions for cabal in favour of this or that prelate who would regard translation as promotion. Thus Eusebius, bishop of Berytus, had procured the see of Nicomedia, and with it a high position in the imperial court: and the Council was not the less likely to bear this in mind after its recent experience of his Arianizing tenacity. Its language on the general subject, compared with that of the Council of Arles, shows that the evil had grown rapidly. The Western synod had briefly resolved, 'that presbyters or deacons who transfer themselves to other places be deposed' (c. 21), and generally that all 'ministers should continue in the places where they were ordained' (c. 2). The General Council says, 'Because of the great disturbance and the factions that have arisen, it is thought good that the custom which has been found to exist, contrary to the rule, in some places, be altogether suppressed, so that neither bishop nor presbyter nor deacon shall remove from city to city. If after the decree (ὅρον) of the holy and great Council any (bishop) shall attempt any such thing, or shall lend himself to such a transaction, the arrangement shall be totally annulled' ('cassabitur hujusmodi machinatio,' Philo and Evarestus; 'vacuabitur praesumentis inceptum,' Vetus), 'and the person transferred shall be restored to the church of which he was ordained the bishop or the presbyter.' Observe this use of ὅρος, as in c. 17, 18, 19, Chalc. 4, 14, Ancyr. 19, 23 for a determination or decree of a Council. (Compare ὅρως, Soc. i. 38, ὁρισμῷ for the decision as to Easter, ib. i. 10, and ὤρυσαν, ib. ii. 8.) Ὅρους is used by Athanasius (de Synod. 13) for the Nicene doctrinal 'definitions;' so ὅρος for the Nicene Creed, by Cyril of Alexandria (Explan. Cap. 1), and Sozomen (vi. 23, compare ὅρον τῆς πίστεως, Soc. ii. 20); and again, for the doctrinal formulary of Chalcedon. Like κανών, it represents the idea of definiteness and fixedness. Is then this fixed 'determination' to be understood as absolutely forbidding all translation? The 14th Apostolic canon, which perhaps is post-Nicene, expressly recognises an exception: 'when, in the judgment of many bishops, some greater benefit could be secured to the people of the place' whither the person would be transferred: for instance, when the bishop of an obscure town had a gift of preaching which would tell powerfully on the society of a metropolis. This exception would have been allowed by the Nicene bishops, for the orthodox and learned Eustathius of Antioch had recently been translated from Berœa: and Socrates enumerates several approved cases of translation, together with a few that are irrelevant (vii. 36). The chief ante-Nicene precedent was the settlement of Alexander at Jerusalem (Euseb. vi. 11). What the Council meant to strike at was obviously translation associated with worldly motives and tending to scandalous discord, as Rufinus boldly paraphrases, 'Ne de civitate inferiori ad majorem ecclesiam transire quis ambiat.' Such translation was common enough, in the subsequent years, among the Eusebian faction, as Julius of Rome observes in Athan. Apol. c. Ari. 24 (cp. ib. 6); but it is to the credit of Eusebius of Cæsarea that on the ground of this canon he refused to be translated to Antioch (Vit. Const. iii. 61). The Sardican Council, in its very first canon, remarked, with a touch of sarcasm, that no bishop had yet been found to aim at being transferred from a greater city to a lesser; inferred that the 'pernicious abuse' was indicative of a 'passionate' eagerness for more money, or an arrogant craving for more power; and went so far as to resolve that prelates thus offending 'should not even have lay communion,' a sentence so much sterner than the Nicene that Balsamon labours to make the two

Councils refer to two different cases,—the Nicene to that of a bishop removing his see from one place in his diocese to another, the Sardican to the invasion of a vacant church. This gloss refutes itself, and the increase of severity is accounted for by the increase of what the Sardican canon energetically denounces as 'corruptela funditus eradicanda.' It is the Antiochene Council of 341 which in its 16th canon speaks plainly of the case of a bishop without a see, whom it calls a 'vacant' bishop, usurping the see of a vacant church without authority of a complete synod. This case is distinct from that now in question, as to which Tillemont observes with austere terseness, that 'this disorder, though condemned, was still practised, because ambition, being the enemy of the Church, is not subject to its laws' (vi. 673). The Acacian Arians, in 360, found it convenient to put those laws in force against the Semi-Arian Dracontius, 'because he had removed from Galatia to Pergamos' (Soc. ii. 42): while one of their leaders, and one of the worst of the Arians, Eudoxius, imitated Eusebius of Nicomedia by holding in succession three bishoprics, that of Constantinople being the third. The case referred to by St. Basil in Epist. 227 is not properly one of translation: Euphronius, although he was to remove to Nicopolis, would retain the oversight of Colonia. At the second General Council this canon was quoted by the Egyptian and Macedonian bishops as against Gregory Nazianzen's right to that great bishopric: he speaks of them as 'turning up laws that had been long dead' (Carm. de Vit. sua, 1810): but a better answer lay in the fact that he had never taken real possession of the see of Sasima. In the less Arianized West the canon was better observed: Damasus of Rome, in his letter to Paulinus, evidently adopts its language (Theod. v. 11); and Leo repeats the old censure as to bishops 'despising the insignificance of their own cities,' etc. (Epist. 8). The prohibition includes within its scope presbyters and deacons: but it was found impracticable to confine every cleric rigidly, for life, to the sphere of his first ordination. However, Bishop Wilson, in his 'Sacra Privata' for Sunday, seems to deprecate any migration of a pastor from a familiar to an untried field. He himself, as a bishop, refused to leave the Isle of Man for Exeter: and Francis de Sales, in the preceding century, had declined to accept the coadjutorship, with right of succession, to the archbishopric of Paris.

Canon XVI.

This canon is closely linked to the preceding: but it relates not to bishops, but to presbyters and other clerics only, who 'recklessly, and without having the fear of God before their eyes, and without knowing,' i. e. considering, 'the rule of the Church' (which Rufinus expresses by the softer phrase, 'nulla existente causa probabili'), remove themselves from the church to which they belong. Compare Apost. can. 15, Antioch. 3, Chalc. 5. For the expression ἐν τῷ κανόνι ἐξεταζόμενοι, see above on c. 1. Such deserters are not to be received elsewhere, 'but, on the contrary, all possible pressure ought to be put upon them to return to their own dioceses'—for this is the sense of παροικίας. The ecclesiastical use of this word and its cognates must be traced to the Septuagintal use, which represents the idea of sojourning, living (so to speak) in the world, but not belonging to it, in that sense 'living beside it,' like a foreigner staying with the people of a country not his own. So in 1 Chron. xxix. 15, πάροικοι, παροικοῦντες, and in Ps. xxxviii. (our xxxix.) 12, 'I am πάροικος ἐν τῇ γῇ καὶ παρεπίδημος.' So in the New Testament we have πάροικον (Acts vii. 6), and παροικία (Acts xiii. 17), referring to the 'sojourning' of Israel in Egypt: παροικεῖς in Luke xxiv. 18 has the notion of 'lodging.' St. Peter calls human life a παροικία (1 Pet. i. 17), and adopts the Psalmist's words for all Christians (ii. 11), as if to say, 'Remember that your interest in this world is but transitory.' Thus to the earliest Christians this class of words represented the fact, then present in such vivid intensity to those who had given up all things for Christ, that although, in a spiritual sense, they were 'not πάροικοι, but members of God's household' (Eph. ii. 19), yet with respect to life in its secular aspects, 'it was not here that they had an abiding city' (Heb. xiii. 14); they were still 'in via,' not yet 'in patria' (cp. S. Aug. Serm. 256. 3). Such a thought may be embodied in the first words of the first sub-apostolic letter, 'The church of God, ἡ παροικοῦσα 'Ρώμην, to the church of God τῇ παροικούσῃ Κόρινθον,' Clem. Ep. Cor. 1 (see Bp. Lightfoot's note), and in the similar addresses in the letters of the church of Smyrna and of the churches of Vienne and Lyons (Euseb. iv. 15; v. 1), the former of which is also addressed not only 'to the church παροικούσῃ at Philomelium,' but 'πάσαις ταῖς παροικίαις of the holy Catholic Church in every place.' Gradually the idea of 'sojourning' would be merged in the sense of 'Christians' 'dwelling in a particular city or town.' The passages show that the word did not mean originally the church in a village or country district, dwelling near a city: Origen indeed speaks of churches as 'dwelling beside' the non-Christian populations (c. Cels. iii. 29, 30), but he is referring to the churches of towns. It is clear, from the frequent use of παροικία in Eusebius (e.g. i. 1; ii. 24; v. 23; vi. 8, 43; vii. 9), that he ordinarily understood by it what we should call a diocesan church, or a diocese; the same use appears in the Encyclical of Alexander of Alexandria, ap. Soc. i. 6, and in Athanasius' Apology against the Arians, 36, etc. (see Bingham, ix. 2. 1; Suicer, Thesaur. in v.; Sclater, Draught of the Primitive Church, p. 33). The Latin Church writers use the word in this sense, as Jerome, 'episcopum in cujus parochia' etc. (Ep. 109. 2), or as when Augustine says that Fussala 'ad parœciam Hipponensis ecclesiæ pertinebat' (Epist. 209. 2), and our own Bede, 300 years later, that the West-Saxon bishopric was divided 'in duas parochias,' and that Sussex for a time had 'belonged to the parochia of the church of Winchester' (v. 18). For other instances, see Haddan and Stubbs's Councils, ii. 330, iii. 239, 449, 522, 578; and Ducange in v. Yet, as the importance of particular Christian settlements or congregations within a diocese made itself felt, there would be a disposition to describe any one of them as 'the church dwelling' in that place, without prejudice to its dependence on the diocesan church as a whole; in a word, to anticipate our present use of *parish*. Eusebius in one passage would seem to use the word in this sense, when, after mentioning 'Alexandria and the rest of Egypt,' he says that Demetrius had 'received the episcopate τῶν αὐτόθι παροικιῶν' (vi. 2), unless we interpret this of primatial authority over subordinate sees. In the 'Clementine' Liturgy prayer is made for 'our bishop James καὶ τῶν παροικιῶν αὐτοῦ,' which is again repeated in regard to 'Clement' and 'Euodius.' And in the fifth century Theodoret could write to Leo the Great, just as a modern bishop might express himself, to the effect that his see of Cyrrhos had 800 παροικίας (Epist. 113): and see below, Chalc. 17. So in an African canon, 'presbyteri qui parochiæ præest' (Mansi, iii. 959): and in the 21st of the Council of Agde in 506, 'parochiæ' mean recognised country churches (ib. viii. 327), and so in Sidonius Apollinaris, Epist. vii. 6.

But to return to the canon. If the offending clerics refuse to return to their own dioceses, 'they ought to be ἀκοινωνήτους,' not excommunicated in the ordinary sense, but debarred from officiating with their brethren, as Balsamon and Zonaras explain. Compare Eph. 6; Chalc. 20, 23. And 'no bishop shall dare surreptitiously to get hold of a cleric who is duly registered among the clergy (ἐξεταζόμενος, see can. 1) as belonging to another bishop, and to ordain him in his own church without that other prelate's consent' (as the Vetus renders, 'fratre cujus fuerat non præbente consensum'). Here, undoubtedly, the Council had in mind the celebrated case of Origen's ordination in Palestine by the bishops of Cæsarea and Jerusalem, without permission from his own bishop Demetrius (Euseb. vi. 8). So at the 3rd Council of Carthage, bishop Epigonius complains that another bishop, Julian, has admitted a reader of his to the diaconate, against an old rule, now again confirmed, 'ut clericum alienum nullus sibi præripiat episcopus, præter ejus arbitrium cujus fuerit clericus;' and the Council decrees that the cleric in question shall be sent back (Mansi, iii. 888). Innocent I. directs that one bishop shall not ordain a cleric belonging to another unless the latter chooses to signify his consent (ib. iii. 1034). Ἄκυρος is rendered 'infirma' by Philo and Evarestus, and by the Vetus Interpretatio: 'irrita' by other Latin versions. Its force is illustrated by the provision in the 4th canon, that the κῦρος in the case of an episcopal appointment is to rest with the metropolitan. The order now before us is repeated by the Sardican Council (can. 15); and the Dedication Council of Antioch pronounces similarly as to ordinations performed by a stranger bishop in a city or district not under his authority, or appointments by him to cures outside his diocese (can. 22), the case treated in Apost. can. 36. The same council attaches 'invalidity' to a dying prelate's nomination of his successor (can. 23); and the 76th Apostolic canon does the like, in apparent expansion of the Antiochene rule. So the Council of Constantinople in its 4th canon 'invalidates the consecration of Maximus and all ordinations performed by him,' showing by the context that it regarded him as not a bishop, and persons ordained by him as not really ordained at all. Once more, the Council of Chalcedon treats ordination without a title as ἄκυρος, c. 6. The present Nicene canon, if we construe it literally, implies that if the injured bishop should afterwards resolve to promote the offending cleric, he would treat the former ordination as null, and ordain him *de novo*. On this the question arises, Did not the ancients treat some ministrations as invalid, which would afterwards have been treated as only irregular? Later theologians, for instance, would have said of the case before us, '"Quod fieri non debuit, factum valet:" ordination has really taken place: what is lacking is due mission. It is this which the man's rightful bishop has to supply, if he should think good: and until he supplies it, the presbyter illegitimately ordained has no ecclesiastical right to minister.' But, as Hefele observes on the canon of Constantinople, such a distinction did not occur to the Church of this period, which, indeed, had not fully worked out its ideas, or decisively harmonized its local traditions, on the more urgent question of the effect of heresy on the performance of the baptismal act. The state of its mind in regard to some applications of the ecclesiastical and sacramental principles was, so far, somewhat analogous to that of the Ante-Nicene mind as to the drift and contents of the doctrine of the Divine Sonship. But whereas, in the earlier centuries, an inevitable crudeness of thought had produced inadequacy of statement, in the fourth it led to what we may think an excessive stringency. Dreading and abhorring ecclesiastical disorder, the Fathers of the Council took the shortest way of suppressing it. If a bishop did an act involving a breach of discipline, their impulse was to say, 'It is invalid, we disown it utterly,—we esteem it as null.' It has been suggested that this facile cancelling of ordination implies the non-existence of a belief in any 'exceptional spiritual powers' as 'conferred' by the hands of the ordaining bishop (Hatch, Bamp. Lect. p. 133). It rather implies—as the voiding of marriages within the forbidden degrees would be admitted to imply—an exceeding anxiety on the part of the Church to preserve the reality from being confounded with the counterfeit, to vindicate the sanctity of a great ordinance by rejecting what was deemed not to fulfil its conditions. As to ministerial powers, the Church of the fourth century spoke its mind clearly enough in the habitual 'sacerdotalism' of its language, notably in the third book of St. Chrysostom's famous treatise 'On The Priesthood,' and in such a statement as Jerome's, 'Ecclesia non est quæ non habet sacerdotes' (adv. Lucif. 21). And when in the fifth century,—after St. Augustine had formulated the proposition that sacraments schismatically, and therefore 'illicitly,' administered, were realities, but their beneficial effects were suspended until the recipients came over to Church unity (c. Epist. Parmen. ii. s. 29, de Bapt. i. s. 18),—Leo the Great wrote to bishop Rusticus of Narbonne, that bishops unduly elected, 'having received their dignity amiss' ('male accepto honore'), were 'not to be reckoned among bishops,' and that no ordination of clerics by these 'pseudo-bishops' could be held 'rata' unless it were shown to have had the consent of the lawful diocesan, failing which it must be deemed 'vana' (Epist. 167.

1), we may reasonably infer that 'rata' is here used in the sense of 'regular,' and that 'vana' means 'such as can give to the persons thus ordained no right to officiate in the Church.' In the same light may be read the 10th canon of the Council which met at Tours a few days after Leo's death, 'ordinationes vero illicitas in irritum devocamus, nisi satisfactione quæ ad pacem pertinent componantur' (Mansi, vii. 946), as much as to say, 'Clerics unlawfully ordained shall have no status among our clergy, until they reconcile themselves to their legitimate superiors. Then, and not till then, will the Church own them as ministers of hers.' The Chalcedonian canon above quoted may be similarly understood.

Canon XVII.

Another form of clerical secularity had shown itself in the taking of excessive interest on loans. The mind of the Old Testament had been strongly expressed in such passages as Ps. xv. 5 (here quoted from the LXX), Exod. xx. 25, Ezek. xviii. 17, and especially in Nehemiah's exhortation to the rulers to 'leave off the exacting of usury from their brethren' (Neh. v. 7, 10). It must be remembered that interest, called τόκος and 'fenus,' as the *product* of the principal, was associated in early stages of society,—in Greece and Rome as well as in Palestine,—with the notion of undue profit extorted by a rich lender from a needy borrower (see Grote, Hist. Gr. ii. 311 ff.; Arnold, Hist. Rome, i. 282; Mommsen, Hist. R. i. 291). Hence Tacitus says, 'sane vetus urbi fenebre malum, et seditionum discordiarumque creberrima causa' (Ann. vi. 16), and Gibbon calls usury 'the inveterate grievance of the city, abolished by the clamours of the people, revived by their wants and idleness' (v. 314). Thus he who made gain out of his loans, whose 'foul usance' devoured 'the substance of the poor' (Macaulay, Lays of Anc. Rome, p. 125), was regarded as at once avaricious and oppressive: and this moral ground underlies the Biblical condemnation of 'interest.' Although the allusion in Matt. xxv. 27 might seem to sanction a certain amount of τόκος, the early Church adhered to the Hebrew maxims on this subject, which Cyprian recites as simply binding (Testim. iii. 48), and this the rather that even the 'legal and mildest interest' (Hefele) was $\frac{1}{100}$ of the principal, hence called ἑκατοστή or 'centesima,' i. e. 12 per cent. It was payable each month, at what Horace on that account calls the 'tristes Kalendæ' (Sat. i. 3. 87); and Beveridge quotes St. Ambrose, 'Veniunt Kalendæ, parit sors centesimam' (de Tobia, s. 42). This rate of interest was 'the legal' one under the emperors, until Justinian reduced it by half (see Dict. Antiq. p. 527). So it was that, in primitive times, any cleric who lent money on interest was deemed to exhibit a base 'covetousness' and an unchristian 'cruelty' (Bingham, vi. 2. 6). The mischief had existed in Cyprian's time; it is startling to find that among the demoralising results of that 'long peace of the Church' which ended with the Decian persecution was the eagerness shown by 'very many bishops, usuris multiplicantibus fenus augere' (de Lapsis, 6). One of the 'most ancient' of the 'Apostolic canons' (Hefele) had embodied the needful censure in the fewest possible words: 'a bishop, presbyter, or deacon, demanding interest from his debtors, must either desist or be deposed' (Ap. can. 44). The 20th canon of Elvira, not content with censuring clerical usurers, had menaced laymen who should 'persist in that iniquity' with 'expulsion from the Church:' its clause respecting clerics had been copied by the Council of Arles with a special reference to a 'divinely-given rule' (can. 12). The present canon begins by stating the fact that 'many who are registered on the canon or clerical order' (see on c. 1) are yet so 'led away by avarice and a base love of gain, in forgetfulness of the Psalmist's words, as to lend money and then exact,' as interest, 'the hundredth part' of the loan. Thereupon it ordains that any cleric who 'after this decision' (ὅρον, see on c. 15) 'should be proved to take interest by actual bargain' (ἐκ μεταχειρίσεως, which the Prisca renders 'ex hoc contractu'), 'or to transact the matter in any other way, or exact half as much again (of the loan), or (here is the most comprehensive clause of the ὅρος) 'resort to any other device whatever ('aliquod negotiationis,' says a Council of Arles in 452, copying this among other canons) for the sake of base gain, shall be deposed, and have his name struck off the canon.' The word ἡμιολίας, 'half as much again,' has been taken to mean the whole centesima and half of it, but Gothofred explains it of a 'less odious' kind of exaction than ἑκατοστάς, which some might therefore deem allowable, but which also is here forbidden, i.e. an 'increase' on advances of corn or other produce, sanctioned by a law made some two months before the Council (Cod. Theod. ii. 33. 1). He illustrates it by Jerome's words, 'Suppose in winter we give 10 modii, and at next harvest receive 15' (in Ezech. c. 18); and by Rufinus' reference to 'frumenti vel vini ampliationem.' Thus 'hemioliæ' means the amount lent and half as much again. By its allusion to 'any other device,' the Council means to bar out any evasions of its prohibitory enactment, whereby the phrase 'lending at interest' might be avoided (see Balsamon, and cp. Leo, Ep. 4. 4).

The Council might rebuke and menace, but the evil was too strong for legislation. The Laodicene Council, apparently, did not think it practical to say more than that 'persons in orders ought not to lend money, and take interest and what was called ἡμιολίας' (can. 4). Basil had to point out the twofold moral evil connected with it (Epist. 188. 14). Audæus referred to it as one of the scandals which justified his secession from the Church (Theod. iv. 10). Ambrose, in the work above cited, compares 'usuræ' to a viper's brood. Chrysostom uses the same illustration, and, while conscious that he is touching a sore point, exhorts Christians not to exact the ἑκατοστή which the poor debtor could so ill afford to pay. 'Do not,' he says, 'tell me of the exterior laws' as permitting it (in Matt. Hom. 56). Augustine says that one who takes usury is 'rebuked by the Church, and execrated by his brethren' (Serm. 86. 3). The 3rd Council of Carthage forbids any cleric who has lent anything to receive back more than his loan (can. 16). The

Council in Trullo renewed the penalty imposed at Nicæa (can. 10). It is well known that the old religious aversion to interest lingered long after modern habits had disconnected the practice with the temper of an extortioner: and the word had still a reproachful sound when Shakspere could make Shylock say of Antonio,

> 'He rails . . . . . .
> On me, my bargains, and my well-won thrift,
> Which he calls interest.'
> (*Merch. of Venice*, i. 3).

And as we know from the epitaph on John Combe, wrongly ascribed to Shakspere, 'Ten-in-the-hundred' was the old name of opprobrium 'for one who lent money' (Knight's Life of Shakspere).

Canon XVIII.

The last kind of clerical misconduct censured by the Council is of a very different kind. It is presumption on the part of deacons, showing itself in three forms of abuse. The Council of Arles, as we may observe, had already censured the deacons of cities for taking too much upon themselves, and derogating from the dignity of the presbyters (can. 18). But the Nicene canon gives us much more full information.

(1) 'In some places and cities the deacons give the Eucharist to the presbyters:' under what circumstances? The deacons in the time of Justin Martyr were wont to administer the Sacrament in both kinds to the communicants (Apol. i. 65, 67: compare the rubric in St. James's Liturgy, 'The deacons lift up the patens and the cups in order to administer to the people,' Hammond's Liturgies, p. 51). At a later time, it seems, they had the distinctive duty of administering the chalice (Cyprian, de Lapsis, 25: compare the 'Clementine' Liturgy, Hammond, p. 21). The Council of Ancyra refers to their function τὸν ἄρτον ἢ ποτή- ριον ἀναφέρειν (can. 2), which some (as Routh, Rell. Sacr. iv. 132) explain of their 'carrying the elements' for the communion

of the people: but the expression seems more appropriate to their 'bringing up' the bread and wine, contributed by the people, to the celebrant at the offertory (Apost. Const. viii. 12, as an Athanasian fragment says, 'You will see the Levites (deacons) φέροντας ἄρτους καὶ ποτήριον οἴνου, and placing them on the table,' Mai, Nov. Biblioth. Patrum, ii. 584). Later, an African canon, in the series wrongly ascribed to a '4th Council of Carthage,' allows deacons to administer 'the Eucharist of Christ's body even in the priest's presence, if ordered by him to do so' (Mansi, iii. 955). What is it which the present canon censures? Hefele reasonably suggests that when several priests were 'concelebrating' with the celebrant (a custom referred to by Evagrius, i. 13, and in a well-known story in Adamnan's Life of St. Columba, i. 44, and still retained in the Roman Ordinal) the attendant deacon took on himself to administer 'the Eucharist,' or, as it is afterwards called, 'the Body of Christ,' to such priests, who ought to have received it from the chief minister. This was contrary to traditional 'rule and usage,' and also to ecclesiastical propriety—'that those who have no authority to offer (the Eucharistic sacrifice) should give the Body of Christ to those who do so offer it.'

Several points here deserve notice: (*a*) the term προσφέρειν is used absolutely, 'to make the oblation.' No explanation was needed, for—as we have seen above in regard to can. 5, 13—the character of the Eucharist as an oblation was simply taken for granted throughout the Church. On this absolute use compare the 1st canon of Ancyra, whereby priests who lapsed in persecution, but afterwards became confessors, are still forbidden προσφέρειν ἢ ὁμιλεῖν,—the 9th and 13th canons of Neocaesarea, and Athanasius (Apol. c. Ari. 28), λειτουργεῖν ἢ προσφέρειν,— and a similar use of 'offero,' as in Tertullian (de Exhort. Cast. 7), 'et offers et tinguis,'—Cyprian (Epist. 17. 2), 'et offerre pro illis,'—Ambrose (Epist. 20. 4, 5), 'missam facere coepi ... Dum offero, etc.' So too the 15th and 19th canons of Arles. (*b*) The deacons had no authority to 'offer' or celebrate. The Council asserts this with full confidence, and argues from it. The Council of Arles had noticed the fact that in many places deacons took on themselves 'offerre' (having probably, as Hefele suggests, begun to do so in the recent persecution, when priests were often not at hand), and had declared that this ought by no means to be done, 'fieri minime debere' (c. 15). The wording is emphatic: it prepares us for the Nicene canon, and for the statement in Apost. Const. viii. 28, 'A deacon does not offer;' for the argument used on behalf of St. Athanasius, that Ischyras could not have celebrated the Eucharist,—and therefore no chalice could have been wrenched out of his hands by the archbishop's messenger Macarius,—because he was not a presbyter (Athan. Apol. c. Ari. 11, 28, 76): for St. Hilary's remark on the same case, that 'sacrificii opus sine presbytero esse non potuit' (Fragm. ii. 16); for Jerome's categorical assertion that a deacon cannot 'Eucharistiam conficere' (Dial. adv. Lucif. 21), and for his indignation at the arrogance of certain deacons who exalted themselves against those at whose prayer 'Christi corpus sanguisque conficitur' (Epist. 146. 1). In the Ancyran canon already referred to we may observe in passing that ἀναφέρειν cannot reasonably be taken to mean 'offering the Eucharist.' Had the Council meant this, it would have said προσφέρειν simply, as in can. 1. There is also a passage in which St. Ambrose dramatically represents St. Laurence as declaring himself to have received from his bishop Sixtus 'Dominici sanguinis consecrationem, consummandorum consortium sacramentorum' (de Offic. i. c. 41): but the context, in which Laurence is made to say to Sixtus, 'You had never been wont to offer the sacrifice sine ministro' (i.e. without his deacon to 'serve' him) suggests that by 'consecrationem' is here meant the benedictory administration of the chalice (referred to in the 25th Laodicene canon), whereby the assistant would share with the celebrant in the 'completion' of the mysteries (Bingham, ii. 20. 8). It may be added that when Rufinus, reading new matter into his text from the practice of his own time, makes this canon tell deacons that *they* ought not to distribute the Eucharist when presbyters are present, but must minister 'illis agentibus,' whereas, if no presbyter is present, 'tunc demum etiam ipsis licere dividere,' he does not say 'conficere,' and he must be understood as referring to the administration of a previously consecrated and 'reserved' Eucharist. (c) The Eucharist is called 'Christ's Body' with a simple absoluteness which involves the belief in a real and unique mystery. It is parallel language to that of the Liturgies, specially the 'Clementine,' in which the celebrant and deacon when administering say 'The Body of Christ,' and 'The Blood of Christ, the cup of life,' and the communicant responds, 'Amen,' probably quite a primeval form: or St. Mark's, 'The holy Body,' 'The precious Blood of our Lord and God and Saviour.' Here is implied what the canon asserts, that 'Christ's Body is given,' just as plainly as the 13th Neocæsarean or 25th Laodicene canon speaks of 'giving the bread;' so Basil, Epist. 199. 27, 'Nor let him distribute to others the Body of Christ.' In other words, the relation between the 'outward' and the 'inward parts' of the Sacrament was believed to be prior to actual reception: the communicant was expected, by an act of faith, to recognise what was given to him as being what the Church called it, and so to 'distinguish' it from ordinary food (1 Cor. xi. 29). Lastly (d), that which is imparted is called 'the Eucharist,' which is elsewhere identified with the 'oblation,'—see on can. 13. Dionysius, in his rendering of this canon, twice paraphrases the Eucharist by a phrase which had been used by Philo and Evarestus, 'gratiam sacræ communionis' ('gratiam' being used for 'gift'), and once by 'sacra oblata.'

(2) The second abuse was, that in some instances deacons have presumed to 'touch the Eucharist' (the Prisca says, 'Corpus Christi'), i. e. communicate, even before 'the bishops' did so. Apparently this refers to cases in which some bishop was present but not celebrating. He ought then to have received the Sacrament immediately after the celebrant: but the celebrant's deacon occasionally anticipated him. 'Let all this, then, be done away; and let the deacons keep within their

own lines, knowing that they are under-officers of the bishop, and inferior to the presbyters.' The word ὑπηρέτης is full of history. It is applied by St. Paul to Christian ministers in their relation to Christ (1 Cor. iv. 1), by St. Luke to John Mark in his relation to Paul and Barnabas (Acts xiii. 5). St. Ignatius applies it to deacons in relation to the Church (Trall. 2): the Ancyran Council calls the diaconate an ὑπηρεσία (can. 10): and the Nicene phrase before us calls up the image of a primitive deacon ever within call of his bishop, ready at once to do his bidding (see e. g. Athan. Apol. de Fuga, 24), go on his errands (ib. Apol. c. Ari. 67), bring him information, act as an organ of communication with his laity, take troublesome business off his hands, be his 'ear, eye, mouth, soul' (Apost. Const. ii. 44, cf. ib. 28, 30, iii. 19). He is also said ἐξυπηρετεῖσθαι not only to the bishop, but to the presbyters (ib. 20), and indeed to the poor, as an almoner (ib. 19). But as the deacons, especially those of great cities (where they were often fewer than the presbyters, Euseb. vi. 43, Neocæs. 15,—yet see Apost. Const. iii. 19), rose to a higher status in the Church, the designation of ὑπηρέτης was, so to speak, passed down to the subdeacon: already the Council of Neocæsarea had so applied it (can. 10); the Laodicene Council afterwards did the like in five canons (c. 21, 22, 24, 25, 43): so did the author of the nine Declarations wrongly ascribed by Gelasius to the Nicene Council (Mansi, ii. 885); while Sozomen gave it a yet lower application to the lighter of the church lamps (vi. 31). The deacons, proceeds the canon, must be content to 'receive the Eucharist in their proper turn, after the presbyters and from the hands of the (celebrating) bishop or presbyter.'

(3) And here comes in the third complaint. According to usage, the bishop sat on a throne or raised seat (see Athan. Apol. de Fuga, 24; not on a lofty tribunal like Paul of Samosata's, Euseb. vii. 30) in the semi-circular apse of the sanctuary or 'bema,' and the presbyters occupied a tier of lower seats on each side of him, ('synthronus,' 'consessus,' compare Euseb. x. 5, 'the second throne'), while the deacons 'stood near at hand'

(Apost. Const. ii. 57) within the bema, usually on the north or right side, in what Goar calls the 'dextera pars sacri tribunalis' (Euchol. p. 17, and Beveridge on this canon), so as to be near the Diaconicon, which was like a N.E. chapel, opening into the sanctuary, and served as a sacristy (like the Western 'secretarium') where the deacons could keep the sacred vessels, etc. Compare Bingham, viii. 6. 10, 23. The prohibition to the deacons to sit referred to the bema, and not to this their own special apartment (Beveridge, Annot. p. 85), which a later canon forbade the subdeacons to enter (Laodic. 21). Gregory of Nazianzus gives a description of this arrangement in his poetical 'Dream' respecting his church called Anastasia, and describes the deacons under the name of ὑποδρηστῆρες (compare ὑπηρέτης) as 'standing in shining vestures, resembling the brightness of angels' (Somn. 11), these vestments being like tightly girded albs (Apost. Const. ii. 57). It appears that some deacons disdained this modest posture, and forced their way, in contempt of 'rule and good order,' into the 'consessus' of the presbytery. The canon ends with a menace: if any deacon should, 'even after the publication of these decrees (ὅρους), refuse to obey them, he should be made to cease from ministering as a deacon.' Yet, says Hefele, 'even after the Nicene Council, complaints continued to be made of the pride of the deacons:' and in that letter already quoted, wherein Jerome discharged what Bingham calls his 'angry humour' (ii. 20. 1) against their self-assertion in regard to presbyters, he tells us that 'as abuses grow up by degrees,' he had seen a Roman deacon sitting (in church) among the presbyters when the bishop was absent, and also, at a private entertainment, 'giving his blessing to presbyters;' but he is careful to say that at Rome, doubtless on ordinary occasions, when the bishop was present, ancient usage was observed; 'presbyteri sedent et stant diaconi.' It should be added that the Laodicene Council forbade a deacon to sit down where a priest was present (i.e. out of the church as well as within it), unless bidden by him to do so (can. 20).

Canon XIX.

The difficulties which this canon has presented are chiefly due to its lax and, as it were, colloquial wording. It reads somewhat like the first draft of a resolution struck off in debate, and not yet elaborated into form.

It begins,—'Concerning those who had *Paulianized*,' that is, had been adherents of the sect which traced itself to Paul of Samosata, bishop of Antioch, deposed for heresy (after long and patient investigation) by a Council held at that city in 269. His system combined two great forms of erroneous speculation, and illustrated the connection between the 'Socinian' and the 'Sabellian' points of view (compare Wilberforce on the Incarnation, p. 173). Briefly it came to this,—that Jesus was not God really incarnate, but a man morally deified;—and that the Divine Logos was not substantive or personal, but an attribute of God, as reason is of man. (*a*) He started, it seems, as an inheritor of that Psilanthropism of which first Theodotus, and then Artemon, had been the exponents; he admitted the miraculous birth of Christ, but took Him to be essentially a human person, who, as such, was 'from beneath' (Euseb. vii. 30), and who, by constant advance ($\pi\rho o\kappa o\pi\eta$) in spiritual insight and moral excellence, became, in a titular sense, God's Son, as being in signal measure the recipient and organ of His Logos. (*b*) That Logos, according to Paul, was not a real and pre-existent Son, but an impersonal Divine activity (see the letter of six bishops to Paul in Routh's Rell. Sacr. iii. 290, and Epiphan. Hær. 65. 1), which had poured itself forth in movements of inspiration, dwelling richly in the prophets, more fully in Moses, and with exceptional completeness in the Christ. Thus, as Malchion, the able Catholic disputant, pointed out at the close of a long cross-examination, in which, having caused minutes to be taken down, he followed Paul up through every track, baffled all his resources of verbal elusion, and 'brought him to a stand' (Evans, Biogr. Early Church, ii. 341), he could not and 'did not admit that the Only-begotten Son was personally one (οὐσιῶσθαι) with the Saviour' (Routh, iii. 302): in effect, he denied the Trinity and the Incarnation, and the 'divinity' which he ascribed to Christ was but human goodness in its supreme development under a special influence from on high.

Paul had been ecclesiastically condemned, and ultimately ejected from the cathedral and bishop's house at Antioch. But the school which had gathered round him, fostered by the sophistical acuteness and diplomatic shrewdness which were associated with his deepseated misbelief, carried on his traditions, and contributed to the upgrowth of the next great heresy (see Newman, Arians, p. 7). The learned presbyter Lucian of Antioch adhered to this sect during three episcopates (Theod. i. 4); and although he rejoined the Church, and ultimately died a martyr, yet the earliest Arians called themselves after him 'fellow-Lucianists' (ib. i. 5), and for years after the Nicene Council it was necessary for Catholics to attack the 'Samosatene's' errors (Athan. de Decr. Nic. 10. 24, Orat. i. 25, iii. 51), and for Semi-Arians to disown his view of Christ (Ath. de Syn. 24. 26); while the influence of his theology was so plainly seen in the heretical activity of Photinus, that Rufinus could explain the position of the Paulianists by adding, 'qui sunt Photiniani.' The Council had heard that some of these Paulianists had 'fled to the Catholic Church' as a refuge from error: on what terms were they to be admitted? (1) 'A decision has been promulgated' (by the Council) 'that they are in all cases to be re-baptized.' The word ἀναβαπτίζεσθαι (like ἀναβαπτισθέντες below) is clearly used in a popular sense, as by Cyril of Jerusalem in his Introductory Catechetical lecture, 'Only certain heretics ἀναβαπτίζονται,' and he then guards the phrase from misconception,—'because their former baptism οὐκ ἦν βάπτισμα' (c. 7); and also by Basil, who virtually explains 're-baptism' to mean the administration of the baptism of the Church (Epist. 199. 47). What is meant is that the persons in question are to be baptized *de novo*. Their former baptism is regarded as void: therefore, strictly speaking, the baptism to be administered to them on their coming over to the Church would be, in the Council's eyes, their only real baptism,—as Cyprian had said that converts from heresy, when baptized in the Church, according to the African as against the Roman custom, were *not* 're-baptized,' because, from the African point of view, they had never been previously 'baptized' at all (Epist. 71. 1 : 73. 1). To go through the form of baptizing a person who was believed to have already received real baptism was always regarded as a sacrilege, or as Apost. can. 47 says, a 'mockery of Christ's Cross and death,' which would have no sacramental effect. That baptism was, and could be, but *one*, was just as much a first principle with those who treated the baptism of heretics as a nullity, and therefore, in the popular sense, 're-baptized' converts from heresy, as with those who acknowledged such baptism to be valid. It was in the Eastern churches, where the former opinion prevailed, that the 'oneness' of baptism was asserted in the Creed, in parallelism to the 'oneness' of the Father, the Son, the Spirit, and the Church (Bp. Phillpotts, Letter to his Clergy in 1851, p. 26). But why was the baptism of Paulianists disallowed? Did they not use the right form, 'In the Name of the Father,' etc.? Athanasius, who must have been well informed on this point, tells us that they did so; but, he adds, the grossness of their heresy made the sacred words of none effect (Orat. ii. 43). So that, on this showing, a heretic who administered baptism with the right form, but not with the right faith, would be held not to have conferred a valid baptism. This was in accordance with the Eastern view (Apost. can. 46, 68), but not with the Western, which had expressed itself at the Council of Arles (A.D. 314), to the effect that a convert from heresy should be asked to repeat his creed, and if it should appear that he had been baptized 'in Patre et Filio et Spiritu Sancto,' he was only to receive imposition of hands : ' but if, in reply to the question, non responderit hanc Trinitatem, baptizetur' (can. 8). Now, if we take this canon in its natural sense simply (instead of reading into 'hanc Trinitatem' the idea of 'a right faith as to the Trinity,' when the context points to the sacred threefold Name), we see that it indicates the opinion held by Stephen of Rome in the third century, that 'the majesty of the Name' invoked at every baptism in which the right form was used carried with it the full sacramental reality (Cypr. Epist. 74. 5), and afterwards worked out at length by St. Augustine, who boldly affirmed that a right belief on the part of the baptizer was of the utmost importance for his own salvation, but of none at all 'ad sacramenti quæstionem' (de Bapt. iii. 14. 19), and whose allusions to a 'plenary Council' which upheld the anti-Cyprianic view are most reasonably understood of the great Western Council of 314 (cf. de Bapt. ii. 10. 14, iv. 5. 7, etc.), though Tillemont refers them to that of Nicæa (vi. 675). This view was so thoroughly taken for granted at Rome, that Innocent I. and Augustine, assuming that it had been sanctioned at Nicæa, inferred that the Paulianists did not baptize 'in nomine Patris,' etc. (Innoc. Epist. 22. 5; Aug. de Hæres. 44). But, as we have seen, there is good evidence that they did so: and if they did so, then a discrepancy between the decisions of Arles and Nicæa becomes too evident for denial; and Hefele is not justified in saying, twice over, that the latter Council 'was here 'applying' or 'adopting' the decree of the former; it was rather taking the opposite line. And St. Basil's subsequent ruling in the Eastern sense, as to the Encratites, is a comment on the intention of the fathers of Nicæa (Epist. 199. 47). He expressly says, that although these Encratites were baptized 'into Father and Son and Holy Spirit,' their baptism ought not to be recognised, because they consider God to be the Maker of evil, i.e. that their heresy vitiates their use of the right form. He also disallows the baptism of the Montanists (Epist. 188. 1). as did the Council of Laodicea (can. 8). See below on Constant. 7, and comp. Transl. of Tertull. Lib. Fath. p. 288.

(2) The second provision in this canon (ignored by Rufinus) relates to ex-Paulianist clergy (on ἐν τῷ κλήρῳ ἐξητάσθησαν, see can. 1). If their previous character has been 'blameless and irreproachable' (on ἀνεπίληπτοι, see can. 9), then, after they have received baptism *de novo*, they are to be 'ordained by the bishop

of the Catholic Church' in the district. Their previous baptism being null, their previous ordination is also null; for, of course, an unbaptized person is incapable of receiving holy orders. 'But if on inquiry they should be found unfit' to receive Catholic ordination, 'it is proper that they should be deposed.' Here καθαιρεῖσθαι is used popularly—as the Greek commentators say, καταχρηστικῶς—like ἀναβαπτίζεσθαι above: it means not that, being regarded as ordained, they are to be deprived of their orders —for, by the hypothesis, they had never really been ordained; but simply that they are to be refused ordination,—and are to remain in the position of lay Churchmen. The Prisca expresses this by adding 'et sint in ordine laicorum:' the Vetus, by adding 'vel abjici.' Dionysius simply renders καθαιρεῖσθαι by 'abjici.'

(3) The third sentence is matter of much difficulty. Accepting the text περὶ τῶν διακονισσῶν—for the reading διακόνων, found in Gelasius of Cyzicus, and followed by Philo and Evarestus, the Vetus, and Isidore, has the look of a conjectural emendation and introduces a puzzle of its own (which Hefele does not remove) by mentioning deacons after clerics—we must first consider generally the office of deaconesses. It is traced up to Phœbe of Cenchreæ (Rom. xvi. 1): it is discernible in the allusion to a 'list' of widows, as of an order, in 1 Tim. v. 9, in the term 'ministræ' applied to the two Christian women whom Pliny the younger examined under torture (Epp. Traj. 96), and perhaps in what St. Ignatius says of 'the virgins who are called widows' (Smyrn. 13); for although Tertullian thought it most anomalous that a virgin should sit among the widows of the church (de Veland. Virgin. 9), yet later writers (Apost. Const. vi. 37, Epiphan. Expos. Fidei, 21) tell us that a deaconess might be either a virgin or a widow who had been but once married. On the duties of deaconesses, see Bingham, ii. c. 22. They had (1) to assist in the instruction, and attend the baptism, of female catechumens: (2) to take messages from the bishop to Churchwomen: (3) to look after them in church. The senior members of their order are probably alluded to, under the name of πρεσβύτιδες, in the 11th Laodicene canon (see Hefele,

and compare Epiphan. Hær. 79. 4). We find St. Basil writing a doctrinal letter to two deaconesses of Samosata (Epist. 105). St. Chrysostom's friend Nicarete refused to let him appoint her a deaconess, 'to preside over the Church virgins' (Soz. viii. 23); but the more celebrated Olympias had been so appointed by his predecessor (Soz. viii. 9), and his biographer Palladius (Dial. p. 36) tells us how two deaconesses fell weeping at his feet when he took farewell of his church in the Whitsunweek of 404. Theodosius I., following St. Paul's rule as to widows, endeavoured to fix the age for admission into the order at 60 years; but see below, Chalc. 15, allowing them to be appointed at æt. 40. Sozomen mentions a deaconess named Nectaria (iv. 24) and another, Eusebia, of the Macedonian sect (ix. 2). In the fifth and sixth centuries several Gallican synods forbade them to be ordained, but this was not to forbid their appointment: the order lasted on in the West until the 10th century or later, and at Constantinople until the latter part of the 12th. For the now obsolete Eastern rite of ordaining them, see Goar, Eucholog. p. 262. The canon proceeds, 'Touching the (ex-Paulianist) deaconesses, and generally all who are reckoned on the clerical staff (for this use of κανόνι, see can. 1), the same standard is to be retained.' Here the word τύπος is used as synonymous with ὅρος, as Athanasius speaks of τύποι, meaning Church decrees (Encycl. 1). Compare Eph. 8: see too Gregory of Neocæsarea, can. 5 (Routh, Rell. Sac. iii. 262). The special notion of the word is that of a pattern to be observed; and, like ὅρος, it is used in a dogmatic sense, as in the 'Type' of Constans II. It means a rite in Basil, de Spir. Sanct. 74. Here the Council says in effect, What we have just laid down as to (ex-Paulianist) priests or deacons is to apply to deaconesses also, and to all who have held any official position within the sect. But what of the next words, 'We have mentioned the deaconesses,' etc.? The phrase τῶν ἐν τῷ σχήματι ἐξετασθεισῶν has been variously rendered by Latin translators, as 'in eadem specie,' 'in hoc ordine,' 'in eodem habitu,' 'in habitu' (as in later ritual terminology σχῆμα was used for the monastic habit, Goar, p. 489). It must be understood to mean, in their visible status or rank of deaconesses (compare c. 8). But it is added that 'they have no sort of χειροθεσία.' Here the question arises, Were not then deaconesses ordained with imposition of hands? St. Basil speaks of the body of a deaconess as consecrated (Epist. 199. 44): imposition of hands is prescribed in their case in Apost. Const. viii. 19, and is proved by Chalc. 15 to have been practised in the fifth century; compare the Constantinopolitan rite already referred to, and the appointment of St. Radegund in Gaul by imposition of bishop Medard's hands in 544. Hence it has been proposed (1) to distinguish between some Paulianist deaconesses who were thus ordained, and others who had merely the σχῆμα (see Beveridge) of this female diaconate: (2) to assume that all Paulianist deaconesses were appointed without imposition of hands: (3) to date the introduction of this ordination of deaconesses, within the Church or outside it, after the Nicene era: (4) to say that the imposition of hands then received by deaconesses was only a solemn benediction, as Hefele argues, adding that, according to can. 8 and the decree about the Meletians, 'the Nicene fathers took χειροθεσία as synonymous with mere benediction,' yet imputing to them by his argument the use of χειροθεσία in two senses, (*a*) a reconciling benediction, (*b*) ordination; for here it is said, 'they have no imposition of hands,' which he interprets as 'no proper ordination.' The opinion (2) seems simpler than either (1) or (3), and the wording favours it, as if special attention were called to the fact that *Paulianist* deaconesses had in no sense been ordained. The general purport of the passage may be stated thus: 'All ex-Paulianist officials, including deaconesses, are to be dealt with by the method now prescribed. We mention these deaconesses, however, merely as having been so regarded in their former sect. But in fact we refer to them *ex abundanti*, for they stand outside the class of persons whose "ordination" is to be performed *de novo* after their conversion; they have never had any imposition of hands, so that these women must in all respects be reckoned among the laity.'

CANON XX.

This last canon, which is passed over by Rufinus, and omitted in the Antiquissima, touches a point of ritual observance. The Council remarks that 'there are some persons who bend the knee in prayer on the Lord's day, and on the days of the Pentecost.' We must observe at the outset, that τῆς Πεντηκοστῆς here means the whole period of fifty days from Easter to Whitsunday inclusive, as when Tertullian says that Pentecost is a very ample period ('latissimum spatium') for 'making arrangements about baptisms' (de Bapt. 19); he speaks again of 'the period of Pentecost as spent in solemn rejoicing' (de Orat. 23), and observes that all the several solemnities of the Gentiles will not make up a Pentecost (de Idol. 14). So Eusebius calls the whole 'venerable festal period of seven weeks' by the name of Pentecost (Vit. Const. iv. 64); Basil speaks of 'the seven weeks of the sacred Pentecost' (de Sp. Sancto, 66); the 38th Apostolic canon, of 'the fourth week of the Pentecost;' Epiphanius, of the whole Pentecost of 50 days (Exp. Fid. Cath. 22); Chrysostom, of the order for reading the Acts in the Pentecost (in Princip. Act. Hom. 4. 3); Jerome, of not fasting 'in Pentecoste' (Epist. 41. 3). Hilary uses 'Quinquagesima' in the same sense, (Prolog. in Psal. s. 12); and so does the 1st Council of Orleans (can. 25, A.D. 512), and Ven. Bede (H. E. iii. 27).

The custom of standing in prayer was 'inherited from the Jewish Church, in which it was the rule to pray standing, except in a time of mourning' (Scudamore, Notitia Eucharistica, p. 182). Not only the self-complacent Pharisee, but the penitent Publican, are described in our Lord's parable as standing while they prayed: and He 'assumes that this would be the ordinary practice of those to whom He spoke, "When ye stand praying,"'—and praying, as the context shows, for the pardon of sins (Mark xi. 25). In the early Church this posture, although not adopted on all occasions of worship, was enriched with new and more sacred associations, and made obligatory, by custom, during the annual Easter festival season, and on Sunday as 'an Easter day in every week,' as symbolizing the participation of the redeemed in the risen life of their Redeemer, and expressing the 'erectness and jubilance and deathless expectation' (Grant's Church Seasons, p. 212) which were inseparable from the commemoration of His victory over death. In Tertullian's time, for instance, it was thought 'nefas' to kneel on the Lord's day, and the same 'exemption' from a posture significant of sorrowful abasement was enjoyed from Easter-day to Whitsunday (de Cor. 3). He even argues against standing on Saturday from the fact that it is on Sunday and in 'the time of Pentecost' that kneeling is traditionally forbidden (de Orat. 23). In the 'Responsiones ad Orthodoxos,' falsely ascribed to Justin Martyr, where the question is asked, 'Since kneeling is the more fitting posture for sinners, why do men stand in prayer on the Lord's days and from Easter to Pentecost?' Irenæus is cited as saying, in his treatise on the Pascha, that this usage began in apostolic times (qu. 115). Peter of Alexandria says simply, 'We keep the Lord's day as a day of rejoicing because the Lord rose again on that day, on which, by tradition, we do not even bend the knee' (can. 15).

This custom, then, as to all Sundays and the fifty days of Easter, the Nicene fathers had inherited, and desired to perpetuate. 'In order that the same observances may be retained in every diocese' (παροικίᾳ, see above on can. 16) 'it has seemed good to the holy Council that men should present their prayers to God' (i.e. during the times specified) 'in a standing posture.'

It is to the great general outlines of ritual observance that this principle of uniformity was intended to apply. In particulars, much diversity was allowed on all hands, as we know from the coexistence of 'five different groups or families of Liturgies,' characterized by an 'extraordinary unity' in idea and general structure, but also by an 'extraordinary variety of order, not only in minor details but of' such 'important parts of the service' as 'the great intercession' (see Hammond's Liturgies, pp. xvi. xxxvii); from St. Augustine's language on the difference between Roman and Milanese usage as to whether Saturday should be kept as a fast or a feast, and his full recognition of a class of observances as to which 'every man should do quod in ea ecclesia in quam venit invenerit' (Epist. 54. s. 3, 6); and, still later, from the invaluable account of varieties of usage in Socrates, v. 22.

After the Nicene times, we find Hilary asserting that the custom of not praying with prostration during the fifty days had come down from the Apostles (Prol. in Psal. 12). Epiphanius simply says that kneeling and fasting are disused during that period (Exp. Fid. Cathol. 22); Basil observes that Christians were wont to pray standing on the first day of the week, but that 'all did not know the reason,' and he explains that it represents the obligation of 'those who are risen again with Christ to seek the things that are above,' the 'transfer of the mind' from the present to the future, and the restoration of fallen man through the benignity of God (de Spir. Sanct. s. 66). Jerome ranks the custom as to Sundays and the Paschal period among matters of unwritten tradition (Dial. adv. Lucif. 8). An ancient ordinance of the African church ('4th Council of Carthage,' c. 82) alludes to it by saying that penitents ought to kneel even 'diebus remissionis.' Augustine, at the beginning of the fifth century, testifies that the custom of praying at the altar in a standing posture on Sundays, and from Easter day to the day of Pentecost 'in token of the Resurrection,' and 'of the rest and gladness' procured through it, was observed in Africa; but whether it was observed everywhere else, he knew not. He illustrates its meaning by combining with it the practice of singing Alleluia in the Paschal season (Epist. 55. s. 28, 32). It lasted on in the West at least until the ninth century: e.g. the 3rd Council of Tours, in 813, excepts from the rule of kneeling in prayer the Lord's days, and those solemnities on which the universal Church is wont to pray standing in memory of the Lord's resurrection' (can. 37; Mansi, xiv. 89). In the East it is retained; compare the 90th canon of the Council in Trullo, ordering that when the priest goes into the sanctuary on Saturday evening, no one is to kneel, 'according to the prevalent custom,' until the 'entrance' in the lychnic (or vesper) office on Sunday. Thus, it is added, should we 'keep festival in honour of the Resurrection (πανηγυρίζειν τὴν ἀνάστασιν) in a complete night and day.' It may be observed that the 29th Arabic 'canon of Nicæa' extends the rule of not kneeling, but only bending forward, to all great festivals of the Lord.

The canon does not mention, but goes far to imply, that custom of standing at the Holy Communion to receive the Eucharist, which to all appearance was taken for granted on all hands. It was indeed usual for the faithful to kneel during the first prayer said after the dismissal of the ordinary penitents: see Chrysostom (on 2 Cor. Hom. 18. 3), that during this prayer they were prostrate on the pavement: and in the 'Clementine' liturgy the deacon proclaims at this point of the service, 'Let all of us, the faithful, bend the knee.' But from the offertory onwards, all stood: so the 'Clementine' represents the deacon as saying just before it, 'Let us stand upright to offer to the Lord.' Compare the similar direction in the Liturgy of St. James, 'Upright all!' (Hammond's Liturgies, p. 32): and St. Mark's (ib. p. 179), and there are, later on, repetitions of 'Let us stand,' as in St. James's Greek and Syriac, St. Chrysostom's, the Armenian, the Coptic, etc. The very title of the συνιστάμενοι tells us enough, and the Roman canon still describes those who are present at the Mass as 'standing around' ('Memento . . . omnium circumstantium.') 'It was thought the proper position for all who offered sacrifice' (Scudamore, Notit. Euchar. p. 183), as the faithful did in their own way, not only by contributing the elements, but by sealing the 'great oblation' with their Amen. And as sacrifice was consummated by participation (see Scudamore, p. 400) they kept the same posture at the moment of communion: thus Tertullian speaks of 'standing at God's altar' and 'receiving the Lord's Body' (de Orat. 19), and Dionysius of Alexandria tells a remarkable story about a man who had long been accustomed to 'stand beside the table, and stretch forth his hand to receive the holy food' (Euseb. vii. 9; laymen were wont to come up to the altar for Communion, compare Gregory Nazianzen, Orat. 17. 12, Chrys. in 2 Cor. Hom. 20. 3, and Martene, de ant. Eccl. Rit. i. 430). Rather more than twenty years after the Council, Cyril of Jerusalem instructed his catechumens, when they made their Communion for the first time, to 'receive the Body of Christ' in the palm of the right hand, to 'draw near to the cup, not stretching out the hands, but stooping ($κύπτων$), and saying the Amen in token of worship and reverence' (Catech. 23. 21, 22). To this day, communicants in the Eastern Church thus stand bending forward (compare an old Ethiopic form, 'Ye who stand, bend your heads,' before the prayer of access; Hammond, p. 236). In the Latin Church 'some traces of the ancient practice remain' (Scudamore, p. 636), notably in the case of the priest's own communion at Mass, and of the deacon's at a solemn papal celebration.

The Puritans of 1604 quoted this canon as against 'kneeling at the Sacrament' (Neal, Hist. of Purit. i. 429); but this was an 'economic' argument, designed to impress an antiquarian king. Any imagined parallel between their position and that of the Nicene fathers, on the question of kneeling at a Sunday Communion, is destroyed by a consideration of the 'animus' of the respective parties. The Council vetoed a ritual innovation which seemed to symbolize an ill-timed sorrow; the Puritans broke with existing Church order as prescribing what they deemed an undue reverence. The aims being thus different, the resemblance of the cases is purely superficial, and indeed vanishes when it is remembered that they who thus endeavoured to utilise a Nicene canon themselves preferred to communicate sitting, a posture further removed than kneeling from that which, as described above, was familiar to Christians of the Nicene age.

'These,' says Tillemont, 'are the twenty canons of this celebrated Council which have come down to us, and also the only Canons which it made; at any rate, no ancient writer has reckoned more than twenty of them. Theodoret mentions no others (Theod. i. 8); the African church, having asked for copies of the Nicene canons from the churches of Alexandria, Antioch, and Constantinople, received only these twenty, which we still have; and the twenty-two of Rufinus contain nothing more than do these twenty commonly reckoned, being only distributed in another way' (vi. 674). Rufinus, indeed, using the strange freedom which he allowed himself as an abbreviator, inserted into the last of his canons the Nicene decision about the calculation of Easter, which was not properly a canon. Although Gelasius attributes to the Council nine constitutions, clearly post-Nicene, on prayer, manual labour, the clerical orders, the unlawfulness of laymen going into the ambon, baptism, the Eucharist, resurrection, the one Church, providence, yet he clearly distinguishes them from the true canons, which he twice reckons as twenty (Mansi, ii. 30, 31). These only are included in the ancient Greek and Latin collections, or recognised by the Greek commentators; Hincmar of Reims, in the ninth century, expressly says that 'it is manifest' that no others are Nicene (adv. Hincm. Laud. c. 21); and the additional Arabic canons, which would make up the number to 84, as edited by Echellensis (Mansi, ii. 982), betray their own lateness of origin, and were probably called Nicene through uncritical carelessness, attributing to the First General Council other decrees contained in collections wherein that Council's canons had, of course, the foremost place (so Hefele, and compare Chr. Justellus as to the 'Code of Canons of the Universal Church,' Biblioth. Jur. Can. Vet. i. 16). Neale says that this Arabic compilation was probably made shortly after the rise of the Mahometan empire (Hist. Alex. i. 109).

But there are some passages of ancient writers which have been relied on as proving that there were other Nicene canons than those which we possess. They are, however, to be explained by a reference to laxity of expression, or to mistake. Thus—Julius of Rome, when he wrote to the Eusebians that the Nicene fathers decreed that one Council's resolutions might be reviewed by another (Athan. Apol. c. Ari. 22), means only that they acted on this principle by considering the Arian question *de novo*, after it had been determined by the synod of Alexandria. When Ambrose told the church of Vercellæ that the Nicene fathers 'tractatus addidisse' to the effect that no digamist ought to be ordained (Epist. 63. 64) was apparently 'misled by the manuscript which he was then using,' and in which a canon on this subject was wrongly set down as Nicene (see the Benedictine note in loc.): just as the Roman series of canons, in the fifth century, confounded Sardican canons with Nicene, and led the Roman bishops, first in ignorance, as in the cases of Zosimus and Boniface, and afterwards, in spite of authentic information (as in the case of Leo, Epist. 43), to quote as Nicene what was really Sardican, as Gregory of Tours long afterwards called a canon of Gangra Nicene (Hist. Fr. ix. 33). Jerome had 'read' somewhere that the Nicene Synod recognised the book of Judith as part of scripture (Præf. ad lib. Judith), he may have been deceived by some catalogue of scripture books ascribed by a 'pia fraus' to the great Council (see Vallarsi's note, Op. x. 21); or he may have found a citation of the book in some professed account of Nicene discussions (Hefele). It is incredible that the Council should have 'canonized' a book which later catalogues, such as the Laodicene, ignore. On this whole subject, see Hefele, sect. 41.

NOTES ON THE CANONS OF CONSTANTINOPLE.

CANON I.

THIS canon is part of a 'Tome' or doctrinal formulary which, as we know from the letter of a Council held at Constantinople in the year 382, had been drawn up by the Council of Constantinople, properly so called, in 381 (Theod. v. 9). It has been thought that when the Council of Chalcedon informed the Emperor Marcian that the bishops who assembled at Constantinople had written to the Westerns against the Apollinarian heresy (Mansi, vii. 464), it alluded to this document. But it was at the meeting of 382—which may, indeed, be called an adjourned session of this council—that a letter to the Westerns was drawn up, and the perfect humanity of the Redeemer affirmed in it, as appears from the letter itself, and the last paragraph of Theod. v. 9.

The present canon begins by ordaining that 'the πίστις of the 318 fathers who assembled at Nicæa in Bithynia shall not be set aside, but remain in force (κυρίαν).' By πίστις is here meant belief as formulated in a document, in other words, a confession of faith, or a creed. The word is so used in a letter of the Council of Ariminum, ap. Athan. de Synod. 10, τὴν συγγραφεῖσαν πίστιν, by St. Athanasius in Tom. ad Antioch. 5, and by St. Basil when he speaks of Hermogenes, 'the man who at the great Council wrote the great and impregnable πίστιν,' Epist. 81; and, as we shall see, in a celebrated decree of the Council of Ephesus, can. 7. Socrates also repeatedly speaks of a πίστις as composed, drawn up, presented, and read (ii. 18, 19, 45).

The number 318, by which the Nicene fathers have been often described, is traceable to Athanasius in one of his later treatises, (ad Afros, 2; he had previously reckoned them as about 300, Hist. Arian. 66; de Synod. 43; cp. Apol. c. Ari. 23, 25). It was adopted by Epiphanius (Hær. 69. 11), Ambrose (de Fide, prol.), and later writers—all the more readily because of its coincidence with the number of Abraham's trained homeborn servants who successfully pursued the captors of Lot (Gen. xiv. 14).

But here a question arises. The Council of Chalcedon ascribes to this Council of Constantinople, under the name of 'the 150 fathers' (Mansi, vii. 109), that recension of the Nicene Creed which has practically superseded the original form, with the restoration of the Nicene phrase 'God from God' in East and West alike, and with the addition of the 'Filioque' and the change of 'and' into 'of' before the name of Mary, in the West only. But is this statement compatible with the formal ratification of the Nicene Creed in the canon now before us? It may be answered that the members of the Council of A.D. 381 would not consider themselves to be in any sense invalidating, but rather confirming and perpetuating, the formulary of A.D. 325, when they adopted, with hardly any change, a development of it which had been embodied just eight years previously in the 'Ancoratus' of Epiphanius, and therein described as the creed of the Church, set forth by 'bishops more than 310 in number' (Ancor. 120, 121). This creed was in effect the Nicene confession expanded, in view of present doctrinal requirements, by means of material borrowed from what might be called the Creed of Jerusalem, as it may be collected from the Catechetical Lectures of Cyril delivered in 347 or 348. It may seem strange that Epiphanius should use such language respecting a formulary which was not *verbatim* identical with the Nicene: but he is not to be judged by our notions of accuracy, and it is, on the other hand, practically incredible that he should not have known the wording of the Nicene symbol itself, which had been solemnly exhibited, as accepted by three

Semi-Arian deputies, before an orthodox council at Tyana in Cappadocia, six years before he wrote his 'Ancoratus' in Cyprus for a church in Pamphylia. (Cp. Basil, Epist. 226, 3: 244, 7: Soz. vi. 12.) It is true that these deputies, in their letter to Liberius, alter the Nicene wording in one clause of the creed, so as to read, 'And in one Only-begotten God, the Lord Jesus Christ' (Soc. iv. 12): but for the rest they commit their 64 brethren to that wording. And if any of the prelates at Constantinople could have taken this 'Epiphanian' symbol for the Nicene in a literal sense, Gregory of Nyssa, whose brother, St. Basil, had embodied the Creed of 325 (omitting Θεὸν ἐκ Θεοῦ) in a letter to the Antiochene church, written in 373 (Epist. 140. 2), or Pelagius of Laodicea or Zeno of Tyre (cp. Mansi, iii. 568), who had sat in the synod of Tyana, could have at once corrected the mistake, and shown in what sense that symbol could be called Nicene—a sense sufficient for their purpose, although it might fail to satisfy a modern standard of precision. It is remarkable that Basil in 377 had written to Epiphanius, to the effect that 'not the smallest addition' could be made to the Nicene Creed except on the divinity of the Holy Spirit; some proposed additions on the Incarnation he had declined even to consider (Epist. 258. 2). On both these points the 'Epiphanian' creed contained additions which the Council, according to the received opinion, saw reason to adopt. It has, again, been objected that, between the years 381 and 451, this recension of the creed, which we call Constantinopolitan, is never alluded to; in other words, no 'Creed of the Second Council' appears to have been known; Socrates says merely that the Nicene Creed was 'confirmed' (v. 8). The Western churches, the Alexandrian church, the Council of Ephesus, the Antiochene party opposed to that Council (comp. Mansi, iv. 1341, 1375), recognise the original Nicene Creed and no other (cp. Lumby, Hist. of Creeds, p. 72). But the authority of the Council of Constantinople itself was ignored by the West and by Egypt (see Neale, Hist. Alex. i. 209, Le Quien, Or. Chr. ii.

405): the Council of Ephesus was largely under the influence of the great prelate whom his enemies called 'the Egyptian:' and the Syrian churches, however keenly opposed to 'Apollinarianizing' tendencies, might not have had occasion to consider or adopt the recension before us, which in one passage, relating to the Nativity, bears token of hostility to Apollinarian mysticism. At any rate, none of the bishops at Chalcedon appear to have challenged the assertion of the imperial commissioners that 'the 150' made an 'ecthesis' of the faith (Mansi, vi. 937); and when in the next session the same commissioners caused the present Creed to be read as what 'the 150' had thus put forth, 'all the bishops exclaimed, This is the faith of all' (Mansi, vi. 957): and the whole Council, in its 5th session, solemnly adopted it as forming, with the original Nicene Creed, a 'wise and salutary symbol' (Mansi, vii. 112). It was quite possible in ancient times for persons to be zealously attached to the Nicene formulary, and yet to use, side by side with it, some other formulary agreeing with it in doctrine, but not altogether in language,—as was probably the case with Charisius (see below on Eph. 7), and certainly with Gregory of Tours, who prefixes to his 'Historia Ecclesiastica Francorum' a 'credo' of his own as 'quod in ecclesia credi prædicatur.'

Admitting, then, the received statement as to the sanction given by this Council of 'the 150' to our present 'Nicene Creed' (with the exceptions above named), we observe that the anathemas against Arianism, appended to the Creed in its earlier form, are 'conspicuously absent' from this. The Epiphanian Creed, of which the 'Constantinopolitan' is almost a reproduction, was accompanied by these denunciations, which reappear in a somewhat enlarged form at the close of the very paraphrastic 'Nicene Creed' in the Armenian Liturgy (see Hammond, Liturgies, p. 147). But the 'Constantinopolitan' formulary has them not. From this fact some rather large inferences have been made, which, however, would seem to be disposed of by the observation, that the Nicene censures were, for all practical purposes, superseded by new ones of a somewhat different but very definite type, which form the bulk of the present canon. There it is ordained that 'every heresy' shall be 'anathematized,' and in particular seven, being those of the following sects.

(1) 'The Eunomians or Anomœans.' These were the ultra-Arians, who carried to its legitimate issue the original Arian denial of the eternity and uncreatedness of the Son, while they further rejected what Arius had affirmed as to the essential mysteriousness of the Divine nature (Soc. iv. 7, comp. Athan. de Synod. 15). Their founder was Aetius, the most versatile of theological adventurers (cp. Athan. de Synod. 31, Soc. ii. 45: and see a summary of his career in Newman's Arians, p. 347); but their leader at the time of the Council was the daring and indefatigable Eunomius (for whose personal characteristics, see his admirer Philostorgius, x. 6). He too had gone through many vicissitudes from his first employment as the secretary of Aetius, and his ordination as deacon by Eudoxius: as bishop of Cyzicus, he had been lured into a disclosure of his true sentiments, and then denounced as a heretic (Theod. ii. 29); with Aetius he had openly separated from Eudoxius as a disingenuous time-server, and had gone into retirement at Chalcedon (Philostorg. ix. 4). The distinctive formula of his adherents was the 'Anomoion.' The Son, they said, was not 'like to the Father in essence:' even to call Him simply 'like' was to obscure the fact that He was simply a creature, and, as such, 'unlike' to His Creator. In other words, they thought the Semi-Arian Homoiousion little better than the Catholic Homoousion: the 'Homoion' of the more 'respectable' Arians represented in their eyes an ignoble reticence: the plain truth, however it might shock devout prejudice, must be put into words which would bar all misunderstanding: the Son might be called 'God,' but in a sense merely titular, so as to leave an impassable gulf between Him and the uncreated Godhead (see Eunomius' 'Exposition' in Valesius on Soc. v. 10). Compare Basil, Epist. 233, and his work against Eunomius; and Epiph. Hær. 76.

(2) 'The Arians or Eudoxians.' By these are meant the

ordinary Arians of the period, or, as they may be called, the Acacian party, directed for several years by the essentially worldly and unconscientious Eudoxius (already referred to on Nic. 15). His real sympathies were with the Anomœans (see Tillemont, vi. 423, and compare his profane speech recorded by Socrates, ii. 43): but, as bishop of Constantinople, he felt it necessary to discourage them, and to abide by the vague formula invented by Acacius of Cæsarea, which described the Son as 'like to the Father,' without saying whether this likeness was supposed to be more than moral (cp. Newman, p. 317), so that the practical effect of this 'Homoion' was to prepare the way for that very Anomœanism which its maintainers were ready for political purposes to disown.

(3) 'The Semi-Arians,' meaning, not the original maintainers of the Homoiousion, whose leaders might seem to be separated from the Nicene standing-ground by little more than a dread of the Homoousion, and were at one time addressed by St. Athanasius as 'brothers' whose 'meaning' was orthodox (de Syn. 41); but the remnant of their party after its disintegration in A.D. 367 (see Newman, Arians, p. 391). Some frankly adopted the Nicene faith; others, who either 'remained nonconformist,' or, like Eustathius, recalled their profession of conformity (Basil, Epist. 244. 7), became specially distinguished by the theory which in this canon, as in St. Basil's 263rd Epistle, draws down on them the opprobrious title of 'Pneumatomachi,' while their ordinary name in theological history is 'Macedonians,' after Macedonius the Semi-Arian bishop of Constantinople, who, according to Socrates, 'declined to take in the Holy Spirit εἰς τὴν θεολογίαν τῆς Τριάδος' (ii. 45). They held fast, and passionately emphasized, that denial of the proper Divinity of the Holy Spirit which had repeatedly, in its earlier manifestations, attracted the vigilant censures of Athanasius (Letters to Serapion, Tom. ad Antioch. 3, Ad Afros, 11), and, as it came more boldly to the front, had been condemned by synods at Rome and in Illyricum (Soz. vi. 25, Theod. iv. 9). Some of them were still virtually Arian in regard to the Son (Basil, de Sp.

Sanct. s. 6, 13); others became sound on that head (Greg. Naz. Orat. 41. 8): but with all of them the Spirit was only a creature, inferior to the Son, the chiefest of 'ministering spirits,' —not to be glorified with the Father and the Son (see Basil, de Spir. Sanct. s. 65, Epist. 125. 3, etc.). Their chief stronghold was the Hellespontine district (Soc. iv. 4). They were earnestly resisted by St. Basil, as by St. Gregory Nazianzen (Epist. 58, Orat. 31, though he acknowledges their high personal character, Orat. 41. 8): see too Didymus and St. Ambrose 'de Spiritu Sancto,' and Epiphanius, Hær. 74. Their bishops had been invited to the Council, 'reminded of the deputation which they had sent by Eustathius to Liberus bishop of Rome,' and urged to accept the Homoousion; but refused to do so, quitted Constantinople, and exhorted their adherents to stand out against the Nicene creed (Soc. v. 8). It was by way of excluding their characteristic error that the Epiphanian creed, and so the 'Constantinopolitan,' declared the Holy Spirit to be τὸ Κύριον, the Lord or Sovereign Spirit, and ζωοποιόν, the Giver, not the mere transmitter, of life (Newman, Arians, p. 405), and to be associated with the Father and the Son in adoration and doxology. Compare the majestic invocation of the Holy Spirit in St. Mark's Liturgy (Hammond, Liturgies, p. 187), manifestly composed as a safeguard against Macedonianism. It is remarkable that the Spanish king Leovigild (A. D. 570-587) clung to Macedonianism after professing to give up Arianism (Greg. Turon. Hist. Fr. vi. 18).

(4) 'The Sabellians,' whose theory is traceable to Noetus and Praxeas in the latter part of the second century: they regarded the Son and the Holy Spirit as aspects and modes of, or as emanations from, the One Person of the Father (see Newman's Arians, p. 120 ff.). Such a view tended directly to dissolve Christian belief in the Trinity and in the Incarnation (see Wilberforce on the Incarnation, pp. 112, 197). Hence the gentle Dionysius of Alexandria characterized it in severe terms as involving 'blasphemy, unbelief, and irreverence, towards the Father, the Son, and the Holy Spirit' (Euseb. vii. 6).

Hence the deep repugnance which it excited, and the facility with which the imputation of 'Sabellianizing' could be utilised by the Arians against maintainers of the Consubstantiality (Hilary, de Trinit. iv. 4, de Synod. 68, Fragm. 11; Basil, Epist. 189. 2). No organized Sabellian sect was in existence at the date of this anathema: but Sabellian ideas were 'in the air,' and St. Basil could speak of a revival of this old misbelief (Epist. 126). We find it again asserted by Chilperic I., king of Neustria, in the latter part of the sixth century (Greg. Turon. Hist. Fr. v. 45).

(5) 'The Marcellians,' called after Marcellus bishop of Ancyra, who was persistently denounced not only by the Arianizers, but by St. Basil, and for a time, at least, suspected by St. Athanasius (see Epiphan. Hær. 72. 4) as one who held notions akin to Sabellianism, and fatal to a true belief in the Divine Sonship and the Incarnation. The theory ascribed to him was that the Logos was an impersonal Divine power, immanent from eternity in God, but issuing from Him in the act of creation, and entering at last into relations with the human person of Jesus, who thus became God's Son. But this 'expansion' of the original Divine unity would be followed by a 'contraction,' when the Logos would retire from Jesus, and God would again be all in all. Some nine years before the Council, Marcellus, then in extreme old age, had sent his deacon Eugenius to St. Athanasius, with a written confession of faith, quite orthodox as to the eternity of the Trinity, and the identity of the Logos with a preexisting and personal Son, although not verbally explicit as to the permanence of Christ's 'kingdom,'—the point insisted on in one of the Epiphanian-Constantinopolitan additions to the Creed (Montfaucon, Collect. Nov. ii. 1). The question whether Marcellus was personally heterodox—i. e. whether the extracts from his treatise, made by his adversary Eusebius of Cæsarea, give a fair account of his real views—has been answered unfavourably by some writers, as Newman (Athanasian Treatises, ii. 200, ed. 2), and Döllinger (Hippolytus and Callistus, p. 217, E. T. p. 201), while others, like Neale, think

that 'charity and truth' suggest his 'acquittal' (Hist. Patr. Antioch. p. 106). Montfaucon thinks that his written statements might be favourably interpreted, but that his oral statements must have given ground for suspicion.

(6) 'The Photinians,' or followers of Marcellus' disciple Photinus, bishop of Sirmium, the ready-witted and pertinacious disputant whom four successive synods condemned before he could be got rid of, by State power, in 351. (See St. Athanasius' Historical Writings, Introd. p. lxxxix.) In his representation of the 'Marcellian' theology, he laid special stress on its Christological position,—that Jesus, on whom the Logos rested with exceptional fulness, was a mere man. See Athanasius, de Synodis, 26, 27, for two creeds in which Photinianism is censured: also Soc. ii. 18, 29, 30, vii. 32. There is an obvious affinity between it and the 'Samosatene' or Paulianist theory (see on Nic. 19).

(7) Lastly, 'the Apollinarians,' who adopted and developed the theory of Apollinaris, bishop of Syrian Laodicea; which, like Marcellianism, arose out of a onesided antipathy to Arianism, and was at this time being disseminated with extraordinary activity in the East. Its primary proposition was, that in the Incarnate Son the Logos was instead of a rational human mind; its second proposition denied the human origin of His body, and represented it as formed out of the Divine essence. See Tillemont, vii. 602 ff.; Newman's Church of the Fathers, p. 157, and Tracts Theological and Ecclesiastical, pp. 257 ff.; also Later Treatises of St. Athanasius (Lib. Fath.), p. 78. Athanasius had written against these errors (ad Epictetum, C. Apollin.); Basil had pointed out their far-reaching unsoundness (Epist. 263); and Gregory Nazianzen was deeply impressed with their fatal effect on the faith of unwary Churchmen (Epist. 101, 102, 203). The Epiphanian creed had emphasized the reality of Christ's manhood: 'And was incarnate of the Holy Spirit *and* the Virgin Mary' (compare Marcellus' formulary of A. D. 341, Epiphan. Hær. 72. 3). This was adopted in the 'Constantinopolitan' symbol, and so it appears in the Greek and

Latin forms of this creed, as recited to catechumens, in the Sacramentary of Pope Gelasius; later, the West adopted the Aquileian distinction of 'de Spiritu . . . ex Maria.' One main point of interest in Apollinarianism is the occasion which it gave, by reaction, to the Nestorian theory of a mere 'association' between the Word and a personally human Christ.

CANON II.

This canon developes the Nicene legislation (Nic. 4 and 6) as to the territorial arrangements of the Christian hierarchy. It presupposes the conformation of ecclesiastical to civil boundaries: the secular scheme of thirteen 'dioceses,' each including so many provinces, in each of which so many cities were dependent on the metropolis, is adopted for convenience by the Church (Bingham, ix. 1. 3, 4). The civil ruler of a 'diocese,' called in 'the Oriens' a count, in Egypt a prefect, elsewhere a 'vicar' or vice-prefect (Gibbon, ii. 313), had his counterpart in a great prelate who in the next century was called an exarch (Chalc. 9), or, in the case of a few preeminent sees, a patriarch, —a title which some Easterns deemed to belong specially to the bishop of Antioch (Arab. can. 8, Mansi, ii. 955, cp. Neale, Introd. East. ch. 1. 126). The president or proconsul of a province was similarly reflected in the religious sphere by the metropolitan: and each suffragan of a metropolitan in his own παροικία, or, as we should now say, diocese (cp. Nic. 16), corresponded ecclesiastically to the temporal authorities of his city and district. The word διοίκησις, diœcesis, at first applied to any one of the smaller districts of the empire, as when Cicero says that three Asiatic διοικήσεις had been attached to his province of Cilicia (ad Famil. xiii. 67), or Strabo says that the Romans arranged τὰς διοικήσεις in which they established courts of justice (Geogr. xiii. 4. s. 12, cp. s. 17), had in the fourth century a certain elasticity of meaning, retaining always, of course, the notion of a certain area placed under one person's administrative control. In this canon it bears its then recently acquired technical sense of a group of provinces, as Gothofred (Cod. Theod. vol. ii. p. 36) defines it, 'provinciarum in unam administrationem collectio;' (cp. Chalc. 9, on which Balsamon says, διοίκησίς ἐστιν ἡ πολλὰς ἐπαρχίας ἔχουσα ἐν ἑαυτῇ, and ib. 28: and see Palladius' use of it, Dial. de Vita Chrys. p. 53, and the heading of Cyril's third letter to Nestorius, 'The Synod ... ἐκ τῆς Αἰγυπτιακῆς διοικήσεως,' Mansi, iv. 1180). The Council of Arles had apparently used it for a province (see on Nic. 6); so Hincmar used it long afterwards (Op. ii. 249, 310): but in some African canons its import is narrowed to what we should now call a parish or a particular portion of a bishop's district,—a place dependent on his see (3rd C. Carth. c. 42–44, 46, Mansi, iii. 887 ff., cp. also ib. iii. 803, 818); and so Sulpicius Severus speaks of St. Martin as visiting 'diœcesim quamdam,' as it is usual for bishops 'visitare ecclesias suas' (Epist. i. 10), and so the Council of Agde in 506, 'presbyter dum diœcesim tenet.' and Gregory of Tours (Hist. Fr. v. 5), 'dum diœceses ac villas ecclesiæ circumiret.' It might have seemed natural to transfer the term from the part to the whole of a παροικία, and so come nearer the original use; and so in the record of the Conference of Carthage in 411, while 'diœcesis' is sometimes used for a place under a bishop's jurisdiction (Collat. i. c. 128, 133, 142, 163, 176), it seems elsewhere to mean what we should call his 'diocese' (ib. c. 116, 117, 126), and so Augustine uses it in his 'Breviculus Collationis,' i. 12, 'Victoriani Mustitani catholici episcopi, ... in ipsa autem diœcesi Mustitana.' So it is used by the 1st Council of Tours, c. 9, and apparently by Leo in Epist. xii. 10, and so by Sidonius Apollinaris in Epist. vii. 6, although in Epist. ix. 16 it has the narrower sense. As found in Adamnan's Life of St. Columba, i. 35, it is considered by Dean Reeves (note in loc.) to have no technical sense at all.

We now see what the canon means by forbidding prelates stationed outside a particular 'diocese' (for this, as Valesius says, must be the sense of ὑπὲρ διοίκησιν, compare ὑπεροπίοις) to meddle with churches 'internal to it,' and therefore 'external' to their own borders, or 'to disturb them in any way.' Nothing of this sort is to take place; 'but on the contrary, according to the canons, the bishop of Alexandria is to administer (οἰκονομεῖν, cp. can. 6) the affairs in Egypt only, and the bishops of the East,' i.e. the Oriental 'diocese' properly so called, containing fifteen provinces, of which Antioch was both civilly and ecclesiastically the head, 'to manage (διοικεῖν) the East only, the privileges mentioned in the canons passed at Nicæa being reserved for the church of Antioch' (referring to Nic. 6). 'And the bishops of the diocese of Asia' (containing eleven provinces) 'are to administer the affairs of the Asiatic diocese only, and the bishops of the Pontic diocese' (containing eleven provinces) 'the affairs of the Pontic only, and the bishops of the Thracian diocese' (containing six provinces) 'the affairs of the Thracian only.' It is remarkable that the great sees of Ephesus, Cæsarea in Cappadocia, and Heraclea, the capitals respectively of the Asiatic, Pontic, and Thracian 'dioceses,' are not named, and even in the case of the Oriental 'diocese,' Antioch is only named in a saving clause for its rightful privileges, whereas Alexandria stands out prominently as representing Church authority throughout Egypt; see above on Nic. 6, as to the great powers of the Alexandrian see within its 'diocese.' Compare the celebrated law of Theodosius, promulgated on the 30th of July, 381, and naming certain bishops as centres and types of Catholic communion for the Eastern empire, e.g. 'in the Asian diocese Amphilochius of Iconium and Optimus of (Pisidian) Antioch,' 'in the Pontic diocese Helladius bishop of Cæsarea, and Otreius of Melitene, and Gregory bishop of Nyssa' (Cod. Theod. xvi. 1. 3). This brings us to that assertion of Socrates on which Beveridge relies, but which he distorts (Annotationes, pp. 52 ff. 94), that the Council 'distributed the provinces and appointed patriarchs,' so that 'Helladius, Gregory, and Otreius, obtained the patriarchate of the Pontic diocese' (v. 8). If Valesius is wrong in saying that Socrates meant by patriarchs 'extraordinary legates' sent 'through the dioceses to establish the right faith,' Bingham is not less wrong in understanding him of patriarchs properly so called (ii. 17. 6); and for this plain reason, that he assigns three 'patriarchs' to a single (Pontic) diocese, one of them being the bishop of Nyssa (for Beveridge's contention, that Helladius and the rest are *not* the 'patriarchs' referred to in the preceding clause, Annotat. p. 94, is a mere violence to the text). The statement of Socrates, in fact, is simply based on a confused reading of the law and of the canon: he is attributing to the Council what was in fact decreed by Theodosius, and using 'patriarchs' in the sense of 'eminent bishops.' The first application of 'patriarch' to an occupant of one of the great sees appears in the acts of the Council of Chalcedon, where the commissioners speak of the 'patriarchs of the several dioceses' (Mansi, vi. 953), and where Egyptian memorialists address Leo by that title (ib. 1005, 1011, 1021, 1029). To proceed: the canon forbids bishops to go outside the 'diocese' within which their sees are situate, either for the purpose of ordaining (on χειροτονία, see Nic. 4), or for any other acts of ecclesiastical administration, unless invited.

So much as to the relations of the several 'dioceses,'—or, as we might say, exarchates,—to each other. It will be observed that nothing is said as to Western Church arrangements, because this synod was exclusively Eastern: and as to the Eastern Church—using the term in its wider sense—it is implied, though not expressly asserted, that no appeal is to be made by a bishop resident in one 'diocese' to any great see outside its limits, e. g. by a prelate in Pontus to the see of Antioch. It is observable that when St. Chrysostom's friends protested against the intrusive conduct of Theophilus at the Council of the Oak, they cited, not this canon, but the less explicit 5th of Nicæa (Palladius, Dial. p. 29).

(2) But as to the next division, that of provinces,—'it is manifest,' says the canon, 'that the affairs of each province are to be managed by the provincial synod, according to the Nicene provisions' (Nic. 5).

(3) And those churches which had been planted among the 'barbaric nations,' and lay outside the bounds of the Roman Empire, must be 'administered according to the usage established by, and existing in force from the times of, the fathers,' i.e. they must continue dependent on, and receive assistance from, some great church within the empire, from which they originally received the episcopate (compare Balsamon and Zonaras). Such was the relation of the Ethiopian Church to that of Alexandria, ever since Athanasius had consecrated Frumentius as its first bishop (Soc. i. 19). The Christians of Iberia were, according to their own traditions, much indebted to Eustathius of Antioch (Neale, i. 61), although Le Quien thinks that they were at first connected with Cæsarea in Cappadocia (i. 1335). The church of 'Armenia Major,' the oldest of national churches, constituted about A.D. 302 by St. Gregory the Illuminator, who received the episcopate from the same see of Cæsarea, was subject to it at the date of this Council, when Nierses presided in Gregory's church of Etchmiadzine (Neale, i. 1375: for another local account, see Fortescue's Armenian Church, p. 20). The Persian or Chaldæan Church, which had suffered a terrible persecution under Sapor II. (Soz. ii. 9 ff.), was ruled by Cajuma bishop of Seleucia and Ctesiphon, who, like most of his predecessors, was 'catholicus' or 'procurator' for the bishop of Antioch (Le Quien, ii. 1079; Neale, i. 141). Columban, mistaking the special point of this provision, appealed to it as against interference with the Celtic calculation of Easter (Epist. 3, to Boniface IV.).

CANON III.

This is a brief but momentous provision, connected with the preceding canon, which had ruled that bishops were not to interfere in the affairs of other 'dioceses.' 'However (μέντοι) the bishop of Constantinople is to have honorary preeminence after the bishop of Rome, because Constantinople is New Rome.'

The word πρεσβεῖα by itself, as used in can. 2 and Nic. 6, means 'prerogatives' or 'privileges:' but here the qualifying addition τῆς τιμῆς limits its scope to an honorary precedency or, as the old Latin translators say, a 'primatus honoris,' as distinct from any peculiar authority. There is, so far as this phrase is concerned, no question of supremacy or superiority of power. (2) Such a precedency, or priority of rank, or 'primacy of honour,' is implicitly recognised as belonging to the see of Rome in regard to all other sees whatever, the Constantinopolitan included (even as, in the secular order, Old Rome continued to rank above New Rome, Gibbon, ii. 302). So the Arabic paraphrase of these canons says that 'the bishop of Constantinople sits next after the bishop of Rome' (Mansi, iii. 578), and Zonaras observes that μετά denotes ὑποβίβασμον καὶ ἐλάττωσιν. According to Bede (de Temporum Ratione) it was because the church of Constantinople had been 'writing itself first of all churches' that the emperor Phocas declared the Roman see to be 'the head.' (3) An absolute priority being reserved to the see of Rome, precedency over all other sees is conferred *de novo* on that of Constantinople. (4) The reason given, because the city of Constantine is a 'New Rome' (Soz. ii. 3), implies that the existing precedency of the Roman see has, like that of the Constantinopolitan, a basis simply political, the imperial majesty of Old Rome itself. It was not perhaps unnatural that the ecclesiastics and adherents of a church which, as Pope Gelasius said long afterwards, was not even metropolitical, but a mere 'parœcia' or diocesan church, dependent on that of Heraclea (Mansi, viii. 54), should desire to represent the Roman church as owing its distinction to a circumstance in which their own could share. But the representation, although countenanced by the Fourth as well as by the Second General Council, was not the less unfaithful to the facts. The church of Rome was what it was, the first of all churches, for a variety of reasons ecclesiastical as well as political. It owed much to the name of 'the City,' but much also to the names of Peter and Paul. No other Western church could boast of having been consolidated (to say 'founded' in the proper sense would be untrue) by the personal ministry of those two great Apostles (Irenæus, iii. 3. 2), or, indeed, could call its see distinctively apostolical: no other church whatever, perhaps it may be added, could exhibit 'fasti' so religiously august. These considerations, appealing as they did to the universal instincts of Christian reverence, were reinforced by the traditions of an orthodoxy which had hardly, if ever, been sullied, and of a munificent charity which had won the gratitude of poorer brethren in Greece (Euseb. iv. 23), in Syria and Arabia (ib. vii. 5), and in Cappadocia (Basil, Epist. 70): and, as it has been well said, 'the resultant of these forces was increased in intensity by the respect and influence which naturally attached to the centre of political government' (note in Oxf. Transl. of Fleury, vol. iii. p. 96: compare Robertson, Hist. Ch. i. 226). Theodoret, in his letter to Leo, grounds the precedency of the Roman church on the grandeur of its city, on its own faith, and above all on its possession of the graves of Peter and Paul (Epist. 113). But (5) while we cannot on historic grounds accept the Council's too simple view of a many-sided fact, we must observe that it does not hereby invest the see of the Eastern capital with any new jurisdiction, nor even make it independent of the mother-see of Heraclea (Le Quien, i. 19), which, in the person of bishop Theodore, had recently claimed, with success, the right to consecrate Demophilus for Constantinople (Philostorg. ix. 10), and still retains that privilege in regard to the 'œcumenical patriarch' (see Balsamon in loc., although, on Chalc. 12, he denies it to be a right; and Le Quien, i. 180). Powers, indeed, had been usurped by Demophilus himself, and by Arian predecessors of his in the see of Constantinople (Philostorg. v. 3: ix. 8, 13, Soc. ii. 38): and in the period after the Council similar acts on the part of its orthodox occupants, in the first half of the next century, were not warranted by the new canon, but formed part of a series of precedents which, as we shall see, induced the Council of Chalcedon,—while professedly observant of the lines traced by this Council,—to erect for the see of Constantinople a patriarchal jurisdiction on the foundation of an 'honorary precedency.' Socrates indeed says that Nectarius received authority over Thrace as well as over 'the great city' (v. 8); but, as we have already observed, he is loose in his statements about the proceedings of this Synod, and he was likely enough to read into the canon what he knew from later events. If the Council had deliberately meant to make the see of Constantinople supreme over the bishops of Thrace, its second canon must have been worded differently. Lastly, (6) this decree is prejudicial to the status of the great sees of Alexandria and Antioch, which had previously ranked as second and third in the hierarchy. It was probably intended to guard against such claim to interfere in the affairs of Constantinople as Peter of Alexandria had recently put forward (see next canon, and compare Gregory, Carm. de Vita sua, 862; so Neale, Hist. Alex. i. 206): but we cannot wonder that this exaltation of what Egyptians might call 'an upstart bishopric' above the illustrious 'throne of the Evangelist' aroused that persistent Alexandrian hostility which brought such trouble to the noblest of Constantinopolitan bishops. In regard to the church of Antioch, its peculiar condition at that time rendered it especially dependent on the will of the Council. It was suffering from 'the Antiochene schism,' the dissension between the stricter Catholics, who, ever since the deposition of Eustathius by Arianizers in 331, had held aloof from a line of bishops more or less connected with Arianism, and those who, while retaining their faith, had communicated with the prelates successively in possession, and had welcomed, in 361, the accession of a bishop whose first discourse gave substantial evidence of his orthodoxy. This was the celebrated Meletius, whom the 'Eustathians' had refused to acknowledge because of his Arian appointment; and in the following year they had procured the irregular intervention of the zealous Lucifer of Caliaris to consecrate their own pastor Paulinus. Both prelates were eminently good men: Meletius was recognised by the Asiatic churches, Paulinus by Egypt and the West: and a sort of concordat had been made in 378, to the effect that the survivor should be owned by both sections as bishop of Antioch (Soc. v. 5: Soz. vii. 3). Meletius had died at Constantinople during the Council: Gregory of Nazianzus, as bishop of Constantinople, had exhorted the bishops to accept Paulinus: but party feelings proved too strong for this good counsel, and prompted the resolution that a new appointment should be made. In effect, Flavian, a priest of the Meletian party, was chosen, and ultimately recognised by the West as well as the East. Generally, indeed, the see of Antioch was less 'tenacious' of its rights than any other of the patriarchal thrones (Le Quien, ii. 677), its conduct as to Cyprus (Eph. 8) being an exception.

It should be added that this new order of the great sees was naturally ignored by the West. Although Paschasinus, Leo's legate, observed in the 1st session of Chalcedon that in that Council, 'by God's will,' Anatolius of Constantinople was first, whereas at the Robbers' Meeting his predecessor had been fifth (Mansi, vi. 607), yet he and his brother-legate, Lucentius, in the 16th session, disowned the canons of Constantinople, and Leo himself afterwards contended that the elevation of the see of Constantinople above those of Alexandria and Antioch was a breach of Nicene rules. He also described this canon as 'quorumdam episcoporum conscriptio,' which had never been communicated to the Apostolic see, and had long come to nought (Epist. 106. 2, 5). So, four centuries later, Hincmar of Reims emphasizes the old sequence, 'Rome, Alexandria, Antioch' (Op. ii. 429); and Rome did not admit Constantinople to the second place until a Latin patriarchate had been erected there in the beginning of the 13th century. See, e.g. Gregory the Great in Epist. vii. 34, 'The Roman Church has not received the canons ... of that synod.'

These three canons were read as one 'synodicon' of 'the 150 fathers' at the last session of the Council of Chalcedon (Mansi, vii. 446).

Canon IV.

Maximus, also named Heron, had come from Egypt to Constantinople about the beginning of 380, professing to have been formerly a confessor for the faith, but retaining the white dress and the staff which then marked the Cynic philosopher, and also conspicuous (we may as well have the whole picture) by his flowing red locks (Gregory, Carm. adv. Max. 42: de Vita sua, 754, 768). Probably he was not the Maximus to whom Athanasius and Basil had written in terms of respect (see Tillemont, ix. 444). Gregory of Nazianzus, then acting as missionary bishop at Constantinople, was attracted by his apparent earnestness, received with unsuspecting simplicity his own account of his antecedents, publicly eulogized him in a discourse still extant (Orat. 25), and treated him with a kindness which was heartlessly abused. 'He shared my house and board, my teaching, my counsels' (de Vita sua, 811; cp. Tillemont, ix. 445). Maximus repaid him by intriguing with one of his presbyters to secure the bishopric for himself; prevailed on Peter of Alexandria to send over some Egyptian bishops (preceded by auxiliaries of a rougher type); and arranged for his own consecration on a certain night, in the church called Anastasia,—Gregory being ill at the time. Day broke before the ceremony was completed: first some of the clergy, then a miscellaneous crowd, entered the church: the intruders had to take refuge in 'the sorry dwelling of a flute player' (Greg. de Vita sua, 909), where they cut off the Cynic's long hair, which, after all, was false. The outrage was promptly punished: Maximus was driven out of the city,—sought in vain for countenance from Theodosius, who, says Gregory, 'spurned him like a dog' (ib. 1009),—returned to Egypt, and tried to domineer over Peter; but, as Tillemont says (ix. 456), the eyes of 'ce bon viellard' were opened by the insult, and he resumed his friendly relations with Gregory.

Such was the 'disorderly procedure' of Maximus, which provoked the Council to declare by this canon that he was not, and never had been, a bishop,—that all clerics, of whatever degree, who might have been ordained by him had in truth received no ordination, all episcopal acts done in his favour or by him being pronounced invalid (see on Nic. 16).

Maximus, however, having been expelled from Egypt, made his way into Northern Italy, presented to Gratian at Milan a large work which he had written against the Arians (as to which Gregory sarcastically remarks—'Saul a prophet, Maximus an author!' Carm. adv. Max. 21), and deceived St. Ambrose and his suffragans by showing the record of his consecration, with letters which Peter had once written in his behalf. To these prelates of the 'Italic diocese' the appeal of Maximus seemed like the appeal of Athanasius, and more recently of Peter himself, to the sympathy of the church of Rome; and they requested Theodosius to let the case be heard before a really General Council (Mansi, iii. 631). Nothing further came of it: perhaps, says Tillemont, those who thus wrote in favour of Maximus 'reconnurent bientôt quel il était' (ix. 502): so that when a Council did meet at Rome, towards the end of 382, no steps were taken in his behalf.

These four canons are all that were passed by the Council of 381. No others are ascribed to it by the Latin collectors, although the Dionysian version reckons them as three, the Isidorian as six: and the canons reckoned as 5th and 6th must be assigned to a Council held at Constantinople in 382, at the summons of Theodosius, who preferred this plan to the Latin one of a General Council to be held at Rome (compare Ambrose, Epist. 14).

It was to this new meeting of Eastern prelates, which might be called a second session of the Council of Constantinople, that Gregory of Nazianzus, who in his despondency had abdicated the see of Constantinople in the preceding year, was invited, but declined to attend (Epist. 131), protesting (with evident allusion to the recent rejection of his own advice) that he had never seen any good result of a synod, but adding that he had determined to 'retire into himself,' and was, besides, so ill as to be 'fit for nothing.' The bishops, when they met without the advantage of his presence, had before them a letter from Western prelates requesting them to attend a General Council to be held at Rome. Theodoret gives their reply (v. 9); it is not free from a certain apparent disingenuousness (see Tillemont, x. 150), but it pleads inability to visit the West, or to do more than send a synodical letter. The Council then passed two more canons.

CANON V.

'In regard to the "tome" of the Westerns, we have recognised those at Antioch who confess one Godhead of Father, Son, and Holy Spirit.' The sentence is too concise to be self-explanatory. The word 'tome,' indeed, is easily understood to mean a doctrinal formulary, such as the Athanasian 'Tomus ad Antiochenos,' the 'Tome' of Proclus of Constantinople to the Armenians,—the 'Tome' of Leo the Great, otherwise called his 28th Epistle,—the 'Tome' which, according to Philostorgius (vii. 2), was drawn up against Aetius the Anomœan: and so this very Council, in its letter to the Western bishops (Theod. v. 9), refers them to one 'tome drawn up by the Council which assembled at Antioch' (in 379), and to another 'put forth by the Œcumenical Synod at Constantinople' (in 381). But what was the Tome of the Westerns? It was clearly a doctrinal letter sent not long previously by a Western synod to the Easterns,—i. e. to such prelates as had now met at Constantinople,—and touching at least indirectly on the dissension at Antioch. These conditions appear to exclude the series of anathemas against various errors sent by Damasus to Paulinus, the date of which is uncertain (Theod. v. 11),—the letter of a Roman synod of 371–2 to the Easterns (Mansi, iii. 459),—and the letter of an Italian Council, inviting the bishops to attend a Council at Rome (Theod. v. 9: see Hefele, s. 102). It seems most probable that the canon refers to a document framed by a Roman Council, not, as Hefele thinks, in 369, but as Mansi considers, in 377 (iii. 466: cp. Maran, Vit. S. Basil. c. 37. s. 2), and of which a fragment remains, concluding with an assertion of Nicene faith, and a rejection of Macedonian, Marcellian, and Apollinarian error (Mansi, iii. 461). This document, we know, was accepted by a large Council held at Antioch under the presidency of Meletius, nine months after St. Basil's death (Greg. Nyssen, Op. ii. 187), i.e. in September 379 (not 378), when a corresponding statement, called in this Council's letter a tome, and in the 'Libellus Synodicus' a sacred definition (ὅρος θεῖος, Justellus, Biblioth. ii. 1189; Mansi, iii. 486), was drawn up and probably sent to Rome in return (Tillemont, viii. 367). It is unnatural and unnecessary to identify, as Hefele does, 'the tome of the Westerns' with 'the tome made at Antioch.' The Council, therefore, seems to resume the position taken three years before, at Antioch, and to say, 'We quite agree with the Westerns as to the errors which they denounce: we are as much opposed as they can be to every form of Arianism, and to all Macedonian irreverence towards the Holy Spirit: and from that point of view we recognise the orthodoxy' (as ἀποδέχεσθαι is used in Athanasius' Tom. ad Antioch. 3. 6) 'of all those at Antioch, whether belonging to the Eustathian or to the Meletian section, who have a sound belief as to the Trinity in Unity.' It is intended as a contribution to the cause of peace, which, as Westerns might well think, had been gravely injured by the refusal of the Council of 381 to acknowledge Paulinus as the successor of Meletius. Westerns might ask, 'Is not some tenderness towards Arianism at the bottom of this "animus" against one who has spent a life in resisting Arianizers?' The canon was meant to answer, 'None at all.'

Canon VI.

This, the longest canon in our series, treats of charges brought against orthodox bishops. Its language betokens an inevitable result of the protracted Arian controversy, and, to speak more particularly, of the tactics pursued by the Arian party from their first attack on Eustathius and on Athanasius Accusation—bitter, obstinate, relentless—had become a weapon ready to hand at any time. The atmosphere of ecclesiastical society was hot with suspicion, misrepresentation, denunciation. 'A bishop,' wrote Chrysostom about this period, 'has to look round him on all sides, lest some one should find a weak point in his conduct, and strike home there. For all are standing round him, ready to wound and overthrow him ... If he happens to make some little oversight, all his good deeds will not help him against the tongues of accusers ... and they who stand near him and minister with him are the very men whom he has most reason to dread' (de Sacerd. iii. 14). So, later, when he had had personal experience of episcopal difficulties, he declared that 'nobody was afraid to accuse or misrepresent a bishop' (in Act. Hom. 3. 4). So the Council says that 'many persons, with a view to disturbing and upsetting the good order of churches which but for them would be left at peace, and casting a slur on the reputation of bishops (ἱερέων), are given to hatching accusations in a hostile and malignant spirit against the orthodox prelates who are administering the churches.' The verb οἰκονομεῖν in this place, as in can. 2, and Euseb. iv. 4, and when Basil wishes that his brother Gregory might οἰκονομεῖν a church suited to his own temperament (Epist. 98. 2), has obviously the sense of spiritual stewardship, derived from Luke xii. 42, 1 Cor. iv. 1. Used thus absolutely, it cannot be referred to the mere distribution of Church alms (Hatch's Bamp. Lect. p. 41); when a merely 'economic' function is intended, the context shows it, as in Chalc. 26. Observe also the special use of ἱερεύς for a bishop, in whose office the Christian priesthood was, so to speak, concentrated (compare Tertullian, de Bapt. 17, 'summus sacerdos qui est episcopus'). St. Chrysostom's work 'on the Priesthood,' written to account for his own avoidance of the episcopate, illustrates this use, as does ἱερωσύνης in Eph. 2, and Cyprian's frequent employment of 'sacerdos' for 'episcopus,' e. g. Epist. 59. 7.

To guard against the evil complained of, it is ordered that no charges against bishops shall be 'received from anybody without inquiry:' that is, a distinction must be drawn. (1) Those who complain of personal wrong must be heard, and no questions asked as to their antecedents or their religious profession. The words are worthy of an Ecclesiastical Council: 'In such cases we must not inquire as to the accuser's person or his religious profession' (θρησκείαν, used for a 'cult,' as in the imperial edicts translated in Euseb. ix. 1. 9; x. 5). It is absolutely necessary that the bishop's conscience should be clear, and that he who says he is wronged should have justice, whatever be his religious profession. So the Council of Hippo in 393 ruled that no one whose personal conduct was culpable should be allowed to accuse a bishop, 'nisi proprias causas, non tamen ecclesiasticas, dicere voluerit' (Mansi, iii. 920). The distinction is not recognised in Apost. can. 75, which rules that a heretic is not to be admitted as a witness against a bishop: and compare can. 96 in the series called that of the 'Fourth Council of Carthage.' But (2) it is otherwise, the Council proceeds in effect, as to charges of an 'ecclesiastical' nature. Then the accuser's personal position is an important element in the case: and we must refuse a hearing to persons who have no ecclesiastical 'locus standi.' Such are (a) 'heretics, under which name we include (α) persons formerly excommunicated, (β) persons anathematized by ourselves,' (i.e. by Constant. 1. above), (γ) 'those who profess to hold the sound faith, but have gone into schism and formed congregations in opposition to our canonical bishops:' (b) churchmen either (α) previously excommunicated for some fault, or (β) accused of some fault, from which they have not yet cleared themselves. Compare 2nd C. of Carthage, can. 6, 'Si criminosus est, non admittatur ut accuset' (Mansi, iii. 694).

Here several points require attention. (1) Ἀποκηρυχθέντας refers to the greater excommunication, as Alexander says of the original Arians, ἀπεκηρύχθησαν ἀπὸ τῆς ἐκκλησίας (Soc. i. 6), and Gregory Nazianzen says that Damasus made the Apollinarians ἀποκηρύκτους (Epist. 102); comp. ἐκκήρυκτον in Euseb. vi. 43. (2) The reference to the anathema (see Bingham, xvi. 2. 8) pronounced against heretics may be illustrated from the anathematisms at the end of the original Nicene Creed. (3) The term 'heretics' is here used in a wide sense, so as to include schismatics, as in the records of the Conference of Carthage, i. 126, 139; whereas Athanasius (Ep. ad Ægypt. 22), and Basil (Epist. 188. 1), when they distinguish heretics from schismatics, use the term strictly. (4) 'Ἀντισυνάγοντας is illustrated by the ancient technical sense of συνάγειν (Euseb. vii. 11, Athan. Apol. c. Ari. 20, Antioch. 5), συνάγεσθαι (Euseb. iv. 15, Athan. Apol. c. Ari. 8), and σύναξις (Cyril, Catech. 10. 14; Athan. Apol. de Fuga, 24; Tom. ad Antioch. 9; Soc. v. 22; so Chrysostom speaks of the daily συνάξεις, In Act. Hom. 29. 3). Compare the similar use of 'colligere' (Tertull. de Fuga, 14), and 'collecta' united with 'Dominicum' (the Holy Eucharist) in Ruinart's Act. Mart. SS. Saturn. Dativ. etc. Socrates uses παρασυνάγων for holding a congregation apart from the bishop, vii. 5. (5) For κανονικοῖς (ἡμῶν ἐπισκόποις) it has been proposed by Beveridge (and see Routh, Scr. Opusc. i. 421) to read κοινωνικοῖς, 'the bishops who are in communion with us,' in accordance with κοινωνικούς in the letter of this Synod to the Westerns (Theod. v. 9). We find τοὺς κοινωνικοὺς τῆς ἐκκλησίας in the 15th of bishop Isaac's charges against St. Chrysostom, for 'persons in communion with the Church,' and furnished with commendatory letters (Photius, Bibl. c. 59).

Such persons, then, as are not thus disqualified, are to bring their complaints before the provincial synod. 'But if it shall happen that the provincial bishops are not able' to settle the case, let it go up to a synod of the whole 'diocese' assembled for that purpose; and 'the accusers must in the first instance give written guarantees that, in case they are convicted of calumny, they will accept for themselves the same penalty which the bishop would incur if they made their accusation good. But if any one intrude upon the Emperor's attention, or trouble the secular law courts, or an Œcumenical Council, thereby disregarding these provisions, and putting a slight on the bishops of the "diocese," such a person is not to be admitted as an accuser.' The Council of Antioch had provided that if the bishops of the province could not agree in their verdict, the metropolitan should invite some other bishops from the neighbouring province to clear up uncertainties, and in conjunction with his comprovincials arrive at a decision (c. 14). The present canon makes more regular provision for such a contingency: and the 9th canon of Chalcedon went a step beyond the lines here traced by allowing an appeal from the provincial synod, not only to the 'exarch' of the 'diocese,' who probably would convoke a synod of the ' diocese' to hear it (compare a law of Gratian, 'a suæ diœceseos synodis audiantur,' Cod. Theod. xvi. 2. 23), but to the see of Constantinople. The phrase, 'troubling the emperor's ears,' is borrowed from the 11th canon of Antioch. What the Council here means is that no one who carries an ecclesiastical accusation against a bishop before the civil authority shall afterwards be allowed to fall back on the spiritual tribunal.

Canon VII.

What is called the 7th canon of Constantinople is not a canon at all, though Balsamon and Zonaras treat it as such. It is unknown to the Latin translators: it is absent from the collection of Symeon Logothetes (Justellus, Biblioth. ii. 717), and,—what is more,—from that of John Scholasticus of Antioch, who lived in the reign of Justinian (ib. ii. 502). It is acknowledged by Photius in his Nomocanon (ib. ii. 794), and by Alexius Aristenus, who even divides it into two: and it is embodied in the 95th canon of the Council in Trullo in 692, but without any reference to synodical enactment. As it stands here, it has not the form of a canon: it ordains nothing, it only recites a usage,—doubtless the usage of the church of Constantinople,—as to the mode of receiving converts from the different sects. Beveridge considers it to be a slightly abridged and altered form of a letter still extant, addressed by some cleric of Constantinople to Martyrius, patriarch of Antioch, about A.D. 460.

It begins by pointedly separating all heretics as such from 'the portion of those who are being saved' (σωζομένων, from Acts ii. 47, 2 Cor. ii. 15). It then enumerates those sects from which converts are received according to the usage in question, without being baptized *de novo* (see on Nic. 19). These are (1) Arians: (2) Macedonians: (3) Sabbatians, or followers of Sabbatius, a converted Jew who had joined the Novatians, been ordained presbyter, exhibited Judaistic leanings as to the Paschal festival, and ultimately, about the end of the fourth century, formed a sect of his own upon that basis, and procured for himself episcopal consecration (Soc. v. 21, vii. 5, 12; Fleury, 19. 35; Newman's Arians, p. 17). His followers called themselves Protopaschites, or 'observers of the original Pasch.' Theodosius II., in a law of 413, describes them as 'deserters from the Novatian body' (Cod. Theod. xvi. 6. 6). (4) Novatians who call themselves Cathari (see on Nic. 8) and ἀριστέρους, or, as we should rather read, ἀρίστους, or as the letter to Martyrius actually has it, and as Routh would read in this passage, καθαρωτέρους (Scr. Opusc. i. 424). (5) Quartodecimans or Tetraditæ. This latter name is explained by Balsamon to mean that Quartodecimans were accustomed to fast during their Easter, as Catholics did on Wednesdays: but it is more reasonable to understand it of those who, although not holding entirely with the Quartodecimans, ended their ante-paschal fast with the fourth day in Holy Week (Routh, i. 425: he compares Laodic. 50). (6) Apollinarians.

Converts from these sects are received on giving 'libelli,' or written professions of orthodox belief, such as the sectarians of Lydia did when they adopted a Nestorian creed as if it were Nicene (see on Eph. 7), and such as the Trullan canon requires also from ex-Nestorians. They anathematize every 'heresy,' that is, 'every sect, which does not hold what the Catholic Church holds.' They are then anointed with chrism on forehead, eyes, nostrils, mouth, and ears, the officiant saying, 'The seal of the gift of the Holy Spirit'—the form of administering Confirmation in the Eastern Church to this day (see Goar, Euchologion, p. 356; Neale, Introd. East. Ch. ii. 1002).

The other sects, whose baptism is treated as null, are (1) the Eunomians 'who baptize with one immersion only;' an evident allusion to their custom of baptizing into the death of Christ rather than into the threefold Name (Soc. v. 24, comp. Apost. can. 50): (2) 'Montanists, here called Phrygians:' (3) Sabellians, 'who teach the absolute identity of the Son with the Father' (υἱοπατορία, compare Arius' letter to Alexander, Athan. de Synod. 16, and see Card. Newman, Ath. Treat. ii. 475, ed. 2), 'and do other grievous things,—and, generally, all the other sects, for there are many of them, especially those who come from Galatia' (alluding to the Marcellians). Converts from any of these are received as Gentiles, then on the first day are 'made Christians.' This bold anticipative use of the name Christian is found in Sulpicius Severus: a great crowd, near Chartres, begged St. Martin 'ut eos faceret Christianos:' and 'at once, in the middle of the plain, cunctos imposita universis manu catechumenos fecit' (Dial. 2. 4): so St. Augustine (de Catechiz. Rud. s. 14), 'Nobis dicitur, Veni, loquere huic; vult Christianus fieri:' and compare Martene, de Ant. Eccl. Rit. i. 37. Some understand 'fieri Christianos' in Elviran can. 39 in this sense; yet see Hefele in loc. But the next words, 'on the second day we make them catechumens,' indicate a distinction between 'Christians,' as here used, and 'catechumens.' Probably by 'making them Christians' is meant merely their reception as applicants: compare a passage in the Euchologion (p. 335) as to a Jewish convert. When the proselyte makes his solemn abjuration of Judaism, 'we make him a Christian, that is, we reckon him as a Christian unbaptized, such as are those children of Christians who are about to be baptized. On the second day we number him with the catechumens, saying over him the prayer which we say over children catechumens,' the prayer being that in the Greek Order for making a catechumen, which prays that 'the old error' may be removed from the person who has been permitted to fly to the Name' of the Holy Trinity, and that his 'name may be written in the book of life.' Compare the corresponding prayers (from the Gelasian Sacramentary) at the beginning of the Sarum 'Ordo ad faciendum Catechumenum.' Both these offices begin with signing of the cross and imposition of the hands. 'Then on the third day we exorcise them, after breathing thrice on their foreheads and into their ears.' So in the Greek rubric above cited: 'And on the next day we use the prayers of the exorcisms,' two of which exorcisms, in the Greek office, are addressed to Satan, commanding him 'by the salutary Passion' and 'the awful coming' to 'depart from the newly-enrolled soldier of Christ:' (compare the Sarum exorcisms before and after the prayer which still remains in our Baptismal Office, 'Deus, immortale præsidium,' etc.). In the Greek rite, 'the priest breathes thrice on the catechumen's mouth, forehead, and breast, praying that every unclean spirit may be expelled: and the renunciations follow. The statement concludes, 'And so we catechize them, and make them come for a long time into the church, and listen to the Scriptures, and then we baptize them' (see on Nic. 2). On this view, we need not interpret the passage as making out three classes of catechumens. The higher stage, that of the φωτιζόμενοι, is indicated by the last words.

On a survey of this remarkable passage, we are struck with the distinction drawn between Arians and Sabellians on one hand, and Arians and Montanists on the other. St. Athanasius, who not unnaturally regarded Arianism as the worst of heresies, expressly declares Arian, Paulianist, and Montanist baptism to be no true baptism at all (Orat. ii. 43): yet here it is expressly said that Arians on their conversion are merely anointed, which implies the validity of their previous baptism. Why, we may ask, is Arianism thus treated more tenderly than Sabellianism? and why is Montanism, in this respect, ranked with Sabellianism? Because they were both believed to strike at that distinct identity of one or more of the Divine Persons which

Arianism, deadly as it was, had left unimpaired. Sabellianism unquestionably merged the hypostatic existence of the Son and of the Holy Spirit in that of the Father, and thereby made void the baptismal form. And several of the Fathers supposed the Montanists to regard their founder as an incarnation of the Third Person. This is Basil's meaning when he asks, as if the case were too plain for argument, 'How can we be expected to admit the baptism of those who baptize into Father and Son and Montanus?' (Epist. 188. 1). He was mistaken as to their real belief, according to which Montanus was but the instrument of a fuller outpouring of the Holy Spirit than had been vouchsafed to the Apostles. So Augustine (Hæres. 26): and Epiphanius accordingly pronounces the Montanists orthodox in regard to the Trinity (Hær. 48. 1, comp. Tillemont, ii. 470). But the mistake will explain the peculiar stringency with which Basil and the Council of Laodicea (can. 8) insisted that converts from 'the so-called Phrygians' must be treated as men not yet baptized.

NOTES ON THE CANONS OF EPHESUS.

Canon I.

This canon is addressed to those bishops who, 'on account of their own church-affairs or of their health, had remained at home' instead of attending the Council, and is designed to inform them as to 'the resolutions which had been formulated' (τετυπωμένα). 'We make it known to your Holinesses .... that if any metropolitan of a province (lit. of the province, i.e. his) has revolted against the holy and œcumenical Council, and gone over to the revolters' meeting, or hereafter should join them, or has held or holds the opinions of Celestius, he is deprived of all power to take steps against his orthodox comprovincials, in that he is hereby synodically cast out from all ecclesiastical communion, and is in a state of ecclesiastical incapacity' (ἀνενέργητος ὑπάρχων, cp. Chalc. 6): so that, instead of possessing any powers, he is to be 'subjected to his own comprovincials and the neighbouring metropolitans, being orthodox, even to the extent of being deposed from the rank of the episcopate.' For βαθμός see Eph. 2, 3, 5, 6, Chalc. 2, 10, 12, 18, 22, 27, 29. It seems to refer to 1 Tim. iii. 13 (see Chrys. in loc.: but see also Theodoret and Bp. Ellicott in loc.). In order to appreciate the bitter phrase 'sanhedrin of apostasy' or 'of revolt,' we must review the circumstances under which the Council of Ephesus was opened, and Nestorius of Constantinople was deposed.

Celestine of Rome and Cyril of Alexandria had agreed, in the preceding autumn, that, if Nestorius should not make a satisfactory declaration of his belief in regard to the doctrine of the Incarnation, he should forfeit the communion of their respective churches. Accordingly, Cyril wrote his third letter to Nestorius by way of exposition of that doctrine, and appended to it twelve 'anathemas,' which the bishop of Constantinople was required to sign. But before this document could be delivered, Theodosius II., at the request of Nestorius, had convoked an œcumenical synod to meet at Ephesus, on the following Whitsunday (June 7, 431), for the determination of the question. Celestine and Cyril were obliged to acquiesce. But it was found impossible to open the Council on the appointed day: Nestorius and Cyril, with their respective adherents, had arrived, but many prelates were still absent. A fortnight passed; the delay was felt to be wearisome and even dangerous to health; conferences with the Nestorian section only made matters worse by producing plainer avowals of heresy (Mansi, iv. 1181, 1229); and still John of Antioch had not come. The line which he would take was matter of some anxiety: for, having read the twelve anathemas apparently apart from the letter which would have explained their drift, he had deemed them virtually Apollinarian. At last, probably on Sunday the 21st of June, Cyril received a very courteous letter from John, to the effect that he and his fellow-travellers were making all possible haste, and expected to arrive in four or five days' time (Mansi, iv. 1121). The right course surely would have been to wait for the fulfilment of this expectation: but Cyril maintained that 'the Orientals' were seeking to gain time. Probably, also, there was in his mind an unexpressed conviction that their presence in the synod would be perilous to the cause of orthodoxy, an apprehension which made him take advantage of their non-arrival to declare that the bishops assembled had been waiting more than long enough (see Neale, Hist. Patr. Alex. i. 259, calling this a 'weakness of faith'). His influence prevailed,—or rather, perhaps, his proposal was welcomed by prelates who were eager to set to work, that they might the sooner return home. Accordingly, in spite of remonstrances from Nestorius, from sixty-eight other bishops, and from the imperial commissioner Candidian, the majority, consisting of 158 prelates, met in St. Mary's church early on Monday morning, June 22. Candidian made another effort: he read to them the emperor's letter, directing that the doctrinal question should be settled 'without any disturbance' (not, as Cyril soon afterwards quoted it, 'without any delay'), and 'by the common resolution of all' (Mansi, iv. 1120); he begged them to wait only four days more for the bishop of Antioch, whom he had ascertained to be within a comparatively short distance of Ephesus: but he argued and entreated in vain. Having desired him to withdraw, the bishops went through the business of summoning Nestorius (who declined to appear before them), comparing his written statements with the Nicene Creed and Cyril's 'second letter,' taking evidence as to his recent language, hearing a number of quotations from approved writers, and finally deposing him in the name of Christ,—in the course of that long midsummer day. On the Friday, apparently,—somewhat later than the time which he had indicated,— John of Antioch arrived with only some sixteen bishops (Tillemont, xiv. 768): and immediately, 'without taking off his cloak' (Mansi, iv. 1333), he constituted a synod of his companions and of others already at Ephesus. This company of forty-three prelates, after listening to Candidian, 'deposed' Cyril and his friend Memnon of Ephesus on charges of violence, heterodoxy, and precipitancy, and broke off communion with the other bishops. 'Hereby,' says Tillemont (xiv. 411), 'the "Easterns" who accused St. Cyril of an irregular proceeding were guilty of one yet more irregular.' Having thus made quick work, they admitted the delegates sent from the Council, but gave them no answer, and suffered them to be ill treated by attendant soldiers. In consequence, John was put out of communion,—the Council not knowing as yet of the sentence passed against its two leaders. At the fourth session, on the 17th of July, that sentence was the subject of a formal memorial; whereupon the Council thrice cited John to appear, and on his non-appearance excommunicated him, with thirty-four of his supporters, including that same Paul of Emesa who at the close of the next year was the medium of a reconciliation between Cyril and John. So stood matters between the majority at Ephesus and the minority, —here described as a 'synod of revolters,'—when this canon was framed. It is clear from this and the next succeeding canon that the Council was by this time uneasy as to the stedfastness of some of its own members—and not without reason. The course taken in disregard of protests was open to manifest objections: it was confessedly exceptional, and might be represented as disorderly and unfair: the Emperor was likely to be indignant: and bishops who at the time had so strongly acquiesced in the resolution to open the Council might think it expedient to retrace their steps.

The mention of Celestius is a remarkable link between the Eastern and Western Church history, as between the Christology and the anthropology of the period. That keen-witted and pertinacious disciple of Pelagius (see Anti-Pelagian Treatises of St. Augustine, Introd. p. xvi) had come to Constantinople with four bishops who had been 'deposed and driven out of the West' as Pelagians (Fleury, 25. 2). Nestorius, while expressing himself publicly in orthodox terms on the subject of the Fall, gave them hopes of favourable treatment, although he might have known that they had been repelled by his predecessor Atticus (Mansi, iv. 1026): but a memorial drawn up by the advocate Marius Mercator in 429 procured their second expulsion from Constantinople, and Nestorius thereupon sent to Celestius a letter of sympathy. Cyril and Memnon, in their memorial, had linked together the Nestorians and the adherents of Celestius or Pelagius (ib. 1320); and the Council repeatedly, in letters to the Emperor (ib. 1329, 1424) and to Pope Celestine (ib. 1333), asserts that among the supporters of John were 'adherents of Celestius' heterodoxy,' or 'Pelagians, whose opinions were adverse to true religion,' etc., an assertion which is not supported by the list of the 'Easterns,' and probably rests on hostile conjecture (Tillemont, xiv. 441). On the 'affinity,' as Prosper calls it (c. Collat. s. 58), between these two rationalising theories, see Christ. Remembrancer, July 1851, p. 175. Both had been held by Theodore of Mopsuestia: both were attacked by Marius Mercator, and condemned by the Third Council, which read the Roman decisions against Pelagianism, and 'deemed it right that they should remain in force' (Mansi, iv. 1337). This is alluded to by Prosper in his rhetorical vein (c. Collat. l. c.). 'By means of this man (Celestine) the Eastern churches were cleared of a double pest,' etc.

CANON II.

It is similarly ordered that if any provincial bishops have absented themselves from the Council, attached themselves to 'the revolt,' or even attempted to do so, or, after signing the deposition of Nestorius, have turned back to the assembly of revolters, they are to be 'alien from the episcopate' (ἱερωσύνης, see above, Const. 6), and to 'fall from their rank' (βαθμοῦ, c. 1), i. e. to incur deposition. Compare the terms of the sentence on Nestorius, 'that he be ἀλλότριον from the episcopal dignity' (Mansi, iv. 1212).

CANON III.

It is 'thought right that any clerics in any city or country who have been suspended from their sacred ministry' (ἱερωσύνης is here used in its wider sense) 'on the score of their orthodoxy, by Nestorius or his supporters, should regain their proper rank: and, generally, clerics who agree with the orthodox and Œcumenical Council' are forbidden to render any obedience to bishops who have revolted or who may revolt from it.

Canon IV.

'If any clerics should revolt, and dare either publicly or privately to hold with Nestorius or Celestius, it is thought right' (δεδικαίωται = δίκαιον ἔδοξε, Balsamon) 'that they should stand deposed by the Council.'

Canon V.

'All who have been condemned by the Council or by their own bishops for malpractices (ἀτόποις πράξεσι, comp. Luke xxiii. 41), and have been uncanonically restored to communion, by Nestorius,—according to his general line of indifference,—or by his adherents, are to gain nothing by such an irregular restitution, but to remain deposed as before.'

Nestorius is here charged with ἀδιαφορία (compare ἀδιαφόρως in Nic. 12, Chalc. 4): and it is not unlikely that he had been tempted to secure adherents by some laxity of discipline (see Tillemont, xiv. 437). We find Cyril complaining that he had given encouragement to the calumnious malice of some Alexandrians, whom their own 'Pope' had justly censured for grave offences (Mansi, iv. 888, 1005). And he was also charged with allowing clerics from foreign dioceses, in violation of canons, to haunt Constantinople, and with using their agency against orthodox monks (ib. 1108).

Canon VI.

The Council here threatens all who shall aim at unsettling its decisions with deposition if they are bishops or clerics, with excommunication if laymen. On this distinction see Bingham, xvii. 1. 2.

The allusion to laymen indicates a fear of the court influence of men like Candidian, and Count Irenæus, a personal friend of Nestorius. It was to be expected that they would do their utmost to back up the 'Orientals' under John of Antioch, and to exasperate Theodosius against Cyril. Thus we find the Council writing to Theodosius that Candidian had taken pains to preoccupy his mind, and hindered him from seeing the authentic report of its proceedings; and that Count Irenæus, who had been staying at Ephesus as a friend of Nestorius, had terrified the bishops by assaults which imperilled many lives,—a rhetorical amplification of the rough usage incurred under his auspices by their delegates (Mansi, iv. 1421, 1425). It was after this that Irenæus, on his return to Constantinople, induced the court to pronounce against Cyril, until the arrival of Cyril's own physician altered the feelings of men in power, and led to the mission of Count John, the high treasurer, empowered to settle the dispute by sanctioning the sentences passed in *both* synods.

CANON VII.

This, as Dioscorus of Alexandria said at Chalcedon (Mansi, vi. 632), is not properly a canon, but a 'determination' (ὅρος). Its occasion was remarkable; on the 22nd of July, just a month after the deposition of Nestorius, the Council was holding a sixth session, when Charisius, priest and church-steward (see below on Chalc. 26) of Philadelphia, came forward and told the following story. A priest named James had come into Lydia from Constantinople, with letters of commendation from two other priests named Anastasius and Photius, who were in fact Nestorians. He exhibited to some unsuspecting clerics of Philadelphia an 'exposition of faith differing from the Nicene.' This was a lengthy formulary, sound as to the Trinity, but unsound as to the Incarnation, in that it represented Christ, in true Nestorian fashion, as a man conjoined (συνημμένῳ) to the Eternal Son, and made to share in His honour by being entitled Son in a special sense, and worshipped on account of his relation to God the Word. Thus Christ was viewed as a human person, associated with the Divine Person of the Son by a bond only closer in degree than that which linked all holy men to God. (The formulary is attributed by Marius Mercator to

Theodore bishop of Mopsuestia, the great rationalizing theologian who had originated Nestorianism, and who was revered for ages by the far-spread Nestorian sect as 'St. Theodore the Expositor.') A bishop named Theophanes, together with certain clerics, approved of this creed, and permitted some nineteen Quartodecimans and five Novatians to make their profession by it on joining the Church. Charisius, being better informed, denounced it as heterodox: whereupon he was himself, as if heterodox, suspended from his functions. He therefore appealed to the Council, handing in a copy of the 'counterfeit creed,' with the written declarations of the beguiled converts, and a statement of his own belief, which was a variation of the Nicene Creed with a conclusion somewhat resembling that of the Apostles'. Having heard the case, the Council came to this memorable resolution, that 'no one should be allowed to present, or write, or compose ἑτέραν πίστιν than that which was definitely framed (ὁρισθεῖσαν) by the holy fathers at Nicæa, with the aid of the Holy Spirit; and that those who presumed to compose πίστιν ἑτέραν, or bring it forward, or offer it to persons desiring to come over to the knowledge of the truth, either from Heathenism, or from Judaism, or from any heresy whatsoever, should, if bishops or clerics, be deposed—if laity, be anathematized:—also, that the like penalties should be incurred by all who held or taught what was contained in the exposition produced by Charisius,' i.e. the Nestorianizing creed.

Here the main point to be settled is the sense of ἑτέραν πίστιν It has been explained as a belief contrary to the Nicene, or a creed expressing doctrine inconsistent with the Nicene. But this is to explain it away. Πίστις, here as in Constant. 1, means a formulary of doctrine which can be 'written' and 'presented,' —in short, a creed: and ἑτέρα, applied to a creed, must bear the sense of verbal difference, not merely of doctrinal opposition. For an illustration, see Soc. ii. 18; three Semi-Arian deputies, having reached the court of Constans, suppress the πίστις published at Antioch, and present ἑτέραν,—which is, in fact, not opposed in meaning to the Antiochene creed, but a briefer formula to the same purpose. So here we must admit that the Third Council, being resolved to guard against all intrusion of heresy, insists on the Nicene Creed, as settled in A.D. 325. There is to be no mistake, no loophole of evasion, such as might have been left open had the bishops allowed the use of any number of creeds, provided they could be shown to harmonize doctrinally with the Nicene. Instead of this, they say in effect, 'The Nicene Creed, that and no other, shall be used at the reception of converts.' The decree does not touch the case of a doctrinal formulary which is *not* used for that purpose, but serves to explain and guard the Creed's true meaning (see Cyril, Epist. 1 to Acacius of Melitene); and it was only by omitting the crucial words, 'present to those who wish to come over,' that Dioscorus, at the Latrocinium, could contend that it excluded such a statement as Flavian's (Mansi, vi. 907). It has, then, no bearing whatever on the 'second letter' of Cyril to Nestorius, on the formulary of reunion agreed upon by Cyril and John of Antioch, on the 'Tome' of St. Leo, on the 'Definition of Chalcedon,' or,—to come nearer home,—on the so-called Athanasian Creed. None of these documents are used as the ἑτέρα πίστις is supposed to be used. What then does the decree exclude? (1) The Apostles' Creed as a baptismal symbol, or the 'Constantinopolitan' recension of the Nicene; but the Council of Chalcedon, adopting the prohibition, made it refer to ἑτέραν πίστιν than the Creed in its Nicene and its Constantinopolitan forms, considered as one (see above on Constant. 1). It has indeed been said that this Council enlarged the area of the πίστις than which no 'other' was to be tolerated, by including its own 'Definition' of doctrine; but this is not so. A clear distinction is drawn in that Definition between the Creed and mere expository statements; the Chalcedonian use of ἑτέραν πίστιν means any other creed than 'the symbol of the fathers' (Mansi, vii. 116). Then (2) it must be said that this prohibition, as framed at Ephesus and reworded at Chalcedon, would bar the insertion into the body of the Creed itself of any additional phrases explanatory or other; so that the 'Filioque' or 'et Filio' would have been, in the view of these Councils, an unlawful addition, apart from all question as to its orthodoxy. But if we could imagine a General Council adopting the 'Filioque,' it would then be treated as part of that πίστις from which no variation was to be permitted, just as the Fourth Council recognised those additions to the Nicene symbol which were utterly ignored by the Third. The prohibition would tell against the slightly amplified Creed which is recited during the elevation of the Sacrament in the Mozarabic Liturgy, and still more against the Creed as it stands in the Armenian (Hammond, Liturgies, pp. 337, 145).

Canon VIII.

Again we have the word 'canon' loosely applied to a resolution or ψῆφος, passed on July 31; the date in the Acts, 'pridie Kalendas Septembris,' appears to be wrong, for 'the Council assembled no more after the arrival of Count John' the Emperor's second commissioner, who reached Ephesus at the beginning of August (Fleury, 25. 57).

The resolution relates primarily to the church of Cyprus. It had at this time some fifteen or sixteen bishoprics in cities, and, according to Sozomen, some of its villages had bishops over them (vii. 19). The metropolitan see was at Salamis or Constantia, as it had been called in memory, perhaps, of Constantius. Troilus, the late metropolitan, had died in the spring of the current year: and Dionysius, the 'dux' or commander-in-chief for 'the Oriens,' had written, on the 21st of May, to the 'president' of Cyprus and the clergy of Constantia, forbidding any election until instructions had been received from the expected Council. However, 'the bishops of Cyprus,' says Tillemont, 'either anticipated or disregarded this order' (xiv. 446); and Rheginus, the metropolitan thus appointed, came to Ephesus independently of 'the Easterns,' and distinguished himself by an exceptionally violent speech, in which he apostrophised the deposed Nestorius as worse than Cain, and confidently predicted his condemnation at the day of judgment (Mansi, iv. 1245). He now came forward, with two of his suffragans named Zeno and Evagrius, and stated his case; appealing not only to 'the Nicene "canons" and constitutions,' meaning evidently Nic. 6, but to 'apostolic canons,' by which Hefele thinks he must have meant the 36th of the series called apostolical. He then presented the letters of Dionysius. They were read, but the Council requested some further explanation. Zeno affirmed that Dionysius had been prompted by the bishop and clergy of Antioch. John had by this time been suspended from communion by the Council: and some of the members asked 'what was the object of him of Antioch?' 'To subjugate our island,' replied Evagrius: 'to secure the prerogative of ordaining our bishops, contrary to canon and to custom.' Here, then, was the point: the Council thrice inquired, 'whether any bishop of Antioch had been known to ordain a bishop in Cyprus,'—whether it was certain that no such right had existed when the Nicene Council (in its 6th canon) reserved all the rights of the see of Antioch,—whether the last three metropolitans, including 'the venerable Epiphanius,' had been consecrated by the insular synod? Positive replies were unhesitatingly given. No case could be produced in which the bishops of Antioch had thus intervened: never from the apostolic age had any extraneous hand 'imparted to Cyprus the gift of ordination.' One side had thus been fully heard: but the other side could not, under the circumstances, be heard at all. The Synod did not refuse, as a modern assembly would probably have refused, to give a judgment; but it took care to prefix a hypothetical saving clause. 'If it has *not* been a continuous ancient custom for the bishop of Antioch to hold ordinations in Cyprus—as it is asserted in memorials (λιβέλλων here used in its old sense of petitions, Juvenal, xiv. 193, not as in Constant. 7) and orally by the religious men who have come before the Council,—the prelates (προεστῶτες, cp. Euseb. iv. 23, v. 24, vi. 8) of Cyprus shall enjoy, free from molestation and violence, their right to perform by themselves the ordinations of bishops' for their island.

Such was the first part of their resolution relating to what is called the 'jus Cyprium.' Was that 'right' well-grounded? If John had been acting in unison with the Council, he might have maintained, as Alexander his next predecessor but one (the prelate who had the happiness of closing the 'schism of Antioch') had maintained in a letter to Innocent of Rome, that when it was necessary to guard against Arianism the Cypriot bishops had begun to hold consecrations by themselves, 'without consulting any one else,' in virtual transgression of Nicene law, and had kept up this habit when the excuse for it was at an end (Innoc. Epist. 18. 2). What evidence he could have produced for his own claim we know not: Fleury (25. 57) and Neale (Introd. East. Ch. i. 125) seem to think that he could have made his case good; but Balsamon (himself a successor of John) and Zonaras ascribe the Antiochene claim to a purely secular circumstance, the appointment of the prefect of Cyprus by the 'dux' of Antioch: and Tillemont (xiv. 447), and still more distinctly Newman (note in Transl. of Fleury, iii. 114), set it aside. Some fifty years afterwards, it was revived by Peter 'the Fuller,' patriarch of Antioch; but the opportune discovery in the neighbourhood of Constantia of the body of St. Barnabas, with a copy of St. Matthew's Gospel on his breast, was held by the authorities at Constantinople to establish beyond question the 'autocephalous' position of the insular church (Tillemont, xvi. 380), which was solemnly recognised by the Council in Trullo (can. 39), when Justinian II. had constrained his Christian subjects in Cyprus to emigrate to a new city, 'Justinianopolis,' on the Hellespont (Finlay, Hist. Greece, i. 388). After an interruption familiar to the compilers of the Arabic canons (37 or 43, Mansi, ii. 964, 994), it was again acknowledged when Balsamon wrote, ranking the Cyprian church with other autocephalous churches (on Constant. 2), and is still retained to the present day (cp. Neale, i. 128, Le Quien, ii. 1043).

But the resolution expands into a general order, affecting all the 'dioceses' and their subordinate provinces everywhere. No prelate is 'to take possession of any province which has not been from the first subject' to his own see; and any one who has thus 'seized upon and subjected' a province is to restore it; lest the canons of the fathers be transgressed, and the arrogance of secular power creep in under the cover of priestly' (i. e. episcopal) 'office,' ('under the pretence of reverence due to the priesthood,' Tillemont, xiv. 447), 'and we thus lose by degrees that liberty which our Lord Jesus Christ, the Liberator of all men, bestowed upon us by His own blood. It is therefore the pleasure of the holy and Œcumenical Council that the rights belonging from the first to each province be secured to it intact and inviolate, according to the custom which of old time has prevailed; and each metropolitan is permitted to take a copy of this act for his own security.'

The emphatic words, ἐξουσίας τῦφος κοσμικῆς, are remarkably like some other words addressed a few years before to Celestine of Rome by the African bishops in Council, at the close of the great case of the appellant presbyter Apiarius. The 'Nicene canon,' to which the Roman bishops had referred as permitting them to receive that appeal, had been proved by authentic copies, received from Constantinople and Alexandria, to be not Nicene, (it was, in fact, Sardican): and Apiarius himself had confessed before the Council all the crimes for which he had been degraded in Africa. It was then that the African prelates exhorted Celestine to respect the true Nicene decree, which had provided that all causes should be decided in the countries where they had arisen (see Nic. 5); and concluded, 'Do not send clerics of your own, at any one's request, to execute orders of your own, ne *fumosum typhum sæculi* in ecclesiam Christi, quæ lucem simplicitatis, et humilitatis diem, Deum videre cupientibus præfert, videamur inducere' (Mansi, iv. 516). Now it so happened that Africa was represented at Ephesus by a single Carthaginian deacon named Besulas, the deputy of his bishop Capreolus, the successor of that Aurelius who had presided in the African synod of 424. If the Roman delegates were present when the Cyprian case came on, Besulas would hardly, perhaps, have quoted his church's stringent admonition to their principal: but in their absence he might have done so. If he did not, the coincidence is among the most remarkable on record. Be this as it may, the decree securing the existing rights of all provincial churches against invasion on the part of powerful neighbour-prelates has often been quoted as against the pretension of Gregory the Great (Bede, i. 27) to 'commit to the charge' of Augustine, as archbishop, 'all the bishops of Britain,' i.e. those of the old British church which had been represented at Arles and Ariminum, and had not been included within that proper and original patriarchate of Rome, which, as we have seen above (on Nic. 6), did not even extend into Northern Italy. (See Bingham, ix. 1. 6, 10; Johnson's Vademecum, ii. 137; Hallam, Middle Ages, ii. 226, ed. 2; Palmer, Treatise on the Church, ii. 419, etc.) The gradual enlargement of the area of Roman jurisdiction was unquestionably inconsistent with this canon; but it must in fairness be added that the Ephesine prohibition was set aside by the Council of Chalcedon when it formally subjected three 'dioceses,' including twenty-eight metropolitan churches (Bingham, l.c.), to the see of Constantinople (Chalc. 28). This resolution is quoted as canon 8 in John Scholasticus' 'Collectio,' tit. 1. (Justellus, Bibl. Jur. Can. Vet. ii. 509), although he reckons the Ephesine canons as seven (ib. 502). In his Nomocanon it is referred to as the 7th (ib. 603), which shows that he omitted what we reckon as can. 7, probably as irrelevant to his purpose (Dict. Chr. Ant. i. 399).

NOTES ON THE CANONS OF CHALCEDON.

Canon I.

THIS canon reaffirms and upholds in force all the canons 'passed in each Council' of the Catholic Church (in the East) up to that time; i.e. those of Nicæa, Constantinople, and Ephesus, and those also of the local Eastern synods of Ancyra, Neocæsarea, Antioch (i.e. the Council of the Dedication in 341, regarded *pro tanto* as a legitimate Church synod, see Hefele, s. 56), Gangra, and Laodicea. We know that when the Council of Chalcedon assembled, a collection of such canons was current. Thus, in the fourth session of Chalcedon (Oct. 17, 451), the archdeacon of Constantinople read from 'a book' the 5th canon of Antioch, and it was accepted by the Council as 'a canon of the holy fathers' (Mansi, vii. 72); in the tenth, the 4th Nicene was read (ib. 93), and again in the fourteenth from a book in which it occurred as 'Chapter 6' (ib. 308; 'an old error,' probably, for 4). In the sixteenth, the same archdeacon produced a book containing the 6th Nicene, and three canons of Constantinople as one 'synodicon' (ib. 444); whereas in the fourth session he read the 4th and 5th canons of Antioch as 'canons 83 and 84' of a then-existing code (ib. 84); and, in the eleventh session, the 16th and 17th of Antioch were read as 'canons 95 and 96' (ib. 281). Christopher Justellus, in his preface to what he published as 'the Code of Canons of the Universal Church,' says that 'the Fathers when composing it arranged the several Councils in a definite order of succession, and reckoned the canons in a definite and continuous series, and by an unbroken sequence of numbers' (Justell. Biblioth. Juris Canonici Veteris, i. 16), the order of the Councils being this:—

1.	Nicæa,	Canons 1– 20,
2.	Ancyra,	21– 45,
3.	Neocæsarea,	46– 59,
4.	Gangra,	60– 79,
5.	Antioch,	80–104,
6.	Laodicea,	105–163,
7.	Constantinople,	164–167;

to which, after the Council of Chalcedon, the Ephesine canons were added, 'perhaps' by Stephen bishop of Ephesus, 'cujus exstat,' says Justellus, 'collectio nondum edita, exhibiting the canons of these seven Councils in the same sequence and order as in the vetus codex ecclesiæ universæ, quibus ipse Ephesinos addidit,' as a later collector added the canons of Chalcedon. But, as the Ballerini have shown (de Antiq. Collect. Can. in Append. to St. Leo), the early code was not compiled by the Fathers, but by private students; and the method of continuous enumeration was not used in all copies of that code. At first it consisted of the canons of Nicæa, Ancyra, Neocæsarea, and Gangra, probably compiled by a resident in Pontus: then, before A. D. 400, the canons of Antioch were added by another compiler, belonging to the 'Oriental diocese,' but when quoted against St. Chrysostom, in 403, were repudiated on his part, as the work of Arianizers; at some later time the Laodicene were added. The Constantinopolitan were not in the code as generally received in 451 (Mansi, vii. 441); the Ephesine, not being regarded as properly canons, were not inserted until the sixth century. Stephen's work was a synopsis, not a collection, and he was not the Stephen whose case came before the Council of Chalcedon in its eleventh session, but a much later bishop of that name: (Stephen II. about 692, Le Quien, i. 683): and Justellus 'nullum codicem antiquum habuit qui hanc collectionem, uti ab ipso est edita, contineret,' but compiled, 'suo marte,' what he believed to be 'the primitive code of the universal Church.' (In fact, the Roman church at that time acknowledged no canons but the Nicene, or what passed for Nicene). Nor can the collection, as translated by Dionysius Exiguus in the earlier part of the sixth century, represent the original Greek code. He tells us in his preface, addressed to Stephen bishop of Salona (Justellus, i. 101), that he has 'arranged the rules of the Nicene synod, and thenceforward of all the Councils which preceded or which followed it, as far as the synod of the 150 at Constantinople, in numerical order, that is, from the 1st to the 165th chapter,' (by a peculiar arrangement he made out 156 rather than 167 canons), 'sicut habetur in Græca auctoritate. Tum sancti Chalcedonensis concilii decreta subdentes, in his Græcorum canonum finem esse declaramus' (Justell. i. 110). These canons he called by the familiar Latin term 'regulæ;' he omitted the so-called 5th, 6th, and 7th canons of Constantinople: and while in his recension he followed the older Latin version called the Prisca by omitting the Ephesine canons so called, he inserted the Laodicene which the Prisca omitted, and did not place the Constantinopolitan, as the Prisca did, after the Chalcedonian. In other words, he did not exhibit the oldest series. He also added the Sardican and the African, together with the so-called Apostolical canons, which he supposed to have been published by St. Clement. 'Ex quibus verbis colligimus,' say Voel and the younger Justellus in their preface to the second volume as a whole, 'Synodum Sardicensem a Græcis inter orientales synodos non fuisse relatam,' principally because its canons providing for appeals to Rome were diametrically opposed to the Antiochene canons, etc. The Ballerini, indeed, argue from the letter of the Council of 382, in Theod. v. 9, that the Sardican synod was then acknowledged in the East; but this is improbable in itself, and the passage could not have been written by persons who knew the Sardican canons as they stand, even if the writers could have mistaken a Sardican rule for a Nicene. They seem to be expanding the Nicene canon to which they refer. It is more to the purpose that some Greek collections of the fifth century seem to have contained these canons, for Eutychian collectors of late date admit them (de Ant. Collect. i. 6. 13): and John Scholasticus, who became patriarch of Constantinople in 564, had previously arranged under fifty 'titles' the canons of ten synods, which earlier collectors had arranged under sixty (Justell. ii. 500). His series of canons is, 'Apostolical,' Nicene, Ancyran, Neocæsarean, Sardican, Gangran, Antiochene, Laodicene, Constantinopolitan, Ephesine, Chalcedonian, St. Basil's in his three canonical letters (Epist. 188, 199, 217). In 692 the Council in the Trullus or dome of the palace, in its 2nd canon, confirmed the code in its enlarged form, including (after the Chalcedonian) the 'Apostolical,' Sardican, and also the African canons, together with the canonical directions of various fathers. To these were added the canons of the Council 'in Trullo;' and at last, says the elder Justellus, 'ex iis omnibus tam canonibus quam patrum decretis a Nicæna I. synodo ad Nicænam II. compositus est codex canonum Ecclesiæ Orientalis' (Justell. i. 17). Thus the later Greek collectors, as Photius, Aristenus, and Symeon Logothetes, include both the Sardican and the African canons, although two of them rank the Sardican next after the Chalcedonian, while one arranges the local councils chronologically. Johnson observes that not only the Council of Sardica, but those of Arles and Eliberis (Elvira) and the Carthaginian Councils, 'were not admitted into the code' as received at Chalcedon, 'and probably some of them were never heard of by these holy fathers; and that not one of the canons here ratified by a Council in which the Pope's delegates presided, was made in the Latin Church, or drawn up in that tongue' (Vademecum, ii. 139).

CANON II.

This canon is against simony, and against kindred faults in regard to offices connected with the Church, but not sacred.

The first set of offences is described by supposing (1) a bishop to 'hold a χειροτονία for money,' clearly, an ordination, (see above on Nic. 4, and compare χειροτονίας τῶν ἀρχιερέων, Josephus, B. Jud. iv. 3. 6), 'and bring down into the market that grace which is not to be sold' (Acts viii. 20), 'and ordain for money a bishop, chorepiscopus' (see on Nic. 8), 'presbyter, deacon, or any other of those who are numbered among the clergy,' i.e. subdeacons (often called ὑπηρέται), readers, singers, exorcists, ostiaries, doorkeepers; see Bingham, b. iii., on these inferior orders. For subdeacons see Euseb. vi. 43; Antioch. c. 10; Athanasius, Hist. Ari. 60, on the martyred Eutychius; and a law of Constantine, Cod. Theod. xvi. 2. 7. For readers and singers see below on can. 14. Exorcists are mentioned, as an order, in the 10th canon of Antioch, and in the 24th of Laodicea, which also mentions doorkeepers, as does Epiphanius, Expos. Fidei, 21. These minor orders are enumerated in a law of Gratian, A.D. 377 (Cod. Theod. xvi. 2. 24). It is remarkable that the acolyth, though bearing a Greek name, was a functionary peculiar to the Latin Church. Ordaining for money is of course the grossest form of the sin named after Simon Magus, which Thomas Aquinas defines as 'the deliberate intention of buying or selling a spiritual thing, or something annexed to a spiritual thing' (Sum. Theol. 2ª. 2ᵃᵉ. q. 100). The 40th canon of 1604 defines it as 'the buying and selling of spiritual and ecclesiastical functions, offices, promotions, dignities, and livings.' The 30th (or 29th) Apost. canon, which, referring to the case of Simon Magus, directs that in such cases both the ordainer and the ordained should be deposed and excommunicated, is probably not ante-Nicene: for 'simony was an offence nearly excluded by the nature of the case from the first three centuries of Church history' (Newman, note in Transl. of Fleury, vol. iii. p. 17). But it grew up like a weed when bishoprics became objects of secular ambition. Something like it is depicted in the 2nd canon of Sardica: a man might bribe a few people in some vacant diocese to procure his own election. Athanasius (Hist. Ari. 73) accuses the Acacian Arians of 'sending out bishops as if from a market, on receipt of gold;' and Philostorgius repeats the charge in regard to a somewhat later period (x. 3). The offence itself had been rife among the chorepiscopi of St. Basil's diocese; some of them took money from those whom they had just ordained, and thought that there was nothing wrong in it because the money was not paid before. 'But taking is taking, take it when you will.' He refers to Acts viii. 20, and condemns the transaction as 'an introducing of huckstering into the Church, where the Body and Blood of Christ are put under our charge' (Epist. 53). A great scandal in the 'Asian diocese' had led to St. Chrysostom's intervention. Antoninus, bishop of Ephesus, was charged with 'making it a rule to sell ordinations of bishops at rates proportionate to the value of their sees' (Palladius, Dial. de Vita Chrysost. p. 50). Chrysostom held a synod at Ephesus, at which six bishops were deposed for having obtained their sees in this manner. Isidore of Pelasium repeatedly remonstrated with his bishop Eusebius on the heinousness of 'selling the gift' of ordination (Epist. i. 26, 30, 37); and names Zosimus, a priest, and Maron, a deacon, as thus ordained (ib. 111, 119). A few years before the Council, a court of three bishops sat at Berytus to hear charges brought against Ibas bishop of Edessa by clerics of his diocese. The third charge was thus curtly worded: Ἔτι καὶ ἀπὸ χειροτονιῶν λαμβάνει (Mansi, vii. 224). The 27th Trullan canon repeated this canon of Chalcedon against persons ordained ἐπὶ χρήμασι, doubtless in view of such a state of things as Gregory the Great had heard of nearly a century earlier, ' in Orientis ecclesiis nullum ad sacrum ordinem nisi ex præmiorum datione pervenire' (Epist. xi. 46, to the bishop of Jerusalem; compare Evagrius' assertion that Justin II. openly sold bishoprics, v. 1). It is easy to understand how the scruples of ecclesiastics could be abated by the courtly fashion of calling bribes 'eulogiæ' (Fleury, 26. 20), just as the six prelates above referred to had regarded their payments as an equivalent for that 'making over of property to the Curia' which was required by a law of 399 (Cod. Theod. xii. 1. 163; see notes in Transl. of Fleury, i. 163, ii. 16).

(2) The lesser offence dealt with in this canon is that of promoting for money to some non-ministerial offices.

(*a*) The office of οἰκονόμος, or Church steward, will be more conveniently considered in reference to can. 25, which is devoted to that subject.

(*b*) The ἔκδικος, 'defensor,' was an official advocate or counsel for the Church (see c. 23). The legal force of the term 'defensor' is indicated by a law of Valentinian I., 'Nec idem in eodem negotio defensor sit et quæsitor' (Cod. Theod. ii. 10. 2). In the East the office was held by ecclesiastics; thus, John, presbyter and ἔκδικος, was employed, at the Council of Constantinople in 448, to summon Eutyches (Mansi, vii. 697). About 496, Paul the ἔκδικος of Constantinople saved his archbishop from the sword of a murderer at the cost of his own life (Theodor. Lect. ii. 11). In the list of the functionaries of St. Sophia, given by Goar in his Euchologion (p. 270), the Protecdicos is described as adjudicating, with twelve assessors, in smaller causes, on which he afterwards reports to the bishop. In Africa, on the other hand, from A.D. 407 (see Cod. Theod. xvi. 2. 38), the office was held by barristers, in accordance with a request of the African bishops (Cod. Afric. 97; Mansi, iii. 802) who, six years earlier, had asked for 'defensores' with special reference to the oppression of the poor by the rich (Cod. Afric. 75; Mansi, iii. 778, 970). The 'defensores' mentioned by Gregory the Great had primarily to take care of the poor (Epist. v. 29), and of the church property (ib. i. 36), but also to be advocates of injured clerics (ib. ix. 64) and act as assessors (ib. x. 1), etc.

(*c*) The next office is that of the προσμονάριος, or, according to a various reading adopted by many (e.g. Justellus, Hervetus, Beveridge, Bingham), the παραμονάριος. Opinions differ as to the function intended. Isidore gives simply 'paramonarius:' Dionysius (see Justellus, Biblioth. i. 134) omits the word; but in the 'interpretatio Dionysii,' as given in the Concilia, freedom has been taken to insert 'vel mansionarium' in a parenthesis (vii. 373; see Beveridge, in loc.). Mansionarius is a literal rendering: but what was the function of a mansionarius? In

Gregory the Great's time he was a sacristan who had the duty of lighting the church (Dial. i. 5): and 'ostiarium' in the Prisca implies the same idea. Tillemont, without deciding between the two Greek readings, thinks that the person intended had 'some charge of what pertained to the church itself, perhaps like our present bedells' (xv. 694). So Fleury renders, 'concierge' (l. 28, 29); and Newman, reading παραμονάριον, takes a like view (note in Transl. of Fleury, vol. iii. p. 392). But Justellus (i. 91) derives παραμονάριος from μονή, 'mansio,' a halting-place, so that the sense would be, a manager of one of the Church's farms, a 'villicus,' or, as Bingham expresses it, 'a bailiff' (iii. 3. 1). Beveridge agrees with Justellus, except in giving to μονή the sense of 'monastery' (compare the use of μονή in Athan. Apol. c. Arian. 67, where Valesius understands it as 'a station' on a road, but others as 'a monastery,' see Historical Writings of St. Athanasius, Introd. p. xliv). Bingham also prefers this interpretation. Suicer takes it as required by παραμονάριος, which he treats as the true reading: προσμονάριος, he thinks, would have the sense of 'sacristan.'

Beside these offices, reference is made to all others who are 'of the canon' or body of church functionaries. 'Any bishop who is convicted of having either ordained a cleric, or appointed to one of the inferior posts, for money, for the sake of his own base gain, will imperil his own rank' (on this phrase κινδυνεύειν περὶ τὸν οἰκεῖον βαθμόν see c. 22, Nic. 2: and compare a phrase in Pope Simplicius' Epist. 3, that certain funds are to be spent on certain purposes by a presbyter, 'sub periculo sui ordinis,' Mansi, vii. 974). For βαθμός see c. 10, 12, 18, 22, 27, 29, Eph. 1, 2, 3. 'And the person so ordained, or promoted, for money, shall gain nothing by such ordination or promotion, but shall be excluded from the dignity or from the charge thus obtained.' Hervetus renders φροντίσματος, 'curatione,' Dionysius 'sollicitudine.' 'And if any one shall be proved to have been an agent' or 'go-between (μεσιτεύων) in these shameful and unlawful bargains' ('turpibus et nefariis lucris,' Prisca; 'turpibus et nefandis datis vel acceptis,' Dionysius), 'he too, if he be a cleric, shall be deposed from his own office' (c. 10, 12, 18, 27) : 'if a layman or a monk, he shall be anathematized' (see on Eph. 6). For the antithesis between a cleric and a monk see Jerome, Epist. 14. 8, ' alia monachorum est causa, alia clericorum.' For other cases in which the anathema or greater excommunication is incurred see c. 7, 15, 27.

CANON III.

This canon is against that form of clerical secularity which showed itself in the farming of estates, or carrying on trade for gain. The Emperor Marcian himself, in the sixth session, had proposed a draft canon, in somewhat shorter form, to the same effect (Mansi, vii. 175).

The evil had appeared in the latter years of that 'Long Peace' which did so much to relax the tone of the Church before the fiery trial of the Decian persecution. Reference has already been made to St. Cyprian's indignation against prelates who 'multiplied their usury.' In the same passage (de Lapsis, 6) he speaks of bishops who, ' despising their stewardship of things divine, became procuratores rerum sæcularium, derelicta cathedra, plebe deserta, per alienas provincias oberrantes negotiationis quæstuosæ nundinas aucupari;' and elsewhere he says that he and his colleagues in synod, and their fellow presbyters who sat by them, had been shocked by learning that a bishop had named a presbyter by will to the office of guardian, in spite of a synodical decision of long standing that no one who should thus act towards any of the clergy should be remembered after death in the Eucharistic sacrifice (Epist. 1). A few years later, Paul of Samosata scandalized his Antiochene flock by preferring his title of 'ducenarius' under Zenobia to his spiritual dignity as bishop (Euseb. vii. 30). The adoption of Christianity by the Emperor was sure to attract towards a religion but recently 'illicit' many who had, in fact, no heart for its 'awful seriousness,' its penetrating requirements, and its pure unearthly elevation. They meant to make use of it, not to be moulded by it. Such proselytes could not but form a tone, and insensibly induce ministers of the Church to take up worldly business under the notion of gaining an influence, which they could turn to the service of religion; and thus, instead of spiritualising others, they would themselves be secularised. Canon after canon had given its warning: the 7th and the 20th 'Apostolical,' among the oldest in that series, had forbidden bishops, presbyters, or deacons, to undertake κοσμικὰς φροντίδας, or any clerics to give security, on pain of deposition; the 18th of Elvira, evidently copying from Cyprian, had forbidden them to 'leave their own places negotiandi causa, or to go round the provinces in quest of gainful markets;' the Council of Hippo and the 3rd Council of Carthage had forbidden them to be 'conductores' or 'procuratores,' or to get their living 'ullo turpi vel inhonesto negotio;' and another canon had ruled 'ut episcopus tuitionem testamentorum non suscipiat' (Mansi, iii. 921, 883, 952). Jerome had written to his beloved Nepotianus, 'Negotiatorem clericum, et ex inope divitem, quasi quamdam pestem fuge;' and had asked how clerics, 'qui proprias jubentur contemnere facultates,' could become 'procuratores et dispensatores domorum alienarum atque villarum' (Epist. 52. 5, 16). The 'Tall Brothers' are said to have thought themselves spiritually injured by intercourse with their patriarch Theophilus when they saw him pursuing χρηματιστικὸν βίον (Soc. vi. 7). Antoninus of Ephesus (see on c. 2) had for the time cloaked his misdeeds from Chrysostom's scrutiny, by causing a court magnate whose 'Asiatic' estates, says Palladius, 'he had in charge' (ἐφρόντιζε), to set Arcadius against the bishop's intended journey. Silvanus of Troas, 'finding that his clergy were making gain out of the disputes of litigants,' in the Church court, 'would not again appoint a cleric as judge, but entrusted the cases to one of the faithful laity, whom he knew to love justice' (Soc. vii. 37).

And now the Council of Chalcedon had to do what it could for the abatement of this oft-recurring evil. 'It has come to the knowledge of the holy Council that some who are enrolled among the clergy become, for base gain, farmers of other men's estates,' (Dionysius renders μισθωταί, 'conductores'), 'and contract for managing (ἐργολαβοῦσι) secular affairs; thus neglecting the service (λειτουργίας) of God; while they insinuate themselves into the houses of men of the world, and from covetous motives undertake the management of their property.' On λειτουργία, as here used, observe that it was transferred by the Septuagintal writers from its classical sense of an 'administrative service which citizens rendered to the State,' into the sphere of public divine worship, and used for the 'ministration' of priests or Levites in the tabernacle and the Temple (e.g. Num. xvi. 9, 2 Chron. xxxi. 2, and compare λειτουργέω, Exod. xxxv. 19, etc.). This sense appears in three passages of the New Testament (Luke i. 23, Heb. viii. 6, ix. 21; comp. λειτουργέω in Acts xiii. 2 used of Christian ministers, and λειτουργός applied to Christ as High Priest, Heb. viii. 2); and with it the sense of a church's faith as presented to God, Phil. ii. 17; beside which the word is used for kindly attendance on an Apostle of Christ (Phil. ii. 30), and contribution to the wants of fellow Christians (2 Cor. ix. 12, comp. λειτουργός in 3 Kings x. 5, 4 Kings iv. 43). But when St. Paul uses it in either of these derivative senses, his context shows his meaning; whereas, to take the idea of the management of Church finance as the key to the absolute use of the term in Church writers (see Hatch, Bamp. Lect. p. 41) would render their contexts pointless even to futility; as may be seen by trying such an interpretation on passages in Euseb. iii. 22, iv. 1, 5, 11, v. 6, 22, where λειτουργία is used for a bishop's office, or on others in Apost. can. 29, 37, Ancyr. 2, Antioch. 3, and especially the passage in the text, where it includes the functions of all ordained men. Wherever it occurs, it suggests the thought of duty and responsibility; (hence Isidore of Pelusium contrasts it with ἀρχὴ ἀνεξέταστος, Epist. 216; and so far it is akin to οἰκονομία, see on Constant. 6). In each case we have a specimen of a secular term adopted into the family of consecrated terms, and thereby filled with a much larger religious significance than could be narrowed to the least spiritual forms of clerical duty. It was just because λειτουργία had come to represent the whole range of sacred ministrations that men used it, 'par excellence,' for those great acts in which the ideas of service and worship had reached their supreme earthly expression.

The description of clerics finding their way into rich men's houses may remind us of the fierce sarcasm, not avoiding coarse details, which Jerome, in the letter already quoted, discharges against the low-born clerics who by mean arts had made themselves at home in the apartments of rich old men and of old ladies without children (Epist. 52. 6).

The canon proceeds: 'No cleric, and no monk, shall either farm property or business, or intrude himself into temporal administrations (διοικήσεσι), unless (1) he be summoned by law to undertake the guardianship of minors, and cannot get off that trust, or (2) the bishop of his city permit him to manage ecclesiastical business, or the affairs of orphans not otherwise provided for, and of such persons as specially need the aid of the Church, because of the fear of the Lord.' Here are several points: (α) Monks, we see, were not exempt from this temptation. Jerome had known of some who had 'by respectful attentions hunted after the wealth of matrons,' and 'became richer as monks than they had been in the world' (Epist. 60. 11), and of others, 'very many,' who could not do without 'artibus et negotiationibus pristinis, and kept up their old trades under new names' (ib. 125. 16). (β) The phrase ἀφηλίκων ἀπαραίτητον ἐπιτροπήν is illustrated by Cod. Theodos. iii. 17. 4 (A.D. 390): 'Cum tutor legitimus defuerit, vel privilegio a tutela excusetur.' Ἀπαραίτητος recurs in can. 19, 25: cp. Zeno's Henoticon, alluding to death as the ἀπαραίτητον ἐκδημίαν of men (Evagrius, iii. 14). Justinian allowed clerics to become guardians on the sole ground of relationship (Novell. 134 c. 5). (γ) A solicitude for her weaker members had always lain close to the heart of the Church. It was a product of her most sacred and endearing recollections, a continuous response to such a text as Matt. xxv. 40. Moreover, to quote an excellent summary of its manifold activities, 'the Christian communities grew up in the midst of poverty. They had a natural message to the poor, and the poor naturally flowed into them: and the poverty ...... was intensified by the conditions of their existence. Some of their members were outcasts from their homes: others had been compelled by the stern rules of Christian discipline to abandon employments which that discipline forbad. In times of persecution the confessors in prison had to be fed; those whose property had been confiscated had to be supported; those who had been sold into captivity had to be ransomed. Above all, there were the orphans,' and the 'virgins and widows,' whose 'numbers multiplied' under the growing 'tendency towards perpetual virginity and perpetual widowhood .... In addition to these were the strangers ... for, driven from city to city by persecution, or wandering from country to country an outcast or a refugee, a Christian found, wherever he went, in the community of his fellow Christians a welcome and hospitality ... In addition to the poor, the widows and orphans, and the travelling brethren, there was the care of such of the church officers as, having no means of their own, were dependent on the Church funds for their subsistence' (Hatch, Bamp. Lect. pp. 42–45). It is true, also, that 'of this vast system of ecclesiastical administration the ἐπίσκοπος was the pivot and the centre;' although he was so in virtue of his relation to the more directly spiritual work of the Church. In the passage before us, it is the bishop who is supposed to entrust the cleric or monk in question with the duty of administering the charitable funds (comp. Jerome, Epist. 52. 9). Early Christian writers refer frequently to this eleemosynary organization. Tertullian says that Christians make voluntary contributions once a month, as they may be able: 'Hæc quasi deposita pietatis sunt. Nam inde ... egenis alendis humandisque, et pueris ac puellis re ac parentibus destitutis, jamque domesticis senibus, item naufragis, et si qui in metallis' (i.e. condemned to penal servitude in mines), 'et si qui in insulis' (i.e. banished to islands), 'vel in custodiis,—duntaxat ex causa Dei sectæ, alumni confessionis suæ fiunt' (Apol. 39). Cyprian speaks of those who are maintained by the Church's supplies (Epist. 2); before his retirement in 250 he placed a sum in the hands of the clergy 'propter ejusmodi casus' (Epist. 5. 1); and when absent from Carthage he repeatedly exhorts them to take diligent care of widows, and the sick, and all the poor, and of foreigners who are in need (Epist. 47); but by the poor he means such of them as have stood firm under persecution (Epist. 12. 2, 14. 2). Cornelius, bishop of Rome in Cyprian's time, speaks in an extant letter of 'more than 1500 persons who are all supported by the grace and loving-kindness of our Lord' (Euseb. vi. 43), through the agency of the church at Rome: compare the story of St. Laurence and the poor as the true 'treasures' of that church (as told by Alban Butler, August 10). For its munificence to foreign Christians see above on Const. 3. The Council of Antioch says (can. 25) that the bishop has to administer (διοικεῖν) church property for the benefit of all who are in need (δεομένους, cp. δεομένων in the text). Athanasius refers to those clerics who had charge of the widows, and assigned to them their places (Hist. Ari. 61); elsewhere he mentions the 'bread of the ministers and virgins' (Encycl. 4), and of orphans and widows (Apol. de Fuga, 6), meaning an allowance of bread provided for them. When Chrysostom lived at Antioch, the church in that birthplace of the Christian name supported 3000 widows and virgins, beside the patients in the hospital etc. (in Matt. Hom. 66. 3). Augustine says that whatever he and his brethren have beyond what is sufficient for themselves is held in trust for the poor (Epist. 185. s. 35); and, when absent from Hippo, reproves his clergy and people for having 'forgotten their old custom as to clothing the poor' (Epist. 122. 2). Isidore says that orphans and widows will accuse a bad bishop at the Judgment, for neglecting them (Epist. iii. 216). Theodoret, in one of his many beautiful letters, says that the Church-people of his 'desolate' little city of Cyrrhos have contributed for the relief of some unhappy African refugees (Epist. 32). Acacius, afterwards bishop of Constantinople, had been head of an orphanage (Theod. Lect. i. 13). About twenty years after the Council, Pope Simplicius lays it down that one fourth of the Church fund is to be bestowed on foreigners and the poor (Epist. 3); and Pope Gelasius at the end of the century (Epist. 9. 27), and Gregory the Great a century later (Bede, i. 27), refer to this rule of a fourfold division as prescribed by Church law. Bingham says that 'all distressed people, the virgins and widows of the Church, together with the confessors in prison, the sick and strangers, ... had relief, though not a perfect maintenance, from the charity of the Church' (v. 6. 3): and compare Milman, Hist. of Christianity, iii. 272; 'To each church were attached numbers of widows and other destitute persons .... The sick in the hospitals and prisons, and destitute strangers, were under their especial care' (i. e. that of the clergy) ... 'The payments seem chiefly to have been made in kind rather than in money,' etc.

These two cases excepted, the undertaking of secular business was made ecclesiastically penal. Yet this is not to be construed as forbidding clerics to work at trades either (1) when the Church funds were insufficient to maintain them, or (2) in order to have more to bestow in alms, or (3) as an example of industry or humility. Thus, most of the clergy of Cæsarea in Cappadocia practised sedentary trades for a livelihood (Basil, Epist. 198. 1); and some African canons allow, or even direct, a cleric to live by a trade, provided that his clerical duties are not neglected (Mansi, iii. 955). At an earlier time, Spyridion, the famous Cypriot bishop,—still one of the most popular saints in the Levant (Stanley's East. Church, p. 126),—retained out of humility (ἀτυφίαν πολλήν, Soc. i. 12) his occupation as a shepherd: and in the latter part of the fourth century Zeno bishop of Maiuma wove linen, partly to supply his own wants, and partly to obtain means of helping the poor (Soz. vii. 28). Sidonius mentions a 'reader' who maintained himself by commercial transactions (Epist. vi. 8): and in the Anglo-Saxon Church, although presbyters were forbidden to become 'negotiorum sæcularium dispositores' (C. of Clovesho in 747, c. 8), or to be '*mongers* and covetous merchants' (Elfric's canons, 30), yet the canons of King Edgar's reign ordered every priest 'diligently to learn a handicraft' (No. 11; Wilkins, i. 225). In short, it was not the mere fact of secular employment, but secularity of motive and of tone, that was condemned: see note in Transl. of Fleury, iii. 393; compare Bingham, vi. 4. 13. It is needless to add that the distinctive character of the priestly order was in no respect affected by such clerical trading as the Church held to be innocent or laudable: and, at the same time, the principle that Christ's ministers ought, if possible, to be maintained by the free-will offerings of the people was upheld, although for lack of means it could not always be carried out, or although reasons akin to those on which St. Paul acted (1 Cor. ix. 18) might in this or that case lead a man to waive his rights in the matter. St. Chrysostom says that teachers ought to be maintained, that they might labour for things spiritual without troubling themselves about things of this life (in 1 Tim. Hom. 15. 2).

Canon IV.

This canon is directed against irregular and anarchical tendencies which had shown themselves among the monks of the East, and had produced results at once scandalous and tragical during the recent Eutychian controversy.

From an early period in the fourth century, men who had embraced that monastic life which seemed to represent in its most intense form the Christian idea of self-renunciation had gained a sort of indefinite prerogative of interposing prominently in behalf of moral and religious interests, and even of rebuking princes or magistrates with the boldness of the great prophet whose garb they had made their own. It was a departure from the strict self-seclusion of the old hermits. A monk was, as such, a 'solitary:' as Jerome had said to one who had left him in the desert of Chalcis, and returned to home life, 'Interpretare vocabulum "monachi," hoc est, nomen tuum; quid facis in turba, qui "solus" es?' (Epist. 14. 6); and to another, 'Quid desideramus urbium frequentiam, qui de "singularitate" censemur?' (Epist. 125. 8). By hypothesis, the monk had quitted the world 'to try to be alone with God, if by any means he might save his own soul' (Kingsley's Hermits, p. 7, cp. p. 134). A monk out of his cell, according to St. Antony, was 'a fish out of water' (Athan. Vit. Ant. 85). Even where community-life was established, the most venerated monks seldom crossed the convent threshold (Mansi, iv. 1428), and Eutyches long adhered to a resolution to remain in his abbey 'as if in a grave' (ib. vi. 700). Yet it was admitted that there were occasions which would force the monk out of his retirement. Antony himself had come down to Alexandria to resist the Arians; and Aphraates, when Valens met him near Antioch and reminded him that he ought 'to stay at home and pray,' had likened himself to a maiden running out of her chamber to put out a fire in her father's house (Theod. iv. 26). When the two commissioners came to Antioch, in the Lent of 387, to inquire into the outrages on the statues of Theodosius, his wife, and his father, it was the hermit Macedonius, surnamed 'the barley-eater,' and his brethren, who commanded rather than entreated them to make an appeal to the humanity of Theodosius (v. 20). Yet, two years later, that emperor was provoked by the lawless violence of some monks in Osrhoene to say to Ambrose (even when on the point of pardoning them at his urgency), 'Monachi multa scelera faciunt' (Ambr. Epist. 41. 27). In 390, indeed, he prohibited the monks from doing what they had done in the affair of the statues: and although ere long he withdrew the prohibition (Cod. Theod. xvi. 3. 1, 2), his son Arcadius made a law in July 398 against 'the audacity' of monks who committed acts of disorder in behalf of persons arrested (ib. ix. 40. 16). For, not to mention the pretended monks who lived in cities by twos or threes without discipline, and were called Sarabaites (Cassian, Collat. xviii. 7), or Remoboth (Jerome, Epist. 22. 34), or those who, as the great monk Isidore of

Pelusium sarcastically puts it, 'haunted cities, attended public shows, and thought a cloak and a staff enough for the "angelical" life' (Epist. 9), Eastern monasticism in general, 'like the Eastern Church as a whole,' was deficient in 'gravity, stability, self-control.' Human passion, 'repressed at one outlet' by austerities so exercised as to wrong the sober name of 'training' ($\mathring{α}σκησις$), 'burst forth with increased fury at another' (Stephens, Life of St. Chrysostom, p. 65). Hence the wild fanaticism of the Anthropomorphist monks of Egypt (Soc. vi. 7), and the 'sedition' raised by Nitrian monks ($\mathring{ε}νθερμον$ $\mathring{ε}χοντες$ $φρόνημα$, Soc. vii. 14) against the prefect Orestes, in the early days of Cyril of Alexandria. In the Nestorian controversy, the monastic body had resisted Nestorius, as it had formerly resisted the Arians (Soz. vi. 27); a letter 'To the Monks' was one of Cyril's earliest polemical writings; Theodosius, in 431, had ordered Candidianus to expel from Ephesus all monks who came to see the Council; and its members had thanked the old abbot Dalmatius for heading a great monastic demonstration in their behalf at Constantinople (Mansi, iv. 1427). But the zeal of simple recluses for the doctrine upheld by Cyril might easily become zeal for the Monophysite perversion of it. Eutyches himself was a highly respected abbot: Armenian monks had gone about the East, 'intimidating the clergy,' and demanding that some anti-Apollinarian writings should be anathematized (Fleury, 26. 37); and, worst of all, at the recent second Council of Ephesus, known in history as the 'Robbers' Meeting,' the tyranny of Dioscorus had been backed not only by military force, but by a Syrian abbot named Barsumas (Mansi, vi. 828), of whom it was said, in his presence, at the fourth session of Chalcedon (Oct. 17), by those bishops who had been thus terrorised, 'He upset all Syria, he brought in a thousand monks upon us,' 'He stabbed the blessed Flavian,' or, 'He stood by and said, "Stab him!"' 'and then their resentment burst forth again in the appalling exclamation, " To the arena with the murderer!"' (ib. vii. 68). It was amid such recollections that the Council, about a week later, listened to the reading of a draft-canon proposed by the Emperor in person for their consideration (ib. vii. 173): it was the first of three, the second and third being those which took shape in canons 3 and 20; and it was expanded into the canon before us, which, after reserving 'due honour for those who adopt the monastic life in good earnest and in sincerity' (εἰλικρινῶς), recites that some 'use the monastic character as a pretext' (προσχήματι wrongly understood by old translators and Greek commentators to mean the monastic 'habit'—'woollen garments,' says the Arabic paraphrase) 'for disturbing the churches and the affairs of the State' (Marcian had said, public affairs), 'roaming about heedlessly (ἀδιαφόρως, see Nic. 12) in the cities, and even undertaking to found monasteries for themselves; compare can. 23. The passage is singularly like one in which Sozomen says that Chrysostom 'commended monks who remained quiet in their own monasteries, and took pains to protect them from injury, and to supply them with necessaries,—but severely reproved those who went out and showed themselves in the city, as persons who brought disgrace upon' monastic 'philosophy' (viii. 9: see this paraphrased in Gibbon, iv. 153, and compare Marcian's letter to the Eutychianizing monks in Palestine, who raised tumults against the Council in 452, when 'it was their duty to be quiet and to obey the priests,' Mansi, vii. 488). Accordingly, it is enacted that 'no one shall build or found a monastery or a house of prayer anywhere contrary to the will of the bishop of the city;' and that all monks in town or country shall be subject to the bishop, 'and give themselves to quietness, and attend to fasting and prayer only, continuing in the places in which they first renounced the world' (this last clause was not in the draft), 'and shall not leave their own monasteries' (not in the draft) 'to meddle either in ecclesiastical or in worldly affairs' (βιωτικοῖς—the draft has δημοσίοις), 'unless they are permitted so to do, for some necessary purpose, by the bishop of the city.'

Here observe (1) the definite assertion of episcopal authority over monks, as it is repeated for greater clearness in the last words of the canon, which are not found in Marcian's draft, 'It is the duty of the bishop of the city to make due provision for the monasteries:' and compare canons 8, 24. Isidore says that the bishop must 'keep an eye on the negligences of monks' (Epist. i. 149). The Western Church followed in this track (see Council of Agde, can. 27, that 'no new monastery is to be founded without the bishop's approval,' and 1st of Orleans, c. 19, 'Let abbots be under the bishop's power,' and also 5th of Paris, c. 12; Mansi, viii. 329, 354, 542, etc.), until a reaction set in against the oppressiveness of bishops, was encouraged by Gregory the Great (Epist. i. 12, ii. 41), the 4th Council of Toledo (c. 51), and the English Council of Hertford (c. 3, Bede, iv. 5, and Bright's Chapters of Early Engl. Ch. Hist. p. 244), and culminated in the system of monastic exemptions, of which Monte Cassino, St. Martin's of Tours, Fulda, Westminster, Battle (see Freeman, Norm. Conquest, iv. 409), and St. Alban's were eminent instances. These exemptions were disapproved by Lanfranc; and St. Bernard treats an abbot's 'Nolo obedire' episcopo' as equivalent to a bishop's 'Nolo obedire archiepiscopo,' and urges that dispensations should not be lightly given (de Considerat. iii. 4). On this subject see Bingham, ii. 4. 1, 2: vii. 3. 14: Guizot, Civiliz. in France, lect. 15: Robertson, Hist. Ch. iii. 218. Compare can. 8, and Justinian, Novell. 131. c. 4.

(2) The phrase τὴν ἡσυχίαν ἀσπάζεσθαι is an appeal to the monks' traditional love of religious tranquillity. It was a word which they themselves loved. Basil had advised his monks to 'perform the work of Christ ἐν ἡσυχίᾳ' (Epist. 226. 4): Chrysostom had dwelt on the profound ἡσυχία of monasteries (on 1 Tim. Hom. 14. 3): compare Theodoret, iv. 25, and Marcian's letter to the monks, v. s. (On the later limited sense of ἡσυχασταί, see Bingham, vii. 2. 14.) It was what Antony had expressed by 'If thou desirest ὄντως ἠρεμεῖν' (Athan. Vit. Ant. 49), and Chrysostom by a like phrase, 'the monk, remaining by himself, οὐ ταράττεται' (de Sacerd. vi. 7). Compare Kingsley's Hermits, p. 126 ff.

(3) Ἀπετάξαντο is the reading followed by the Prisca and Dionysius, and by Balsamon, who adds, 'or were tonsured:' so Routh, Scr. Opusc. ii. 56. See Bingham, vii. 2. 14, on ἀποταξάμενοι as a title given to monks, and compare ἀποτάσσομαι in the ancient baptismal renunciations. The other reading, ἐπετάξαντο, would mean, 'attached themselves to monastic life' ('ordinati sunt,' Isidorian, Hervetus); but it is clearly wrong.

The restless zeal of eastern monks was not moderated by these restrictions. The monks called Acœmetæ were agitators for orthodoxy; while the Eutychian monks raised tumults in Palestine, and long afterwards, by a violent demonstration at Antioch, provoked the inhabitants to 'make a great slaughter of them' (Evagr. iii. 32).

The canon goes on to forbid monks 'to receive into their monasteries a slave for the purpose of living as a monk, against the will of his own master' (cp. Justinian, Novell. 134. c. 34, allowing a master three years to reclaim a slave before his profession as a monk). The draft had been more explicit as to the rights of ownership: it had a clause which the canon omits, to the effect that no monastery was to be founded 'on an estate without the consent of the landowner;' and for the present clause it read, 'nor shall they have authority to receive into their own monasteries slaves, or persons under obligation to serve others (ἐναπογράφους), without their masters' consent.' The canon, as passed, abridges this, but adds that whosoever 'transgresses its decision' (ὅρον, see Nic. 15) 'shall be excommunicated,' for ἀκοινώνητος see c. 8, 16, Nic. 5, Eph. 6, in order 'that the name of God be not blasphemed,' a quotation from 1 Tim. vi. 1,—the thought being, 'Do not give unbelievers a pretext for calling Christianity a revolutionary religion,'—(comp. Apost. Const. viii. 32). The prohibition was based on the principle that no man having a right to 'property' should be deprived of it. The 82nd Apostolic canon, referring to the case of '*our* Onesimus,' makes the master's consent a prerequisite for the slave's ordination, as if to say, 'He who becomes Christ's minister must be free of all dependence on a human master's will.' The 80th canon of Elvira forbids the ordination of a Heathen's freedman. So in 400 the 1st Council of Toledo ordered that none who were 'obligati' should be ordained 'without their patrons' consent.' It was one of the charges against Chrysostom, in 403, that he had ordained to the episcopate persons who were slaves to other men, and not yet emancipated (Photius, Bibl. 59), in violation of a law of Arcadius, A.D. 398 (Cod. Theod. ix. 49. 3). Leo the Great forbade the evasion whereby slaves whom their masters would not emancipate procured for themselves ordination, so that 'dominorum jura, quantum ad illicitæ usurpationis temeritatem pertinet, solvuntur' (Epist. 4. 1). He has no misgiving whatever about these 'dominorum jura;' they had been respected, he knew, in the Epistle to Philemon; and although that Epistle indeed had deposited a seed which was ultimately to destroy them, 'No longer as a slave, but above a slave, a brother beloved,'—yet it took long ages to unfold what lay in those words. And we must not make an ideal estimate of what the ancient Church could effect for the slave. She could preach moderation in the use of legal power, and rebuke a savage misuse of it (e.g. Chrys. in Eph. Hom. 15. 3). One of her earliest and most large-hearted Fathers could say in a work on Christian ethics, 'We ought to treat οἰκέταις as ourselves, for they are men as we are, and God, if you consider, is to all, whether bond or free, ἴσος' (Clem. Alex. Pædag. iii. 12. 92); and that high truth, developed by the faith in a common Redeemer, by equal membership in the Divine 'familia,' by joint participation in the one Eucharist, did gradually, 'here a little and there a little,' extend through legislation the immunities of the slave. Again and again it was pressed home on the Christian conscience; as when Gregory of Nazianzus affirmed that equality was man's natural condition, and that slavery was one of those divisions which sin had introduced (Orat. 14. 26), or Isidore of Pelusium insisted that slavery was but 'accidental,' and that all were one by nature, by the faith, by the coming judgment, and 'could not think that a Christian who knew the grace that had set all men free could keep a slave' (Epist. i. 471, 142). But the 'consideration' of such an idea, in the length and breadth of its opposition to Aristotelian theory and to old Roman practice, was a process not to be hurried; and no one, in 451, foresaw the result. See an Essay on 'Slavery as affected by Christianity,' by E. S. Talbot, since Warden of Keble College, pp. 6–18, 22–44: compare Milman, Hist. of Christianity, iii. 240; and also his Latin Christ. ix. 35, on the 'inestimable merit' of the mediæval hierarchy in 'asserting the absolute spiritual equality of all not in sacred orders,' whereby king and serf in all essentials 'stood on the same level before God.'

Canon V.

This canon declares that 'the canons previously enacted by the holy fathers respecting bishops or clerics who remove from place to place shall have their proper force.' See on Nic. 15. It is supposed by Hefele that the bishops were thinking of the case of Bassian, who, in the eleventh session (Oct. 29), pleaded that he had been violently ejected from the see of Ephesus. Stephen, the actual bishop, answered that Bassian had not been 'ordained' for that see, but had invaded it and been justly expelled. Bassian rejoined that his original consecration for the see of Evasa had been forcible even to brutality; that he had never even visited Evasa; that therefore his appointment to Ephesus was not a case of translation. Ultimately, the Council cut the knot by ordering that a new bishop should be elected, Bassian and Stephen retaining the episcopal title and receiving allowances from the revenues of the see (Mansi, vii. 273 ff.). Among the repetitions of this law against translations compare the fifth 'responsio' of Egbert archbishop of York, 'Desertorem propriæ ecclesiæ interdictum habemus in alia ministrare' (Haddan and Stubbs, Councils, iii. 406); the legatine decrees at Celchyth (or Chelsea?) in 787, c. 6, 'et in illo titulo perseverent ad quem consecrati sunt' (ib. 451): and the 8th of the canons of Edgar's reign, that no priest shall forsake that church to which he was consecrated, but shall have it as his lawful spouse (Wilkins, Concil. i. 225).

Canon VI.

This canon forbids ordination without what we call a 'title' (see above). 'No one is to be ordained at large (ἀπολελυμένως) either presbyter, or deacon, or to any other place in the ecclesiastical order (τάγματι),' that is, no one is to be ordained 'unless he is particularly designated to' (lit. proclaimed in, 'in ecclesia ... mereatur ordinationis publicatæ vocabulum,' Isidorian) 'a church of a city or village, or a "martyry," or a monastery.'

Here ἀπολελυμένως, like ἀπολύτως in the next sentence ('absolute,' Lat. Transl.), is explained, with some confusion of construction, in the clause εἰ μὴ ... ἐπικηρύττοιτο. So the Arabic paraphrase, 'Let no one receive ordination unless there is declared to him a place and an abode where he may dwell' (Beveridge, i. 721): compare the 8th canon of the Synod of London in 1126, 'Nullus in presbyterum, nullus in diaconum nisi ad certum titulum ordinetur: qui vero absolute fuerit ordinatus, sumpta careat dignitate' (Wilkins, Concil. i. 408), and the 33rd canon of 1604, 'It hath long been provided by many decrees of the ancient fathers, that none should be admitted either deacon or priest who had not first some certain place where he might use his function.' There are a few exceptions to this rule. 'Paulinus and St. Jerome, says Bingham (iv. 6. 3), 'seem to have had the privilege granted them of being ordained without affixing to any church.' So Vallarsi says that Jerome accepted the presbyterate from Paulinus on condition 'ut .. nulli ecclesiæ alligatus, susceptum ordinem exercere nunquam cogi posset' (Vit. S. Hieron. c. 12. s. 3), referring to Jerome's words in c. Joan. Jerosol. 41. For Paulinus of Nola's case see his Epist. 1. 10 : 'ea conditione in

Barcinonensi ecclesia consecrari adductus sum, ut ipsi ecclesiæ non alligarer,—in sacerdotium tantum Domini, non etiam in locum ecclesiæ dedicatus.' Another exception was Macedonius the Syrian hermit, whose ordination by Flavian is a curious instance of ignorance on the one hand and trickery on the other (Theod. Relig. Hist. 13). Sozomen mentions two other cases, those of Barses and Eulogius (vi. 34): but they were, in fact, successively bishops of Edessa (Theod. iv. 16, 18). The exception was almost a rule in the ancient Irish Church, in which the episcopate 'was frequently conferred in recognition of the preeminence in sanctity or learning of some distinguished ecclesiastic, who nevertheless continued to live either as a hermit, or as the head of a school in his monastery, without necessarily taking upon him the charge of any district, church, or diocese: but the peculiar functions of his order were never overlooked .... These bishops were always applied to to consecrate churches, to ordain ... to give confirmation,' etc. (Todd's St. Patrick, p. 5, cp. ib. 27: and Skene's Celtic Scotland, ii. 25). But in the English Church, as we have seen, the Chalcedonian canon was respected. It was cited by the Council of Trent (sess. 23, de reform. 16): and it was alluded to in a series of canons drawn up at Edinburgh, in 1727, by five Scottish bishops of what was called the 'Diocesan' party as against those who 'were anxious to continue the anomalous system ... of governing the whole Church by an episcopal "College."' 'The consecrating of bishops at large,' says the synod in its 3rd canon, 'is contrary to the canons and practice of the Church' (Grub, Eccl. Hist. Scotl. iv. 3: comp. ib. iii. 391).

By the word μαρτυρίῳ (see can. 8) is meant a church or chapel raised over a martyr's grave. So the Laodicene Council forbids Churchmen to visit the 'martyries of heretics' (can. 9). So Gregory of Nyssa speaks of 'the martyry' of the Forty Martyrs (Op. ii. 212); Chrysostom of a 'martyry,' and Palladius of 'martyries,' near Antioch (in Act. Apost. Hom. 38. 5: Dial. p. 17), and Palladius of 'the martyry of St. John' at

Constantinople (Dial. p. 25). See Socrates, iv. 18, 23, on the 'martyry' of St. Thomas at Edessa, and that of SS. Peter and Paul at Rome; and vi. 6, on the 'martyry' of St. Euphemia at Chalcedon, in which the Council actually met. In the distinct sense of a visible testimony, the word was applied to the church of the Resurrection at Jerusalem (Eusebius, Vit. Con. iii. 40, iv. 40; Mansi, vi. 564; Cyril, Catech. xiv. 3), and to the Holy Sepulchre itself (Vit. Con. iii. 28). Churches raised over martyrs' tombs were called in the West 'memoriæ martyrum,' see Cod. Afric. 83 (compare Augustine, De Cura pro Mortuis, s. 6).

The canon ends by declaring that 'the holy synod has decided to treat' all ordinations 'at large as null and everywhere void of effect,' (Prisca renders ἄκυρον here 'inefficacem,' Dionysius 'irritam,' Isidorian 'vacuam'), 'to the disgrace of the ordainer.' On χειροθεσία, here used as equivalent to χειροτονία, i.e. ordination, see above, on Nic. 8, comp. Nic. 19; and on the 'annulling' of ordinations see Nic. 15. Leo the Great evidently had this canon in mind when he wrote, some seven years afterwards, to Rusticus, 'Vana habenda est creatio, quæ nec loco fundata est,' etc. (Epist. 167, resp. 1).

CANON VII.

Carrying on to a further point the idea of the 3rd canon, the present canon rules that 'persons who had once been numbered among the clergy, or had once adopted a monastic life, must not enter on the public service or any secular dignity.'

By στρατείαν, 'militiam,' is here meant, not military employment as such, but the public service in general. This use of the term is a relic and token of the military basis of the Roman monarchy. The court of the Imperator was called his camp, στρατόπεδον (Cod. Theod. tom. ii. p. 22), as in Constantine's letters to John Archaph and the Council of Tyre (Athan. Apol. c. Ari. 70, 86), and in the 7th canon of Sardica; so Athanasius speaks of the 'camp' of Constans (Apol. ad Constant. 4), and of that of Constantius at Milan (Hist. Ari. 37): so Hosius uses the same phrase in his letter to Constantius (ib. 44): so the Semi-Arian bishops, when addressing Jovian (Soz. vi. 4): so Chrysostom in the reign of Theodosius I. (Hom. ad Pop. Antioch. vi. 2). Similarly, there were officers of the palace called Castrensians (Tertull. de Cor. 12), as being 'milites alius generis—de imperatoria familia' (Gothofred, Cod. Theod. tom. ii. p. 226). So στρατεύεσθαι is used for holding a place at court, as in Soc. iv. 9, Soz. vi. 9, on Marcian's case, and a very clear passage in Soc. v. 25, where the verb is applied to an imperial secretary. It occurs in combination with στρατεία, in a petition of an Alexandrian deacon named Theodore, which was read in the third session of Chalcedon: he says, "Ἐστρατευσάμην for about twenty-two years in the Schola of the magistrians' (under the Magister officiorum, or chief magistrate of the palace), 'but I disregarded στρατείας τοσούτου χρόνου in order to enter the ministry' (Mansi, vi. 1008). See also Theodoret, Relig. Hist. 12, on the emperor's letter-carriers. In the same sense, Honorius, by a law of 408, forbids non-Catholics 'intra palatium militare' (Cod. Theod. xvi. 5. 42); and the Vandal king Hunneric speaks of 'domus nostræ militiæ' (Victor Vitens. iv. 2).

We must compare the canon with Apost. can. 81 and 83. They had in view such a combination of ecclesiastical and secular functions as was displayed for a time by Paul of Samosata, was tolerated under Alexius Comnenus in the case of one Constantine who, after his ordination as deacon, was retained in the service of that emperor (Beveridge, Annot. p. 39), and became familiar, under mediæval conditions of Western Church life, in the stately forms of prince-bishop, chancellor-bishop, or regent-abbot,—of a Bek, a Wykeham, or a Suger (see Mozley's Essays, i. 124). They forbade this attempt, as it was then considered, to 'serve two masters,' and to mix up 'the things of Cæsar with the things of God,' under penalty of deposition. It was under the same feeling that

Hadrian I.'s two legates, when they saw English prelates 'judging of secular matters in their councils' (i.e. sitting side by side with ealdormen in the courts of the shire, see Freeman, Norm. Conq. iv. 388), rebuked them by quoting 2 Tim. ii. 4 (Haddan and Stubbs, Councils, iii. 452). The present canon, as the Greek commentators observe, is directed against the actual abandonment of clerical duties or monastic discipline for the sake of a secular career. Such desertion had already, under Honorius, been ingeniously punished by a lifelong liability to the much-dreaded burdens of a curialis or municipal functionary (Cod. Theod. xvi. 2. 39). The ecclesiastical penalty now imposed is the severest possible. Clerics or monks who 'dare' thus to give up their vocation, and do not repent (μεταμελουμένους used as in Nic. 11), 'and turn again to that which they once chose for God's sake, are to be anathematized.' See Bingham, vi. 4. 1. The Council of Tours, in 461, repeated this canon of Chalcedon (c. 5, Mansi, vii. 945).

Canon VIII.

This canon should be compared with can. 4. It is intended to guard the episcopal jurisdiction over clerics in peculiar spheres of duty, such as 'houses for reception of the poor,' monasteries, and 'martyries.'

What a πτωχεῖον was may be seen from what Gibbon calls the 'noble and charitable foundation, almost a new city' (iii. 252), established by St. Basil at a little distance from Cæsarea, and called in consequence the Basiliad. Gregory Nazianzen describes it as a large set of buildings with rooms for the sick, especially for lepers, and also for houseless travellers; 'a storehouse of piety, where disease was borne philosophically, and sympathy was tested' (Orat. 43. 63, compare Basil himself, Epist. 94, on its staff of nurses and physicians, and 150. 3). Sozomen calls it 'a most celebrated resting-place for the poor,' and names Prapidius as having been its warden while acting as 'bishop over many villages' (vi. 34, see on Nic. 8). Another πτωχοτροφεῖον is mentioned by Basil (Epist. 143) as governed by a chorepiscopus. St. Chrysostom, on coming to the see of Constantinople, ordered the excess of episcopal expenditure to be transferred to the hospital for the sick (νοσοκομεῖον), and 'founded other such hospitals, setting over them two pious presbyters, with physicians and cooks .... so that foreigners arriving in the city, on being attacked by disease, might receive aid, both because it was a good work in itself, and for the glory of the Saviour' (Palladius, Dial. p. 19). At Ephesus Bassian founded a πτωχεῖον with seventy pallets for the sick (Mansi, vii. 277), and there were several such houses in Egypt (ib. vi. 1013); in the next century there was a hospital for the sick at Daphne near Antioch (Evagr. iv. 35). 'The tradition of the holy fathers' is here cited as barring any claim on the part of clerics officiating in these institutions, or in monasteries or martyries, to be exempt from the jurisdiction of the ordinary. They are to 'abide under it,' and not to indulge selfwill by 'turning restive' 'against their bishop's authority,' (ἀφηνιάζω is literally to get the bit between the teeth, and is used by Aetius for 'not choosing to obey,' Mansi, vii. 72). Those who dare to violate this clearly-defined rule (διατύπωσιν, comp. τύπος in Nic. 19), and to refuse subjection to their own bishop, are, if clerics, to incur canonical censure, if monks or laics, to be excommunicated. The allusion to laics points to laymen as founders or benefactors of such institutions. Balsamon quotes the passage against those who in his own day pleaded what in later language might be called 'founders' wills or statutes,' in defence of their claim to exemption from episcopal authority. The canon is against them, he says: what can they say in rejoinder? 'Nothing at all.' On exemptions see above on can. 4. The present canon is recited and enforced in Pope Zacharias' 8th letter to Pippin, no. 10, 'De clericis qui sunt in ptochiis' (Oct. Saec. Scriptores, ed. Migne, p. 934).

Canon IX.

We now come to the provisions for carrying on ecclesiastical litigation, as between (1) two clerics, (2) a cleric and his bishop, (3) a cleric, or a bishop, and the metropolitan.

(1) 'The arbitrative authority of ecclesiastical pastors is coeval with Christianity;' so Hallam, M. Ages, ii. 210 (ed. 2). Questions between Christians were usually referred to the bishop, in obedience to the text, 1 Cor. vi. 1 ff., and also because the bishop was supposed to be 'best acquainted with the principles of natural justice and Christian equity' (Milman, Hist. Christ. iii. 254). The Apostolic Constitutions direct the bishop to prevent such questions from 'coming before a heathen tribunal.' He is to endeavour to settle them privately: but, failing in this, to take cognisance of them on Mondays (so as to allow time for reconciliation before the next Lord's day) with the aid of presbyters and deacons, as assessors, to examine into the antecedents, conduct, and motives of the accuser, and the characters of the witnesses and of the accused; and after hearing both sides, to pronounce judgment (ii. 37, 45, 47, 49–51). Constantine allowed any two litigants to invoke the bishop's arbitration, and invested it, as between them, with force of law (Euseb. Vit. Const. iv. 27; Soz. i. 9: see Lingard, Hist. Engl. ii. 207). The so-called 'Extravagans' in Cod. Theod. vol. vi. p. 339, which represents Constantine as having extended this legalisation to cases in which one of the parties might resolve to apply to the bishop, is a forgery (cp. Hallam, M. Ages, ii. 211; Lingard endeavours to uphold it as a law of Theodosius, but against all probability). The Constantinian legislation was repeated by Arcadius and Honorius, the latter of whom placed the episcopal award on a level with that of a prætorian prefect, from which there was no appeal (Cod. Theod. vol. vi. p. 341); it is alluded to by St. Augustine (Enarr. in Psal. 25. 13); and Valentinian III., in the opening of a lengthy law of 452, laid stress on the condition that both

parties must agree to make the bishop arbiter (Cod. vol. vi. append. p. 127). Augustine, at Hippo, felt this duty of arbitration to be a heavy burden, although in the face of 1 Cor. vi. 1 he durst not decline it; he describes the importunity of those who pressed their 'selfish cupidity' on his attention; 'instant, urgent, precantur, tumultuantur, extorquent' (Enarr. in Psal. 118. s. 24. 3; cp. Possidius, Vit. S. Aug. c. 19): and elsewhere he represents a Christian of the ordinary type of conduct as claiming his own, but, as a matter of course, 'ecclesiastico judicio, non forensi' (c. duas Epist. Pelag. iii. s. 14). For the precedent set by bishop Silvanus of Troas, in delegating this office to a good layman, see above, p. 132. In Anglo-Saxon times, says Prof. Stubbs, 'the bishop with his clerks would be fully compelled to arbitrate, and were probably frequently called upon to do so' (Const. Hist. of Engl. i. 267).

But what of charges brought against ecclesiastics? Constantine had himself heard the charges of illegal exaction and of treasonable correspondence brought against St. Athanasius, and even that of sacrilege brought against his presbyter Macarius (Apol. c. Arian. 60); and so, when Athanasius received notice to answer a charge of murder before the censor Dalmatius, he made no protest, but prepared to defend himself (ib. 65). The charges both of murder and sacrilege were entertained by a Council of bishops at Tyre, under the presidency of Count Dionysius as the emperor's deputy (ib. 72, 86); and Athanasius' appeal to Constantine from the judgment of that council was in the nature of an 'appel comme d'abus.' A few years later, however, Julius of Rome and the Council of Sardica asserted the principle that ecclesiastical offences, such as sacrilege, should be tried by ecclesiastical judges only (ib. 31, 39): while the Council of Antioch ruled that no ecclesiastic deposed by ecclesiastical sentence should appeal to the emperor, on pain of losing all hope of restoration (c. 12). The distinction between religious and non-religious offences of ecclesiastics, the former being reserved for a Church tribunal, the latter being within the cognisance of the secular courts, was significantly recognised when the general Salianus demanded that the atrocious plot of bishop Stephen of Antioch against bishop Euphrates of Cologne, in the spring of 344, should be dealt with, 'not by a synod, but by the courts,' i.e. should be treated as a crime (Theod. ii. 9). So, when St. Basil claimed to judge of any thefts committed within his church-precinct, he was investing them with the character of sacrilege (Epist. 286). It was in the far West that a more absolute claim began to be made in the name of the Church. The 3rd Council of Carthage, in 397, forbade clerics, whether engaged in civil suits or accused on religious grounds, to plead before 'the public tribunals' (can. 9, Mansi, iii. 882). This was a new point of departure, whereby the African Church aimed at retaining, as obligatory for clerics under a Christian State, the course which had once been morally binding on all Christians under a heathen State; and while she drew this somewhat arbitrary line, she neglected the well-grounded distinction between offences of a religious and those of a non-religious character. But the State for a long time held to that distinction. Constantius indeed enacted, in the September of 355, that all charges against bishops should be tried by 'other bishops' (Cod. Theod. xvi. 2. 12); but, curiously enough, this verbal concession of a momentous point to the Church was apparently meant to shield the Arian bishops, who had recently triumphed in the Council of Milan, from charges brought against them by Catholics in the courts of the empire. It was on a 'question of faith' that Valentinian I. declined to adjudicate (Ambrose, Epist. 21. 4, 5): his son Gratian, by a law of May 17, 376, had ordered all causes pertaining 'ad religionis observantiam' to be heard by ecclesiastical tribunals, but had expressly reserved criminal charges against clerics for the cognisance of State courts (Cod. Theod. xvi. 2. 23): and similarly Honorius in 399, 'Quotiens de religione agitur, episcopos convenit judicare: cæteras vero causas quæ ad . . . usum publici juris pertinent, legibus oportet audiri' (ib. xvi. 1 11); and a later law of his, which begins absolutely enough, 'Clericos non nisi apud episcopos accusari convenit' (ib. xvi. 2. 41), is explained by

Gothofred as referring not to all kinds of charges, but to such as affected a cleric's religious reputation. Similarly when Placidia, in the name of the infant Valentinian III., referred to a recent usurper's attempt to bring the clergy 'indiscriminately' under the secular courts, and 'reserved them for episcopal cognisance,' she was clearly contemplating them, as Gothofred says, '*qua* clerici ... et sic in causis, negotiis, delictis ecclesiasticis, at non *qua* cives, etc.' (see Cod. Theod. xvi. 2. 47). Theodosius II. ordered Candidian to restrain the Council of Ephesus from discussing charges of a pecuniary or criminal kind (Mansi, iv. 1120). What is the position assumed by the Council of Chalcedon? It approaches to that of the African Council: it forbids a cleric who has a 'matter' (πρᾶγμα, 1 Cor. vi. 1, clearly a civil, not a religious suit) against another cleric to 'run away to secular tribunals,'—a phrase which, so to speak, begs the question. Rather, he is 'first to state his case before his own bishop, or, with the bishop's own consent, before persons by whom both parties shall agree to have the rights of the case settled,' (συγκροτεῖσθαι, in the sense of being put on their proper footing; the other reading, συγκροτείσθω, is an evident alteration, which disturbs the construction), i.e. in a word, by referees. In the year after the Council, Valentinian III. declared it to be certain that bishops and presbyters had not by law a 'forum,' and could not take cognisance of causes not affecting religion (Cod. Theod. vol. vi. append. p. 127). Justinian first granted to the clergy, as a 'privilege,' that any 'pecuniary suits' against them should in the first instance be referred to the bishop; but while he excluded secular judges from all cognisance of 'ecclesiastical offences,' he reserved to them their authority over the 'civil crimes' of clerics (Novell. 84; cp. Novell. 134. c. 21: Hallam, ii. 212). Bishops, however, he exempted from all ordinary jurisdiction of 'civil or military judges' (Novell. 134, 8); and Charles the Great went further, ordaining that none of the clergy 'should be drawn, de personis suis, ad sæcularia judicia' (Capit. of 803; see Pertz, Mon. Germ. Hist. Legum, i. 110).

This immunity did not exist in England before the Conquest: the 'laws of the Northumbrian priests' go no further than to forbid a priest 'to bring a cause before laymen which he should bring before ecclesiastics' (c. 5); and bishops and archdeacons were wont to try the civil (not the spiritual) offences of the clergy in the shire-moot and the hundred-moot, side by side with civil judges (Stubbs, Const. Hist. i. 266). But after the Conquest a change was introduced which had the effect of establishing the exemption, and the abuses thus introduced (although not without some compensations, Freeman, Norm. Conq. v. 668) led Henry II. to propose 'that clerical criminals should be tried in the ordinary courts of the country,' and, if convicted, should be first degraded and then delivered over to the law (Stubbs, i. 322, 523). The Constitutions of Clarendon, while disallowing the exemption, admitted that separation of the Church court from the 'court of the hundred' out of which it arose (Freeman, v. 676).

(2) If a cleric had 'a matter against his diocesan or some other bishop,' it was to be tried by 'the provincial synod,' see Nic. 5. Compare also the 17th canon of the African Council of May 1, 418, to the effect that a presbyter censured by his own bishop might bring his case before the neighbouring bishops, and, if dissatisfied with their judgment, might go before the primate of his province, or the council of the whole church of (Western) Africa, but might *not* 'appeal to tribunals beyond sea,' as Apiarius had appealed to Pope Zosimus (cp. Hefele, sect. 119, 120). This decree appears in two forms in the African Code (28, 125).

(3) But what if the question lies between a bishop or a cleric and his metropolitan? In that case, let him appeal 'either (*a*) to the exarch of the "diocese," or (*b*) to the see of Constantinople, and there plead.'

This title of 'exarch' had been used for a metropolitan in the Greek text of the 6th canon of Sardica; but it is here applied to the primate of a group of provincial churches, as it had been used by Ibas, bishop of Edessa, at his trial in 448; alluding to the 'Eastern Council' which had resisted the Council of Ephesus, and condemned Cyril, he said, 'I followed my exarch,' meaning John of Antioch (Mansi, vii. 237; compare Evagrius, iv. 11, using 'patriarchs' and 'exarchs' synonymously). Reference is here made, not to all such prelates, but to the bishops of Ephesus, Cæsarea in Cappadocia, and Heraclea, if, as seems probable, the see of Heraclea still nominally retained its old relation to the bishops of Thrace.

But an alternative is proposed, and it is a momentous one. The complainant may ignore the arbitrative authority of his 'exarch,' and appeal at once to the 'throne' or see of Constantinople. This provision should have prepared the Roman delegates for the formal creation, in what is called the 28th canon, of a Constantinopolitan patriarchate. What was now done for Constantinople went beyond what was done for Rome by the 3rd, 4th, and 5th canons of Sardica. They only gave to the bishop of Rome the right to appoint new judges: here the appeal to the see of Constantinople is absolute, without the slightest reference to Rome. True, the canon was intended for certain Eastern regions only; but Leo himself would have maintained that the chair of St. Peter was the supreme seat of ecclesiastical justice for all Christendom. No such claim, however, appears to have been made by his delegates in opposition to the passing of this canon, which could not have been either proposed or passed by prelates who admitted the high Roman theory. Theodoret, indeed, had appealed to Leo after being deposed at the 'Robbers' Meeting;' but he had not based his recognition of the Roman 'primacy' on the precise ground which Leo would have liked to see taken by a suppliant (see his Epist. 113, and comp. Epist. 116). Notwithstanding Leo's favourable reply, Theodoret was not reinstated until he had satisfied the Council in its 8th session by anathematizing Nestorius (Mansi, vii. 189).

We must now consider what had taken place, since the Council of Constantinople, to increase the practical power of the bishop of that city. (1) As to Thrace, the wording of the

2nd and 3rd canons of Constantinople would surely have been different had it been intended to make the see of Constantinople supreme over Thrace. Socrates indeed speaks of Nectarius of Constantinople as having 'received authority over the great city and Thrace' (v. 8); but as to this assertion see above, p. 95. Chrysostom, however, who succeeded Nectarius, is expressly said by Theodoret (v. 28) to have 'extended his care not only over that city, but also over all Thrace:' and Atticus twice consecrated metropolitans for Philippopolis (Soc. vii. 37). Next (2) as to the 'Asian diocese,' we have seen above (on Chalc. 2) that Chrysostom was invited to visit Ephesus in order to deal with some grave cases of simony (Palladius, Dial. p. 53). He also wrote to the bishop of Nicæa, directing him to visit the church of Basilinopolis as dependent on Nicæa (Mansi, vii. 305). Atticus complied with a request from the people of Troas to provide them with a bishop (Soc. l. c.), and also exercised authority in the affairs of Synnada, the metropolis of Phrygia Salutaris (ib. vii. 3). It appeared, from the statements of bishops in this very Council, that the then bishop of Synnada, and predecessors of his, had been consecrated at Constantinople (Mansi, vii. 448). The metropolitan of Myra, and several successive metropolitans of Aphrodisias, had also been thus 'ordained.' There was some discrepancy of statement, in an earlier session of the Council, as to whether any bishops of Ephesus itself had been consecrated by bishops of Constantinople (Mansi, vii. 293). Sisinnius had consecrated Proclus for Cyzicus; but the Cyzicenes appointed another bishop, who maintained possession (Soc. vii. 28). Again (3) as to Pontus, it appeared at the 16th session that four metropolitans of Amasia had been consecrated at Constantinople. Evidence somewhat varied as to another metropolitan church, that of Gangra: four of its bishops had been consecrated by the bishops of Constantinople, and some three by the bishops of Ancyra. Eusebius, metropolitan of Ancyra, himself consecrated by Proclus of Constantinople, had consecrated one bishop of Gangra at Proclus' request, but had left Proclus to consecrate his successor (Mansi, vii. 448 ff.). The great see of Cæsarea itself was occupied by Thalassius, once a provincial governor, whom Proclus had suddenly chosen and consecrated when, in 438, the people of Cæsarea sent to Constantinople for an exarch (Soc. vii. 48). In a word, the bishops of many venerable sees in Asia Minor had found their advantage in attaching themselves more and more closely to the potent see of New Rome, and had said in effect, as one of them said in words, 'The glory of the throne of Constantinople is our glory' (Mansi, l. c.).

To this it may be added, that when the ordinance of 421, directing that Church disputes in Eastern Illyricum (Macedonia and Achaia) should not be settled without consulting the bishop of Constantinople (Cod. Theod. xvi. 2. 45), had been cancelled by Theodosius II. in consequence of representations from his uncle Honorius, who was stirred to action by Pope Boniface, Atticus, as Neale expresses it, 'turned his attention to the Eastern diœceses' (Introd. East. Ch. i. 28), and obtained from Theodosius, as if by way of compensation, a law ordering that no ordination of a bishop should take place (in the Eastern empire) without the assent of the bishop of Constantinople; but this law was ignored after his death, in the case of Cyzicus (Soc. vii. 28). Again, Flavian of Constantinople had trespassed on the rights of Domnus of Antioch by recognising, as competent accusers of Ibas of Edessa, two clerics whom Domnus had excommunicated for failing to appear in that character at his own synod (Mansi, vii. 217, 220; Tillemont, xv. 473). Herein Flavian had departed from the example set by his predecessor Proclus, who interceded with Domnus on behalf of Athanasius of Perrha, but carefully disclaimed all encroachment on the rights of the Antiochene 'throne' (Mansi, vii. 325).

The rising power of the see of Constantinople was much assisted by the gradual formation of what was called the Home Synod (σύνοδος ἐνδημοῦσα). It had become usual for several bishops to stay for a time at Constantinople, on account of their own church-business; and their meetings under the presidency of the archbishop assumed, however irregularly, the character of a synod. In the 4th session of Chalcedon the imperial commissioners asked whether such a meeting could rightly be called a synod. Tryphon, bishop of Chios, answered, 'It *is* called a synod, and they assemble, and those who are oppressed get right done to them.' Anatolius of Constantinople said that it was 'a custom of long standing for bishops staying (ἐνδημοῦντας) in "the city of the great name" to assemble when the fit time summons them to do so in reference to ecclesiastical questions which come up' (Mansi, vii. 91; see notes in Transl. of Fleury, vol. iii. p. 273, 406; and Le Quien, i. 28). The institution could be turned against the archiepiscopate, as when the emperor Anastasius, in 496, employed 'the bishops ἐνδημοῦντας' to depose Euphemius (Theod. Lect. ii. 12).

CANON X.

This canon is directed against clerical pluralities, viewed as the result of clerical migrations.

'No cleric is to be enrolled at the same time on the clergy-lists of two cities.' The term κατάλογος, for the roll of clerics of all grades, of all who 'belong to the canon,' occurs in Apost. can. 17, 18. It is supposed that the cleric in question has left the church 'in which he was originally (τὴν ἀρχήν, cp. John viii. 25) ordained (ἐχειροτονήθη) and betaken himself to another, presumably as being a greater church,—from desire of vain glory.' Compare can. 5, Nic. 15, and the 1st Sardican canon, against the migration of a bishop from his own city to another, from motives of avarice, or ambition, or love of power. After repeating the Nicene provision that the cleric who has thus migrated must be sent back to his original sphere of duty, and officiate (λειτουργεῖν) there only, the Council contemplates an exceptional case in which the removal has not resulted from self-will, but from the action of authority, and directly that 'one who has been so removed shall take no further part in the affairs of his former church, or of the "martyries," or "houses for the poor," or "hospices," which may be dependent on it.' Here a new institution comes into view, of which there were many instances. Julian had directed Pagan hospices (ξενοδοχεῖα) to be established on the Christian model (Epist. 49). The Basiliad at Cæsarea was a ξενοδοχεῖον as well as a πτωχεῖον; it contained καταγώγια τοῖς ξένοις as well as for wayfarers, and those who needed assistance on account of illness, and Basil distinguishes various classes of persons engaged in charitable ministrations, including those who escorted the traveller on his way (τοὺς παραπέμποντας, Epist. 94). Jerome writes to Pammachius, 'I hear that you have made a "xenodochion" in the Port of Rome,' and adds that he himself had built a 'diversorium' for pilgrims to Bethlehem (Epist. 66. 11, 14). Chrysostom reminds his auditors at Constantinople that 'there is a common dwelling set apart by the Church,' and 'called a xenōn' (in Act. Hom. 45. 4). His friend Olympias was munificent to 'xenotrophia' (Hist. Lausiac. 144). There was a xenodochion near the church of the monastic settlement at Nitria (ib. 7). Ischyrion, in his memorial read in the 3rd session of Chalcedon, complains of his patriarch Dioscorus for having misapplied funds bequeathed by a charitable lady τοῖς ξενεῶσι καὶ πτωχείοις in Egypt, and says that he himself had been confined by Dioscorus in a 'xenōn' for lepers (Mansi, vi. 1013, 1017). Justinian mentions xenodochia in Cod. i. 3. 49, and their wardens in Novell. 134. 16. Gregory the Great orders that the accounts of xenodochia should be audited by the bishop (Epist. iv. 27). Charles the Great provides for the restoration of decayed 'senodochia' (Capitul. of 803; Pertz, Leg. i. 110); and Alcuin exhorts his pupil archbishop Eanbald to think where in the diocese of York he could establish 'xenodochia, id est, hospitalia' (Epist. 50).

The canon concludes by menacing with deposition any transgressors of this decree (ὅρος, can. 14, cp. Nic. 15, 17, 19). Compare can. 20.

M

CANON XI.

This canon distinguishes between two sets of letters to be given to Christians travelling abroad. 'All the poor and those who need help' are, after examination of their character (lit. with a testing, so Dionysius and Isidorian, 'sub probatione'), 'to travel with ἐπιστόλια, that is, with ecclesiastical letters of peace only.' They would be described in these documents simply as Churchmen deserving of charitable aid. More could not be said; whereas in the letters properly called 'systatic' or commendatory (2 Cor. iii. 1, cp. Rom. xvi. 1), more was said in praise of the bearer. For this appears to be the idea conveyed by the words, 'since the systatic letters ought to be granted to those persons who are in high estimation.' Τοῖς οὖσιν ἐν ὑπολήψει ... προσώποις has indeed been understood by the Greek commentators, and by Hervetus in his translation, to mean 'persons whose character has been, or is, open to suspicion.' In favour of this interpretation the 13th Apost. canon may be quoted, which speaks of commendatory letters as given to persons who had been released from Church censure. So Blastaris in his Syntagma, A. 90, says that one of the purposes for which 'systatics' are given is to prove that charges against the bearer are unjust, or that he has been released from excommunication. But the other sense is the more natural, and is adopted by the Prisca, 'bonæ esse opinioni;' by Dionysius, 'honoratioribus personis;'—by the Isidorian, 'in opere clariores;' by Tillemont, 'qui sont d'une bonne réputation' (xv. 697); and by Routh, 'viri honestiores' (Script. Opusc. ii. 110); and it may be illustrated by the use of ὑπόληψις in can. 21, by the language of an Asiatic prelate in the 16th session, λάμπει ἡ ὑπόληψις τοῦ .. ἀρχιεπισκόπου Ἀνατολίου (Mansi, vii. 452), and by Julius of Rome's words to the 'Eusebians,' 'It is out of anxiety for your reputation (τῆς ὑμῶν ὑπολήψεως) ... that I have thought it necessary to write thus' (Athan. Apol. c. Arian. 34).

To understand this, we must observe that all testimonial letters were generally described in the West as 'formatæ,' either as being drawn up in a peculiar form with some particular marks (see Cod. Afric. 23, compare Codex Canon. Eccles. c. 63, in app. ad S. Leon. Op.; Fleury, b. 20, c. 31; Bingham, ii. 4. 5), or as Sirmond thinks (on Sidonius Apollinaris, Epist. vi. 8), on account of the 'forma sigilli qua muniebantur.' They were divided into two classes. (*a*) The inferior were simple attestations of churchmanship, hence called letters 'of peace' (Antioch, c. 7), or letters 'of communion' (Elviran, c. 25; Arles, 7), and also sometimes (as in Antioch. 8, Laodic. 42) 'canonical' letters, because given according to a rule, and according to Antioch. 8 were obtainable from bishops, from chorepiscopi of irreproachable character, but not from country presbyters, except when addressed to neighbouring bishops. So Sozomen tells us that Eunomius received Eutychius when out of communion with the generality of Anomœans, 'and prayed with him, although it is not lawful among them to pray with those who travel without documents which testify, by signs inserted in the letters, and unintelligible to others, that the bearers are agreed with them in belief' (vii. 17). The present canon says that these are the letters to be given to persons in need of charitable aid. (*b*) On the other hand, the letters of 'special commendation,' or 'systatics,' being of higher value, were reserved for persons of exceptional merit, and were also given to clerics about to travel, or to clerics who, with their bishop's leave, were going into another diocese (in which case they were called ἀπολυτικαί, 'dimissory'), see Trullan can. 17; cp. Blastaris, Synt. A. 9, that letters dimissory, whereby the bishop permits a cleric to leave his church and to officiate elsewhere, are also called 'pacific,' because they show that the bond of holy love is not broken between the bishop who gives and the bishop to whom the bearer presents them; and that a cleric who means to travel ought to carry both a systatic and a dimissory letter. In the 13th Apostolic canon the term 'systatics' is applied to letters of communion; so again in the 34th, 'Let no foreign bishop, or presbyter, or deacon, be received without systatics.'

Canon XII.

Previous canons had carefully secured the rights of existing metropolitan sees, and the boundaries of respective provincial churches. But, as we learn from this canon, there were cases in which an ambitious prelate, 'by making application to the government' (δυναστείαις), had obtained what are called 'pragmatic letters,' and employed them for the purpose of 'dividing one province into two,' and exalting himself as a metropolitan. The name of a 'pragmatic sanction' is more familiar in regard to mediæval and modern history; it recalls the name of St. Louis, and, still more, that of the Emperor Charles VI., the father of Maria Theresa. Properly a 'pragmatic' was a deliberate order promulgated by the Emperor after full hearing of advice, on some public affair. We find 'pragmatici nostri statuta' in a law of A.D. 431 (Cod. Theod. xi. 1. 36); and 'pragmatici prioris,' 'sub hac pragmatica jussione,' in ordinances in Append. to Cod. Theod. pp. 95, 162; and the empress Pulcheria, about a year before the Council, had informed Leo that her husband Marcian had recalled some exiled orthodox bishops 'robore pragmatici sui' (Leon. Epist. 77). Justinian speaks of 'pragmaticas nostras formas' and 'pragmaticum typum' (Novel. 7. 9, etc.). The phrase was adopted from his legislation by Lewis the Pious and his colleague-son Lothar (compare Novel. 7. 2 with Pertz, Mon. Germ. Hist. Leg. i. 254), and hence it came to be used both by later German emperors (see, e. g. Bryce's Holy Roman Empire, p. 212), and by the French kings (Kitchin, Hist. France, i. 343, 544). Augustine explains it by 'præceptum imperatoris' (Brev. Collat. cum Donatist. iii. 2), and Balsamon in his comment uses an equivalent phrase; and so in the record of the 4th session of Chalcedon we have θεῖα γράμματα ('divine' being practically equivalent to 'imperial') explained by πραγματικοὺς τύπους (Mansi, vii. 89). We must observe that the imperial order, in the cases contemplated by the canon, had only conferred the title of 'metropolis' on the city, and had not professed to divide the province for civil, much less for ecclesiastical, purposes. Valens, indeed, had divided the province of Cappadocia, when in 371 he made Tyana a metropolis: and therefore Anthimus, bishop of Tyana, when he claimed the position of a metropolitan, with authority over suffragans, was making a not unnatural inference in regard to ecclesiastical limits from political rearrangements of territory, as Gregory of Nazianzus says, ἠξίου τοῖς δημοσίοις συνδιαιρεῖσθαι καὶ τὰ ἡμέτερα (Orat. 43. 58), whereas Basil 'held to the old custom,' i. e. to the traditional unity of his provincial church, although after a while he submitted to what he could not hinder (see Tillemont, ix. 175, 182, 670, and on the principles here involved, compare c. 17). But in the case of Eustathius of Berytus, which was clearly in the Council's mind, the Phœnician province had not been divided: it was in reliance on a mere title bestowed upon his city, and also on an alleged synodical ordinance which issued in fact from the so-called 'Home Synod' (see on i. 9) that he declared himself independent of his metropolitan, Photius of Tyre, and brought six bishoprics under his assumed jurisdiction. Thus, while the province remained politically one, he had *de facto* divided it ecclesiastically into two. Photius petitioned Marcian, who referred the case to the Council of Chalcedon; and it was taken up in the 4th session. The imperial commissioners announced that it was to be settled not according to 'pragmatic forms,' but according to those which had been enacted by the Fathers (Mansi, vii. 89). This encouraged the Council to say, 'A pragmatic can have no force against the canons.' The commissioners asked whether it was lawful for bishops, on the ground of a pragmatic, to steal away the rights of other churches? The answer was explicit: 'No, it is against the canons.' The Council proceeded to cancel the resolution of the Home Synod in favour of the elevation of Berytus, ordered the 4th Nicene canon to be read, and upheld the metropolitical rights of Tyre. The commissioners also pronounced against Eustathius. Cecropius, bishop of Sebastopolis, requested them to put an end to the issue of pragmatics made to the detriment of the canons; the Council echoed this request; and the commissioners granted it by declaring that the canons should everywhere stand good (Mansi, vii. 89-97). We may connect with this incident a law of Marcian dated in 454, by which 'all pragmatic sanctions, obtained by means of favour or ambition in opposition to the canons of the Church, are declared to be deprived of effect' (Cod. Justin. i. 2. 12).

To this decision the present canon looks back, when it forbids any bishop, on pain of deposition, to presume to do as Eustathius had done, since it decrees that 'he who attempts to do so shall fall from his own rank ($\beta\alpha\theta\mu o\hat{u}$) in the Church. And cities which have already obtained the honorary title of a metropolis from the emperor are to enjoy the honour only, and their bishops to be but honorary metropolitans,—so that all the rights of the real metropolis are to be reserved to it.' So, at the end of the 6th session, the emperor had announced that Chalcedon was to be a titular metropolis, saving all the rights of Nicomedia; and the Council had expressed its assent (Mansi, vii. 177; cp. Le Quien, i. 602). Another case was discussed in the 13th session of the Council. Anastasius of Nicæa had claimed to be independent of his metropolitan Eunomius of Nicomedia, on the ground of an ordinance of Valens, recognising the city of Nicæa as by old custom a 'metropolis.' Eunomius, who complained of Anastasius' encroachments, appealed to a later ordinance, guaranteeing to the capital of Bithynia its rights as unaffected by the honour conferred on Nicæa: the Council expressed its mind in favour of Eunomius, and the dispute was settled by a decision 'that the bishop of Nicomedia should have metropolitical authority over the Bithynian churches, while the bishop of Nicæa should have merely the honour of a metropolitan, being subjected, like the other comprovincials, to the bishop of Nicomedia' (Mansi, vii. 313). Zonaras says that this canon was in his time no longer observed; and Balsamon says that when the primates of Heraclea and Ancyra cited it, as upholding their claim to perform the consecration of two 'honorary metropolitans,' they were overruled by a decree of Alexius Comnenus, 'in presence and with consent' of a synod (on Trullan c. 38).

Canon XIII.

A short canon, requiring 'foreign clerics and readers' to produce 'commendatory letters from their own bishops before they are allowed to officiate in any city. See above, c. 11. The 42nd Laodicene canon requires a cleric who travels to carry 'canonical' letters. There is a various reading—ἀγνώστους for ἀναγνώστας—which was evidently followed by the Greek commentators, and is adopted by Justellus (Bibl. Jur. Can. Vet. i. 64), Hervetus (Mansi, vii. 364), and Beveridge. The old Latin translation says 'lectores:' and see Routh, Script. Opusc. ii. 60, and Hefele. The difficulty as to ἀναγνώστας is that it seems to place readers outside the clerical body. See on next canon. Compare the legatine canons of Celchyth (A.D. 787), that no migratory cleric is to be received 'absque ... litteris commendatitiis' (Haddan and Stubbs, Councils, iii. 451).

Canon XIV.

This canon makes provision for the married life of Readers and Singers.

(1) First, then, as to these two minor orders, then existing in distinction from each other. (*a*) The Readers, whose function it was to read the Old Testament lections or 'prophecies,' the Epistles (Hammond's Liturgies, p. 95), and, in Spain and Africa (1st C. of Toledo, c. 2; Cyprian, Epist. 38. 2), the

Gospels, and sometimes other portions of Scripture selected for the occasion by the bishop (Aug. in Ps. 138), formed the oldest of the minor orders. Tertullian mentions them as existing even among heretical sects, which mistook disorderliness for simplicity, and whose deacons of to-day would be the readers of to-morrow (de Præscr. Hæret. 41). Cyprian repeatedly mentions them (Epist. 29, 38. 2, 39. 4): Cornelius of Rome refers to them, without giving their numbers, as on his clerical staff, but as if inferior to subdeacons, and even to acolyths (Euseb. vi. 43): and the 10th Antiochene canon ranks them among those whom chorepiscopi could ordain. We have to think of them as ascending the steps of the 'ambon' (Soz. ix. 2) or 'pulpitum' (Cypr. Epist. 38. 2), taking up the 'codex' containing the portion to be read, and announcing, 'Thus saith the Lord,' etc. (Chrys. in 2 Thess. Hom. 3. 4), whereupon the deacon proclaimed, 'Let us attend:' and Chrysostom, writing at Constantinople, complains that many in the congregation did not even make a show of attending (in Act. Apost. Hom. 19. 5). Readers were appointed, at any rate in some parts of the East (Apost. Const. viii. 2), but apparently not in St. Basil's 'diocese' (Epist. 217. 51), with laying on of hands, in the West by delivery of a 'codex' ('4th c. of Carthage,' so called, c. 8). They were restrained by the Council of Laodicea from wearing the 'orarium' or stole (c. 23); by the 3rd Council of Carthage, from saying, 'Peace be with you,' which they had been wont to do in the third century (Cypr. Epist. 38. 2). Although Gratian places them between exorcists and doorkeepers (Cod. Theod. xvi. 2. 24), their importance in the East is illustrated by the protest of the advocate Eusebius against Nestorius, in which they alone are named between the deacons and the laity (Mansi, iv. 1009). Originally, it seems, persons of some distinction in the Church were made readers, as Cyprian appointed Aurelius and Celerinus in reward for their brave confessorship. Sisinnius, a Novatian reader at Constantinople, gave advice which piloted the Catholic archbishop Nectarius through a crisis full of difficulty (Soc. v. 10).

Meletius had ordained Chrysostom a reader 'as a preliminary step' to employing 'his powers in some sphere of active labour in the Church' (Stephens, Life of St. Chrysostom, p. 23); and Chrysostom had a faithful reader named Paul, who was included with him in the citation to attend the Council of the Oak (Soc. vi. 15). On the other hand, the Alexandrian church, somewhat characteristically, permitted catechumens thus to officiate (Soc. v. 22); and the 1st Council of Toledo allows penitents or subdeacons who had married to be appointed readers, on emergency, and with a restriction,—they were not to read 'the Gospels or the Apostle.' And mere youths were often set to this work,—as Julian (Soz. v. 2 : Socrates dates his appointment a little later, iii. 1), Proclus (Soc. vii. 41), and Theodoret 'when the down on his cheek was thin' (Relig. Hist. 12): so Augustine speaks of boys as 'in gradu lectorum' (de Consens. Evang. i. s. 13), and of a boy-reader as once divinely moved to substitute another passage for that which he had prescribed (Serm. 352): and Ambrose, preaching at his brother's funeral, quotes Psal. xxiv. 4 as having been already recited in the service 'per vocem lectoris parvuli' (de Exc. Fratr. Sat. i. 61): and Victor of Vite (de Persec. Vandal. v. 9) says that at Carthage 'quamplurimi lectores infantuli' (meaning, boys of about seven, cp. ib. 14) were sent into exile by the Arian tyrant Hunneric, A.D. 484. It is to Victor that we owe the most striking of all anecdotes about readers. During the former persecution under Genseric (or Gaiseric), the Arians attacked a Catholic congregation on Easter Sunday; and while a reader was standing alone in the pulpit, and chanting the 'Alleluia melody' (cp. Hammond, Liturgies, p. 95), an arrow pierced his throat, the 'codex' dropped from his hands, and he fell down dead (de Persec. Vand. i. 13). Five years before the Council, a boy of eight named Epiphanius was made a reader in the church of Pavia, and in process of time became famous as its bishop. Justinian forbade readers to be appointed under eighteen (Novel. 134. 13). The office is described in the Greek Euchologion (p. 236) as 'the first step to the priesthood,' and is conferred with delivery of the book containing the Epistles. Isidore of Seville, in the seventh century, tells us that the bishop ordained a reader by delivering to him, 'coram plebe,' the 'codex' of Scripture: and after giving precise directions as to pronunciation and accentuation, says that the readers were of old called 'heralds' (de Eccl. Offic. ii. 11). (*b*) The Singers are placed by the 43rd Apostolic canon between subdeacons and readers: but they rank below readers in Laodic. c. 23, in the Liturgy of St. Mark (Hammond, p. 173), and in the canons wrongly ascribed to a '4th Council of Carthage,' which permit a presbyter to appoint a 'psalmist' without the bishop's knowledge, and rank him even below the doorkeepers (Mansi, iii. 952). The chief passage respecting the ancient 'singers' is Laodic. 15, which forbids any person to sing (as Hefele understands it, to take a leading part in the chant) except 'the canonical singers, who ascend the ambon and sing from the vellum.' Socrates seems to refer to them as ὑποβολεῖς, precentors (v. 22, cp. Bingham, iii. 7. 3). The 75th Trullan canon orders singers not to shout, or 'strain their voices unnaturally.' In the West they have long ceased to exist as an order: but the Euchologion retains a form for their appointment in close connection with the office of reader (p. 233 ff.), just as archbishop Egbert of York, in his 'benedictio lectoris,' has 'in ordinem psalmistarum sive lectorum' (Pontif. Egb. p. 12). Justinian fixed the number of readers in the cathedral of St. Sophia at a hundred and ten, but that of singers at twenty-five only (Novel. 3. 1).

(1) These officials, of both classes, were 'in some provinces allowed to marry' after their appointment. The 27th Apostolic canon concedes this to them 'alone.' The Council of Ancyra permitted deacons to do so if they had stipulated at their ordination for such liberty (c. 10); whereas the Nicene Council, according to a well-known story in Soc. i. 11, adhered to the 'ancient tradition' forbidding the clergy to marry after ordination. The present canon shows that the freedom allowed

to these two minor orders was not universal: but it was maintained by the Council in Trullo (c. 6). Those who make use of it, says the canon, must not marry heterodox wives (the restriction laid on all clerics in the 12th canon of the 3rd Council of Carthage); but if they have done so, and (*a*) have had their children already baptized among heretics, they must bring them into the Catholic communion: (*b*) if such baptism has not been given, they must not allow it to take place, 'and must certainly not give them in marriage to a heretic, or a Jew, or a Pagan, unless the person to be thus united to an orthodox spouse undertakes to adopt the orthodox faith.' Compare the 11th canon of the 1st Council of Arles, that 'puellæ fideles' who marry Pagans must for a time be put out of communion; and the 10th and 31st canons of Laodicea, that Churchmen shall not, in a spirit of indifference ($\dot{a}\delta\iota a\phi\acute{o}\rho\omega s$, see on Nic. 12), give their children in marriage to heretics unless the latter promise to become Christians.' That the mind of the Church was unfavourable to mixed marriages (between Christians and unbelievers) is not to be wondered at: see 2 Cor. vi. 14, and compare Döllinger, First Age of the Church, E. T. p. 371; e.g. Cyprian marks it as a sign of moral decadence that Christians had begun 'jungere cum infidelibus vinculum matrimonii' (de Lapsis, 6). The Trullan Council went so far as to say that a marriage between an orthodox person and a heretic was invalid (c. 72).

CANON XV.

Deaconesses have already been mentioned in Nic. 19. We see here that they are 'ordained' by 'imposition of hands;' compare the collocation of $\chi\epsilon\iota\rho\sigma\tau\sigma\nu\epsilon\hat{\iota}\sigma\theta\alpha\iota$ and $\chi\epsilon\iota\rho\sigma\theta\epsilon\sigma\acute{\iota}a$ in c. 6. The age of forty is fixed as the earliest period for admission into this venerable order, of which, according to Döllinger (First Age of the Church, p. 306), such widows as are mentioned in 1 Tim. v. 9 were primitive members. St. Paul had required them to be twenty years older: and Theodosius I., in a law of 390 (referred to in Soz. vii. 16), had enforced the requirement, with that which related to the 'bringing up of children,' adding that the deaconess must appoint a 'curator' for her sons, if they were under age,—must entrust the management of her property to fitting persons, herself receiving the proceeds,—must not alienate jewels or furniture 'under pretext of religion' (a clause revoked within two months)—and must not make any church, any cleric, or any poor person her heir, such bequest being sufficient to annul the will—a significantly stringent provision (Cod. Theod. xvi. 2. 27). This canon rules that if a deaconess after remaining for some time under 'ministration' (a phrase used in the now obsolete Greek form for ordaining deaconesses, Eucholog. p. 262) shall 'dispose of herself in marriage, and thereby do despite to the grace of God' (i. e. to His favour which placed her in a position of dignity), 'she is to be anathematized with her consort.' St. Paul had spoken of church-widows who married as incurring 'a judgment because they had thereby set aside their original promise' (1 Tim. v. 12). Compare Basil, Epist. 199. 24, and Döllinger, First Age, p. 357.

CANON XVI.

The Council naturally adds that a virgin self-dedicated to the Lord (Δεσπότῃ) God, and likewise those who lead a monastic life (cp. c. 3, 4), cannot lawfully enter into marriage; if they do so, they are to be excommunicated. On the dedicated virgins of the Church, see Cyprian, de Habitu Virginum; Origen, c. Cels. vii. 48, that they lived in celibacy not for the sake of human honour or reward, or from any motive of vainglory, etc.; Athanasius, Apol. ad Const. 33, that the Church was wont to call them brides of Christ; Soc. i. 17, on the personal attention rendered by the empress Helena to the virgins registered on the 'canon' of the churches. After her time, community-life was instituted in Egypt both for men and women; but many virgins, as in earlier days, lived at home (see Bingham, vii. 4. 1). One who thus dedicated herself by a 'public profession' which 'was tantamount to a vow' (T. T. Carter in The Church and the World, p. 372, comp. Ambrose, de Lapsu Virginis, s. 19, 20, 48) and to which the people responded 'Amen,' was 'consecrated' at the altar by the bishop, who put a veil upon her head (Ambrose, de Virginibus, i. s. 65, iii. s. 1, Exhort. Virgin. s. 42). A fillet, or some such ornament, was also assumed: (e. g. Euseb. Mart. Pal. 9); but the hair was not cut off (Soz. v. 10). The bishop delivered an exhortation (Ambrose, de Virginibus, iii. s. 1), and offered up a solemn prayer (de Instit. Virginis, s. 107). The 19th canon of Ancyra had placed virgins who broke their vow of celibacy on the same footing with digamists (see above on Nic. 8, and W. H. Simcox's Beginnings of the Christian Church, p. 403): but this Chalcedonian law is more severe, although it allows the discretionary power of the bishop to mitigate the severity (on φιλανθρωπίας comp. Nic. 12). The first council of Valence, in 374, had been yet sterner (c. 2, Mansi, iii. 493). In the third century Cyprian had said, 'Si perseverare nolunt vel non possunt melius est ut nubant,' etc. (Epist. 4. 2); and Augustine describes the marriage thus contracted as not a mere adulterous connection but a marriage, though entailing spiritual punishment (de Bono Viduit. c. 9, 10). Herein he is plainly at issue with his own teacher, Ambrose (de Lapsu Virginis, s. 21), as well as with Innocent I. (Epist. 2. 12). Canons differed as to the time at which virgins might be consecrated: Basil fixed it as low as sixteen or seventeen, regarding this as the age of discretion, and adding that young girls who were presented before the right age, not on account of any personal choice of celibacy, but for some worldly advantage to their kindred, were not to be lightly accepted until their own wishes could be clearly ascertained (Epist. 199. 18). Ambrose, who was an enthusiast on this subject, admitted that a bishop ought not to be 'rash' in 'veiling a girl,' but urged that maturity of character was the main point (de Virginitate, s. 39). The 3rd Council of Carthage fixed twenty-five as the age for the consecration of virgins or for the ordination of deacons (c. 4), and the 1st Council of Saragossa had already prohibited the 'veiling' of a virgin under forty years old (Mansi, iii. 635). This prohibition was renewed by the Western emperor Majorian, in a law of A. D. 458 (Cod. Theod. vol. vi. app. 2. p. 156).

Canon XVII.

The first point that strikes us in this canon is the use of παροικίας not for what we call dioceses, but for rural portions of such dioceses, dependent on the several episcopal 'churches' or sees (see on Nic. 16: and comp. Soc. i. 27, that the churches of the Mareotis are under [the church of] Alexandria ὡς παροικίαι, and ib. vii. 25 on Atticus' care for the poor τῶν ἐν ταῖς αὐτοῦ παροικίαις). The adjective ἐγχωρίους is probably synonymous with ἀγροικικάς ('rusticas,' Prisca), although Dionysius and Isidorian take it as 'situated on estates,' cp. Routh, Scr. Opusc. ii. 109. It was conceivable that some such outlying districts might form, ecclesiastically, a border-land: it might not be easy to assign them definitively to this or that bishopric. In such a case, says the Council, if the bishop who is now in possession of these rural churches can show a prescription of thirty years in favour of his see, let them remain undisturbed in his obedience. (Here ἀβιάστως may be illustrated from βιασάμενος in Eph. 8: and for the use of οἰκονομεῖν see Const. 2.) But the border-land might be the 'debateable' land: the two neighbour bishops might dispute as to the right to tend these 'sheep in the wilderness;' as we read in Cod. Afric. 117, 'multae controversiae postea inter episcopos de dioecesibus ortae sunt, et oriuntur' (see on Const. 2); as archbishop Thomas of York, and Remigius of Dorchester, were at issue for years 'with reference to Lindsey' (Raine, Fasti Eborac. i. 150). Accordingly, the canon provides that if such a contest had arisen within the thirty years, or should thereafter arise, the prelate who considered himself wronged might appeal to the provincial synod. If he should be aggrieved at the decision of his metropolitan in synod, he might apply for redress to the *eparch* (or prefect, a substitute for exarch) of the 'diocese,' or to the see of Constantinople (in the manner provided by c. 9). It is curious 'that in Russia all the sees are divided into eparchies of the first, second, and third class' (Neale, Essays on Liturgiology, p. 302).

The concluding sentence of the canon is significant. 'If any city has been, or shall be, new-built by imperial authority, then let the arrangement of the ecclesiastical dioceses conform to the civil and public standards.' Here παροικιῶν is used in its ordinary sense for what we should call dioceses: and τύποις is not used technically for authoritative regulations (cp. Nic. 19, and the frequent use of τυπόω in the acts of Chalcedon for to prescribe, decree, or arrange, Mansi, vii. 192, 260, 293, 313), but simply for the models which the political scheme was to furnish to the ecclesiastical; (it is rendered by 'formulis' in the Prisca; compare Julius I. in Athan. Apol. c. Arian. 35, ἄλλος τύπος ἐστὶν οὗτος, 'this is a different form of procedure;' and in the thirteenth session bishop Anastasius of Nicæa is accused of trying to 'confound and break up the imperial and canonical τύπους,' Mansi, vii. 30). The immediate force of the provision is that if a town, suburb, or village, were newly erected into a city, its church should be erected into an episcopal see. So Anastasius of Nicæa asserted that Basilinopolis, once a suburb of Nicæa, had been erected into a city by Julian, or some predecessor of his, and that since that event it had had bishops of its own, ordained by the bishop of Nicæa (ib. 305). But the principle involved in the provision is more momentous, and represents a difference between the Eastern and the Roman ecclesiastical mind. When Valens erected part of Cappadocia into a distinct province, Anthimus bishop of Tyana contended 'that the ecclesiastical divisions should follow the civil' (Greg. Naz. Orat. 43. 58). Basil resisted for a time, but was obliged practically to give way (cp. Tillemont, ix. 182).

The principle which Anthimus asserted, probably from motives of personal ambition, is here upheld by the Council: and it was again sanctioned by the Council in Trullo, c. 38. It had several recommendations: in the case of the partition of a province it prevented collisions between the two provinces on ecclesiastical ground, such as were sure to arise if the Church insisted on treating them as one for her own purposes; and it gave the bishop of the new civil metropolis a much stronger position in presence of the civil governor, whose dignity he could confront by a parallel dignity of his own; see Neale, Essays on Liturgiology, p. 286. The idea of the rule would imply that when a city had risen to commanding importance, its prelate should no longer be subordinate to the bishop of a city more ecclesiastically venerable, but of less account in the civil sphere. Thus 'in the seventh century Seville lost the primacy of Spain to Toledo as the residence of the Visigoth kings' (Neale, p. 290): thus, after the breaking up of the kingdom of Aquitaine in the twelfth century, first one and then another great see shook off the authority of the primatial church of Bourges (ib. 291): and thus Paris, for many ages a suffragan of Sens, became at last, in 1622, an archbishopric. But in earlier times, the Latin church, with a certain superb indifference to political changes, maintained the opposite principle, which Innocent I. thus formulated in reply to a direct question from Alexander of Antioch: 'it has not seemed fitting that the Church of God should change her course ad mobilitatem necessitatum mundanarum' (Epist. 18. 2). In other words, If the Emperor has divided one province into two, it ought still to be one in the eyes of the Church: the civil erection of a new 'metropolis' is no warrant for the appointment of a new 'metropolitan.' This principle covered a case which Innocent had not thought of, the actual detachment of part of an ecclesiastical province from the realm of its former sovereign. Thus the claims of York to metropolitical authority over Scotland, which had a real basis so far as the district south of the Firth of Forth was concerned, were kept up long after the consolidation of the Scottish kingdom as including that territory (see Haddan and Stubbs, Councils, ii. 160; Grub, Eccl. Hist. Scotl. i. 206, 222; Skene, Celtic Scotland, ii. 373): and when in 1266 the Isle of Man and the 'Sudereys' or Hebrides were ceded by Magnus IV. of Norway to Alexander III. of Scotland, any metropolitical rights belonging to the church of Drontheim were expressly reserved (Grub, i. 327). Similarly, in 1472, the first Scottish archbishopric was erected, not at Edinburgh, but in the old primatial church of St. Andrews: and London continues in that subjection to Canterbury which was natural while Essex was a dependency of Kent.

Canon XVIII.

In order to appreciate this canon, we must consider the case of Ibas bishop of Edessa. He had been attached to the Nestorians, but after the reunion between Cyril and John of Antioch had reentered into communion with Cyril on the ground that Cyril had explained his anathemas (Mansi, vii. 240), or, as he wrote to Maris (in a letter famous as one of the 'Three Chapters'), that God had 'softened the Egyptian's heart' (ib. 248). Four of his priests (Samuel, Cyrus, Maras, and Eulogius), stimulated, says Fleury (27. 19), by Uranius bishop of Himeria, accused Ibas of Nestorianism before his patriarch Domnus of Antioch, who held a synod, but, as Samuel and Cyrus failed to appear, pronounced them defaulters and set aside the case (Mansi, vii. 217). They went up to Constantinople, and persuaded Theodosius and archbishop Flavian to appoint a commission for inquiring into the matter. Two sessions, so to speak, were held by the three prelates thus appointed, one at Berytus, the other at Tyre. At Berytus, according to the extant minutes (Mansi, vii. 212 ff.), five new accusers joined the original four, and charges were brought which affected the moral character of Ibas as well as his orthodoxy. The charge of having used a 'blasphemous' speech, implying that Christ was but a man deified, was rebutted by a statement signed by some sixty clerics of Edessa, who, according to the accusers, had been present when Ibas uttered it. At Tyre the episcopal judges succeeded in making peace, and accusers and accused partook of the Communion together (ib. vii. 209). The sequence of these proceedings cannot be thoroughly ascertained, but Hefele (sect. 169) agrees with Tillemont (xv. 474 ff.) in dating the trial at Berytus slightly earlier than that at Tyre, and assigning both to the February of 448 or 449. Fleury inverts this order, and thinks that, 'notwithstanding the reconciliation' at Tyre, the four accusers renewed their prosecution of Ibas (27. 20); but he has to suppose two applications on their part to Theodosius and Flavian, which seems improbable.

'The Council is believed,' says Tillemont (xv. 698), 'to have had this case in mind when drawing up the present canon:' and one can hardly help thinking that, on a spot within sight of Constantinople, they must have recalled the protracted sufferings which malignant plotters had inflicted on St. Chrysostom. They begin by remarking that 'the crime of conspiracy and faction has been absolutely prohibited even by the secular laws; much more ought it to be forbidden within the Church of God.' Here observe the word συνωμοσία, used in Acts xxiii. 13 for the Jews' conspiracy to murder St. Paul, as it had also been used by Thucydides (viii. 54) to describe the oligarchical clubs organized by Pisander. It occurs also in the acts of this Council in connection with the censure pronounced on Stephen of Ephesus (Mansi, vii. 289). The word φρατρία, once venerable as the description of a clan or tribe united by participation in the same religious rites, and by a supposed descent from the same ancestor (Grote, Hist. Gr. ii. 266 ff.), underwent a remarkable deterioration before it could be associated, as here, with the idea of conspiracy, as Socrates also uses it in the form of φατρίας (ii. 3, vi. 4: comp. i. 6, where Meletius is spoken of as συμφατριάζων with Arius. Compare other instances of such 'degeneration of words' in Abp. Trench's Study of Words, p. 30). When the elder Gregory, bishop of Nazianzus, after exhorting the people of Cæsarea to elect Basil, says that if they mean to manage the business κατὰ φρατρίας ἢ συγγενείας, he will have none of it (Greg. Naz. Epist. 41), we see a clearer trace of the original meaning. Zonaras explains the word, as used in this canon, as a συμφωνία in evil deeds; and a deposed patriarch of Constantinople in the thirteenth century significantly described his successor as a 'phratriarch' (Finlay, Hist. Gr. iii. 368). The secular laws are called 'external' to the Church, —a way of speaking derived from such language as the τοὺς ἔξω of 1 Cor. v. 12. So St. Chrysostom, Hom. de Libello Repudii, 1: 'Do not tell me of τοὺς παρὰ τοῖς ἔξωθεν κειμένους νόμους.' The law alluded to is that of Arcadius, A.D. 397, against any one who 'cum militibus, vel privatis ... scelestam inierit factionem, aut factionis ipsius susceperit sacramenta,'—in which law also 'factio' is coupled with 'societas.' A 'factio' was defined to be a 'societas occulta, in exitium aliquod conflata,' or 'malorum consensus et conspiratio' (Cod. Theod. iii. p. 103).

The enactment follows: 'If any clerics or monks be found either forming a conspiracy or a factious association, or concocting plots against bishops or fellow-clerics, let them be wholly deposed from their own rank.' The word τυρεύω, derived from making cheese, and so applied to the stirring up of intrigues, is used by Athanasius, Apol. c. Arian. 72: 'This have they done, in order that ... τυρεύσωσιν ἅπερ αὐτοῖς ἐδόκει,' Apol. de Fuga, 8, ἐφ' οἷς ... καθ' ἡμῶν ἐτύρευσαν κακοῖς: and Soc. ii. 12, that the Arianizers κατὰ τῶν ἐκκλησιῶν πολέμους ἐτύρευσαν. Κατασκευάς is akin to συσκευάς,—comp. Ibas in tenth session of Chalcedon, συσκευὴν ὑπέμεινα (Mansi, vii. 196), and Bassian, ὅτι συσκευὴ ἦν (ib. 277). Athanasius uses the same word in the same sense, Apol. c. Arian. 2: so does Alexander of Thessalonica, ib. 80.

Canon XIX.

This canon renews the Nicene provision (Nic. 5), followed up as it was by the 20th canon of Antioch, for the holding of provincial synods twice a year. 'It has come to our knowledge,' says the Council, 'that in the provinces the Episcopal synods prescribed by rule (κεκανονισμέναι) are not held, and hence many ecclesiastical matters which need correction are neglected.' It is therefore ordered that the canon providing for such synods be duly observed; 'the bishops of each province are to assemble twice a year where the metropolitan may think fit, and to set right any matter that may come before them' (ἀνακύπτοντα, 'si qua fortassis emerserint,' Dionysius). Bishops who are 'residing in their own cities' (i. e. are at home at the time), 'and are in good health, and free from any unavoidable and necessary occupation,' must attend, on pain of incurring 'a brotherly rebuke.' It is observable that four years previously Leo the Great had reminded the Sicilian bishops of the rule of the fathers concerning two yearly assemblies ('conventus') of bishops, and directed them to send three deputies to Rome every year, to arrive on the 29th of September, and to join their brethren in Council (Epist. 16. 7). The excuse of ill-health is recognised by the Council of Tarragona in 516 (Mansi, viii. 543), and is included in the δι' ἀνωμαλίαν of the 40th Laodicene canon (see Hefele). The 2nd Council of Arles ordered that if any bishop, duly warned to attend, were too ill to come, he should send a representative (personam); and added that a bishop who (without such excuse) neglected to attend, or who left the Council before it was dissolved, should be put out of communion, and not be restored except by a subsequent synod (c. 18, 19; Mansi, vii. 880). The word ἀπαραίτητος recurs in c. 3, 25: the Latin versions render it by 'inexcusabilis.' This sentence is adopted in the 8th canon of the Council in Trullo. As we have already seen, it was found necessary to reduce the provincial councils from two to one yearly. Hilary of Arles and his suffragans, assembled at Riez, had already, in 439, qualified the provision for two by adding significantly 'if the times are quiet' (Mansi, v. 1194). The words were written at the close of a ten years' war, during which the Visigoths of Septimania were 'endeavouring to take Arles and Narbonne' (Hodgkin, Italy and her Invaders, ii. 121).

CANON XX.

This canon is the third of those which were originally proposed by Marcian in the end of the sixth session, as certain articles for which synodical sanction was desirable (see above, c. 3 and 4). It was after they had been delivered by the Emperor's own hand to Anatolius of Constantinople that the Council broke out into plaudits, one of which is sufficiently startling, τῷ ἱερεῖ, τῷ βασιλεῖ (Mansi, vii. 177). The imperial draft is in this case very slightly altered. A reference is made to a previous determination (i. e. c. 10) against clerical pluralities, and it is ordered that 'clerics registered as belonging to one church shall not be ranked as belonging to the church of another city, but must be content with (στέργειν) the one in which they were originally admitted to minister (λειτουργεῖν), excepting those who, having lost their own country, have been compelled to migrate to another church,'—an exception intelligible enough at such a period. Eleven years before, the Vandal Gaiseric had expelled the Catholic bishops and priests of Western Africa from their churches: Quodvultdeus bishop of Carthage, with many of his clergy, had been 'placed on board some unseaworthy vessels,' and yet, 'by the Divine mercy,' had been carried safe to Naples (Vict. Vitens. de Persec. Vandal. i. 5: he mentions other bishops as driven into exile). Somewhat later, the surge of the Hunnish invasion had frightened the bishop of Sirmium into sending his church vessels to Attila's Gaulish secretary, and had swept onward in 447 to within a short distance of the 'New Rome' (Hodgkin, Italy and her Invaders, ii. 54–56). And the very year of the Council was the most momentous in the whole history of the 'Barbaric' movement. The bishops who assembled in October at Chalcedon must have heard by that time of the massacre of the Metz clergy on Easter Eve, of a bishop of Reims slain at his own altar, of the deliverance of Orleans at the prayer of St. Anianus, of 'the supreme battle' in the plain of Chalons, which turned back Attila and rescued Christian Gaul (Hodgkin, ii. 129-152; Kitchin, Hist. France, i. 61). The Trullan Council ordered all clerics, who had quitted their churches on account of a barbaric irruption, to return home when the occasion of such migration had passed away (c. 17). The present canon concludes by a warning: 'if any bishop after this decision (ὅρον, cp. c. 4, 14) should receive a cleric belonging to another bishop, the receiver and the received shall be excommunicated until the cleric who has removed' (μεταστάς, Marcian's draft had used the sterner word ἀποστάς) 'should return to his own church.' The patriarchs afterwards acquired a right to take clerics from any of their subject provinces and attach them to their own church (cp. Blastaris, Syntagma, A. 9, E. 11).

On this subject see quotations from the acts of Gallic synods of the fifth, sixth, and seventh centuries, in Pusey on the Royal Supremacy, pp. 84-90, and a reference to this canon of Chalcedon in a Capitulary of 789 (Pertz, Monum. Leg. i. 56).

Canon XXI.

This canon, on the accusation of bishops or clerics, may have been framed with some reference to the 6th canon of Constantinople (i.e. of the Council of 382). If so, the accusations which it presupposes are of an ecclesiastical character. It orders that clerics or laics who come forward as accusers of bishops or clerics shall not be indiscriminately and without inquiry 'admitted as such,' that is, not until their own reputation has been in the first instance scrutinized (on the sense of ὑπόληψις see above, c. 11). On ἁπλῶς καὶ ἀδοκιμάστως compare the 6th canon of the 2nd Council of Carthage, as providing that seniors or bishops might not be attacked 'passim vageque in accusatione' (Mansi, iii. 694; compare Bingham, v. 1. 5). Ibas told his judges at Berytus that Maras, one of his chief accusers, had been excommunicated, not by himself, but by the archdeacon, for insulting a presbyter (Mansi, vii. 232). The Apostolic rule as to two or three witnesses (1 Tim. v. 19), mentioned in Nic. 2, is doubtless taken for granted here. This canon, like several others of the same Council, is reproduced in a Capitulary of 789: 'Item est in eodem concilio, ut laici episcopos aut clericos non accusent, nisi prius eorum discutiatur existimationis opinio.'

Canon XXII.

This is a somewhat startling provision, referring to certain prohibitions in ancient canons (τοῖς πάλαι κανόσιν, instead of which Balsamon and Zonaras followed a corrupt reading, τοῖς παραλαμβάνουσιν); it declares that 'clerics are not allowed, after the death of their own bishop, to seize on the property belonging to him.' Why, we may ask, should they have ever thought such conduct lawful? The idea of the bishop's identification with his church had been perverted into a denial of his personal rights in regard to his private property. The Apostolic canons, while forbidding a bishop to give away any of 'the property of the Church,' had ordered a clear distinction to be maintained between it and his own personal property, over which he was to retain full power, and to dispose of it at will: so that his family might not be injured in the name of the Church, 'for he may have a wife and children,' etc. (c. 39, 40). So the 24th Antiochene canon says that the presbyters and deacons should be 'accurately informed as to what belongs to the Church, and what to the bishop personally, so that at his death the Church may have her own, but not more than her own: for it is just, before God and man, that the bishop should leave what is his own to whom he pleases, and at the same time that the Church incur no loss.' Compare the 12th canon of the Council of Tarragona, in 516, that when a bishop dies intestate, the priests and deacons are to make out a list of all his personal effects; and the 2nd canon of the Council of Valencia, in

524 or 546, that his property is not to be despoiled by 'the rapacious hands' of 'greedy clerics' (Mansi, viii. 543, 620). The 35th Trullan canon directs the clergy to guard both the Church's and the late bishop's property during a vacancy of the see.

The subject is illustrated by the curious Roman custom of stripping and dismantling the cell of a cardinal who had been elected Pope (Ranke, Popes, ii. 235).

Canon XXIII.

This is a sequel to can. 4 on the disorderly conduct of fanatical monks: but it includes clerics within its censure. 'It has come to the knowledge of the holy synod that some clerics and monks, without having received any commission from their own bishop, and even, in some cases, after he has suspended them from communion, betake themselves to Constantinople, and spend a long time there, causing disturbances, troubling the order of the Church, and even upsetting the family life of some persons.' This is evidently aimed at such conduct as that of the accusers of Ibas; see above on can. 18. It is therefore ordered that these persons 'shall first receive due notice from the Advocate (ἐκδίκου) of the most holy church of Constantinople, to depart from the imperial city; but if they impudently persist in the same practices, they are then to be expelled, against their will, by the said Advocate, and to betake themselves to their own homes.' On the office of the Advocate see above, on c. 2.

Canon XXIV.

This canon also is to be read as an addition to a former one. The 4th canon had subjected monasteries to episcopal jurisdiction; and having thus guarded against abuses, the Council proceeds to secure rights. 'Those monasteries which have once been hallowed with the assent of the bishop are to remain monasteries in perpetuity, and all that belongs to them shall be preserved to them, and they shall never be allowed to become secular dwellings:' observe the word κοσμικά, applied to business in c. 3, to tribunals in c. 9, and to civil dignities in Sardic. 7.

The secularisation of monasteries was an evil which grew with their wealth and influence. At a Council held by the patriarch Photius in the Apostles' church at Constantinople, it is complained that some persons attach the name of 'monastery' to property of their own, and while professing to dedicate it to God, write themselves down as lords of what has been thus consecrated, and are not ashamed to claim after such consecration the same power over it which they had before (c. 1, Beveridge, Pand. Can. i. 331). In the West, we find this abuse attracting the attention of Gregory the Great, who writes to a bishop that 'rationalis ordo' would not allow a layman to pervert a monastic foundation at will to his own uses (Epist. viii. 31). In ancient Scotland, the occasional dispersion of religious communities, and, still more, the clan-principle which assigned chieftain-rights over monasteries to the descendants of the founder, left at Dunkeld, Brechin, Abernethy, and elsewhere, 'nothing but the mere name of abbacy applied to the lands, and of abbot borne by the secular lord for the time' (Skene's Celtic Scotland, ii. 365: cp. Anderson's Scotland in Early Christian Times, p. 235). So, after the great Irish monastery of Bangor in Down was destroyed by the Northmen, 'non defuit,' says St. Bernard, 'qui illud teneret cum possessionibus suis; nam et constituebantur per electionem etiam, et abbates appellabantur, servantes nomine, etsi non re, quod olim exstiterat' (de Vita S. Malachiæ, 6). So in 1188 Giraldus Cambrensis found a lay abbot in possession of the venerable church of Llanbadarn Vawr: a 'bad custom,' he says, 'had grown up, whereby powerful laymen, at first chosen by the clergy to be "œconomi" or "patroni et defensores," had usurped "totum jus," appropriated the lands, and left to the clergy nothing but the altars, with tithes and offerings' (Itin. Camb. ii. 4). This abuse must be distinguished from the corrupt device whereby, in Bede's later years, Northumbrian nobles contrived to gain for their estates the immunities of abbey-lands by professing to found monasteries, which they filled with disorderly monks, who lived there in contempt of all rule (Bede, Ep. to Egbert, 7). In the year of his birth, the first English synod had forbidden *bishops* to despoil consecrated monasteries (Bede, iv. 5).

The Council menaces those who permit the secularisation of monasteries with 'the penalties prescribed by the canons,' referring probably to canons which prohibited all acts of sacrilege, Apost. can. 72, 73.

Canon XXV.

The Council has 'heard on all sides that some metropolitans neglect the flocks entrusted to them, and defer the ordination of bishops: it is therefore resolved that such ordinations shall take place within three months of the vacancy, unless some unavoidable necessity (ἀπαραίτητος, see c. 3, 19) shall cause the interval to be extended.' The wording of the canon indicates a considerable development of the authority of metropolitans. The Nicene Council would hardly have spoken so broadly of the flocks of suffragan churches being entrusted to their care. It was, indeed, their duty to provide for those flocks by consecrating a duly elected chief pastor: see Bingham, ii. 16. 12. The 4th Nicene canon, when it assigns to the metropolitan the ratification of an episcopal election, does not expressly require his presence as chief consecrator, but such was the natural arrangement; (cp. Antioch. 19, Sardican 6, Laodic. 12). Leo the Great wrote in 444 to the bishop of Thessalonica, who acted as his vicar for Eastern Illyricum, that all metropolitans in their own provinces 'jus habeant ordinandi' (Epist. 6. 4): and soon afterwards to the bishops of the province of Vienne, that the ordination to a vacant bishopric should be 'claimed by him who was the acknowledged metropolitan of that province' (Epist. 10. 5). So in its thirteenth session the Council read the acts of a synod held at Antioch, which deposed Athanasius of Perrha, and requested his metropolitan, John of Hierapolis, to ordain another bishop, or, as one prelate expressed it, to 'give another president to his church' (Mansi, vii. 345). The metropolitan when thus officiating might be called 'the consecrator,' because he took the principal part in the rite: but the theory which represents the assistant bishops as not really cooperating in the act of consecration is a mere technicalism, the result of Roman centralization, inconsistent not only with the Eastern office, in which the presiding bishop prays that grace may be poured out on the elect, ' by means of the hand of me a sinner and of Thy ministers, my fellow bishops present with me' (Eucholog. p. 302), but with early Western authorities. Thus Bede says that Finan made Cedd a bishop, 'vocatis ad se in ministerium ordinationis aliis duobus episcopis' (iii. 22); and that Wini consecrated St. Chad, 'adsumptis in societatem ordinationis duobus ... episcopis' (iii. 28). So St. Anschar was consecrated by a metropolitan, two other bishops 'adsistentibus ... et pariter consecrantibus' (Vit. S. Ansch. 12): and Hincmar of Reims, writing to his nephew, suffragan, and namesake, says, 'Tuum est autem cum aliis mecum ordinare episcopum' (Op. ii. 408). Compare Martene, de Ant. Eccl. Rit. tom. ii. p. 351; Haddan on Apostolical Succession, p. 221; Lee on Validity of English Orders, p. 240. On the 'decay and revival of the metropolitan jurisdiction' in France, see Robertson, Hist. Ch. ii. 341; iii. 188.

We have seen the word χειροτονία applied to the ordination either of a bishop or a presbyter or a deacon. The word consecration was not in ancient times restricted to the former rite; for instance, Leo uses 'consecrationem' for the promotion of a deacon to priest's orders (Epist. iii. 2). So in the 'Leonine Sacramentary' we find 'consecratio episcoporum' and 'presbyteri,' and 'consecrationis dona' in regard to deacons:

(Muratori, Lit. Rom. Vetus, i. 421 ff.: compare the Gelasian Sacramentary, ib. 623, and see the 6th canon of Celchyth in 787). The interval of three months here permitted was much longer than that which was customary at Alexandria, where the late patriarch's burial was performed by his successor (Liberatus, Breviarium, c. 20)—a practice imitated at Constantinople after the death of Maximian (Soc. vii. 4); but much shorter than that which was sanctioned in Western Africa, where the administrator of the vacant see had to take care that the people provided themselves with a new bishop within the year (Cod. Afric. 74). Times of persecution, of course, might cause a very long interval: the Roman see was vacant a year and a half after the death of Fabian in 250: and the Carthaginian, under Vandal tyranny, twenty-four years, just three years longer than the see of Oxford was kept vacant by the selfish caprice of Elizabeth (1568–1589).

The 'Steward of the Church' (see below) was to 'take care of the revenues of the church widowed' by the death of its bishop, who was regarded as representing Him to whom the whole Church was espoused (see Eph. v. 23 ff.). So in the 'order of the holy and great church' of St. Sophia, the 'great steward' is described as ἐπισκοπεύων καὶ τὴν χηρευομένην ἐκκλησίαν (Goar, Eucholog. p. 269): so Hincmar (l. c.) says, 'Si fuerit defunctus episcopus, ego . . . visitatorem ipsi viduatæ designabo ecclesiæ;' and the phrase, 'viduata per mortem N. nuper episcopi' became common in the West (Lee on English Orders, p. 373). The episcopal ring was a symbol of the same idea. So, at St. Chrysostom's restoration, Eudoxia claimed to have 'given back the bridegroom' (Serm. post. redit. 4). So Bishop Wilson told Queen Caroline that he 'would not leave his wife in his old age because she was poor' (Keble's Life of Wilson, ii. 767): and Peter Mongus, having invaded the Alexandrian see while its legitimate occupant, Timothy Salophaciolus, was alive, was expelled as an 'adulterer' (Liberatus, Breviar. 18).

Canon XXVI.

Although the management of ecclesiastical revenues cannot properly be called a 'primary' function of the primitive bishop (as in Hatch's Bamp. Lect. p. 46), any more than the primitive Church can be called primarily a benefit-club, yet as the eleemosynary system of that Church grew necessarily out of her belief in herself as 'Christ's body mystical,' so the man who, according to 'the earliest theory,' which 'seems to go back to the very beginning of the Christian societies, sat in the Lord's place' (ib. 88, cp. 144), could not but undertake the organization of works of mercy for the relief of those poorer brethren in whom Christ might be 'fed.' Thus regarded, the bishop's temporal οἰκονομία was a fruit of his spiritual (see on Const. 6); it is recognised in Apost. can. 39-41, Apost. Const. ii. 25, Cyprian's Epist. 41. 2, 'ut stipendia ... episcopo dispensante perciperent,' Antioch. c. 24, 25. Of course, as the Church's funds increased, this business grew in importance and extent, so that the bishop was led to devolve its details on his archdeacon; compare the famous story of St. Laurence and the treasures of the church of Rome (Prudentius, Peristeph. 2); and still, as the stream of offerings became fuller, the work of dispensing them became more complex, until the archdeacons could no longer find time for it, and it was committed to a special officer called 'œconomus' or steward (Bingham, iii. 12, 1: Transl. of Fleury, iii. 120). So the Council of Gangra, in the middle of the fourth century, forbids the church-offerings to be disposed of without consent of the bishop or of the person appointed εἰς οἰκονομίαν εὐποιίας (c. 8): and St. Basil mentions the œconomi of his own church (Epist. 23. 1), and the ταμίαι τῶν ἱερῶν χρημάτων of his brother's at Nyssa (ib. 225). And although Gregory Nazianzen took credit to himself for declining to appoint a 'stranger' to make an estimate of the property which of right belonged to the church of Constantinople, and in fact, with a strange confusion between personal and official obligations, gave the go-by to the whole question (Carm. de Vita sua, 1479 ff.), his successor Nectarius, being a man of business, took care to appoint a 'church-steward;' and Chrysostom, on coming to the see, examined his accounts, and found much superfluous expenditure (Palladius, Dial. p. 19). Theophilus of Alexandria compelled two of the Tall Brothers to undertake the οἰκονομία of the Alexandrian church (Soc. vi. 7); and in one of his extant directions observes that the clergy of Lyco wish for another 'œconomus,' and that the bishop has consented, in order that the church-funds may be properly spent (Mansi, iii. 1257). At Hippo St. Augustine had a 'præpositus domus' who acted as Church-steward (Possidius, Vit. August. 24). Isidore of Pelusium denounces Martinianus as a fraudulent 'œconomus,' and requests Cyril to appoint an upright one (Epist. ii. 127), and in another letter urges him to put a stop to the dishonest greed of those who acted as stewards of the same church (ib. v. 79). The records of the Council of Ephesus mention the 'œconomi' of Constantinople, the 'œconomus' of Ephesus (Mansi, iv. 1228-1398), and, as we have seen, (on Eph. 7), the 'œconomus' of Philadelphia. According to an extant letter of Cyril, the 'œconomi' of Perrha in Syria were mistrusted by the clergy, who wished to get rid of them 'and appoint others by their own authority' (ib. vii. 321). Ibas of Edessa had been complained of for his administration of church property; he was accused, e. g. of secreting a jewelled chalice, and bestowing the church revenues, and gold and silver crosses, on his brother and cousins; he ultimately undertook to appoint 'œconomi' after the model of Antioch (Mansi, vii. 201). Proterius, afterwards patriarch of Alexandria and a martyr for Chalcedonian orthodoxy, was 'œconomus' under Dioscorus (ib. iv. 1017), as was John Talaia, a man accused of bribery, under his successor (Evag. iii. 12). There may have been many cases in which there was no 'œconomus,' or in which the management was in the hands of private agents of the bishop, in whom the Church could put no confidence; and the Council, having alluded to the office of 'œconomus' in c. 2 and 25, now observes that 'some bishops had been managing their church property without œconomi,' and thereupon resolves 'that every church which has a bishop shall also have an œconomus from among its own clergy, to administer (οἰκονομοῦντα, see on Constant. 2) the property of the church under the direction of its own bishop; so that the administration of the church-property may not be unattested, and thereby waste ensue, and the episcopate (τῇ ἱερωσύνῃ) incur reproach.' Any bishop who should neglect to appoint such an officer should be punishable under 'the divine' (or sacred) 'canons.'

Nearly three years after the Council, Leo saw reason for requesting Marcian not to allow civil judges, 'novo exemplo,' to audit the accounts of 'the œconomi of the church of Constantinople,' which ought, 'secundum traditum morem,' to be examined by the bishop alone (Epist. 137. 2). In after days the 'great steward' of St. Sophia was always a deacon; he was a conspicuous figure at the Patriarch's celebrations, standing on the right of the altar, vested in alb and stole, and holding the sacred fan (ῥιπίδιον); his duty was to enter all incomings and outgoings of the church's revenue in a chartulary, and exhibit it quarterly, or half yearly, to the patriarchs; and he governed the church during a vacancy of the see (Eucholog. pp. 268, 275). In the West, Isidore of Seville describes the duties of the 'œconomus;'—he has to see to the repair and building of churches, the care of church lands, the cultivation of vineyards, the payment of clerical stipends, of doles to the widows and the poor, and of food and clothing to church-servants, and even the carrying on of church-lawsuits,—all 'cum jussu et arbitrio sui episcopi' (Ep. to Leudefred, Op. ii. 520); and before Isidore's death the 4th Council of Toledo refers to this canon, and orders the bishops to appoint 'from their own clergy those whom the Greeks call œconomi, hoc est, qui vice episcoporum res ecclesiasticas tractant' (c. 48, Mansi, x. 631). There was an officer named 'œconomus' in the old Irish monasteries; see Reeves' edition of Adamnan, p. 47.

Canon XXVII.

This canon throws a lurid light on the recesses of a Christianised society. 'Those who forcibly carry off women even under pretence of marriage' (συνοικεσίου must have this sense, see Isidorian, 'qui sibi rapiunt uxores'), 'or who are accomplices of such persons, or actually take part in the act, are to be deposed if clerics, anathematised if laymen.' The 22nd and 30th 'canons' of St. Basil had imposed penances on persons guilty of this crime.

Canon XXVIII.

The preceding canon is the last of those which are recognised by the Latin translators, by Joseph the Egyptian in his Arabic paraphrase (Mansi, vii. 422), by John Scholasticus in his Collection of Canons (Justellus, ii. 502), and even by Theodore the Reader in his History (i. 4). What is called the 28th canon was passed under the following circumstances.

At the close of the fourteenth session (October 31), Aetius the archdeacon of Constantinople, and chief of the ecclesiastical secretaries (Mansi, vi. 984), who had already in the second session read the Constantinopolitan form of the Creed, gave notice that his church had some matters to lay before the Council, and requested the two episcopal deputies of the Roman see, Paschasinus and Lucentius, to take part in the proceedings (Mansi, vii. 428). In order to appreciate the situation at this critical moment, we must remember (1) that the unquestioned 9th and 17th canons of the Council had already assigned to 'the see of Constantinople' an appellate jurisdiction : (2) that on the very day preceding, after the metropolitical authority of Nicomedia had been formally guaranteed, Aetius had requested that the claim of the see of Constantinople to ordain or to sanction ordinations at Basilinopolis in Bithynia, might not be compromised, and thereupon the imperial commissioners had promised that the subject of that see's right 'to ordain in the provinces' should be discussed at the proper time 'in the holy Council' (Mansi, vii. 313). This official announcement, following on enactments which logically involved the question of a Constantinopolitan patriarchate, had given the Roman delegates fair warning; so that when they heard Aetius' request, they had no excuse for declining it save the technical one which in fact they put forward: 'We have no instructions on the matter.' It is clear that they foresaw the coming discussion, and that, expecting to be outvoted if they took part in it, they deemed it best to secure the dignity of Rome by enabling themselves to say that any resolution which might aggrandise Constantinople was invalid, as having been passed in their absence. Aetius thereupon applied to the commissioners, who answered by directing the Council to take up the question. The Roman delegates heard this, but did not alter their line of conduct: they followed the commissioners out of the church, and the rest of the Council passed at once to the business which Aetius was to bring forward. The third canon of Constantinople was read, and the following resolution (ψῆφος) was carried.

'We, following in all things the determinations' (ὅροις, cp. 4, 14, Nic. 15, 19) 'of the holy fathers, and recognising the canon just read, which was made by the 150 religious bishops' [one text adds, 'who were assembled in the imperial city of Constantine, New Rome, in the reign of the emperor Theodosius of pious memory,' Mansi, vii. 428, Routh, Scr. Opusc. ii. 68: the clause is omitted in Mansi, vii. 369] 'do ourselves also adopt the same determination and resolution respecting the privileges (πρεσβείων) of the most holy church of [the same] Constantinople, New Rome. For the fathers naturally assigned privileges to the see (θρόνῳ) of the elder Rome, because that city was imperial; and, taking the same point of view, the 150 religious bishops awarded the same privileges to the most holy see of New Rome, judging with good reason that the city which was honoured with the sovereignty and senate, and which enjoyed the same privileges with the elder imperial Rome, should also in matters ecclesiastical be dignified like her, holding the second place after her.' Compare the summary of Aristenus and Symeon Logothetes, 'Let the bishop of the New Rome have equal honour with him of the elder, because of the transfer of the sceptre' (Justellus, Biblioth. ii. 693, 720).

Thus far we have little more than a paraphrase of the canon of 381. What was there decreed as to the πρεσβεῖα of Old Rome and of New Rome is here reiterated with some verbal expansion, but with the significant omission of the qualifying τῆς τιμῆς. (Compare the demand of the clerics of Constantinople in the eleventh session, 'Let not the privileges [προνόμια] of Constantinople be lost,' Mansi, vii. 293.) What was there implied as to the political ground of the elder Rome's ecclesiastical precedency is here broadly asserted, and antiquity is cited in its favour; although the bishops had in the second session recognised an ecclesiastical ground for that precedency by exclaiming in reference to Leo's Tome, 'Peter has spoken thus by Leo' (Mansi, vii. 692)—an expression which would be pointless apart from the belief that he sat in Peter's chair;—and so the Council says in its letter to Leo, 'You were the interpreter of Peter's voice to us all' (Leon. Epist. 98). But the resolution proceeds—'*And so that* of the Pontic, the Asian, and the Thracian "dioceses" the metropolitans alone, together with those bishops of the said "dioceses" who live in barbaric territories, should be ordained by the aforesaid holy see of the holy Church of Constantinople; it being understood that each metropolitan in those "dioceses" will, together with the comprovincial bishops, ordain comprovincial bishops, as is prescribed by the sacred canons; but that the metropolitans of those "dioceses," as has been said, should be ordained by the archbishop of Constantinople, after harmonious elections have been made according to custom, and reported to him.'

Here is a great addition to the canon of 381, so ingeniously linked on to it as to seem at first sight a part of it. The words καὶ ὥστε are meant to suggest that what follows is in fact involved in what has preceded: whereas a new point of departure is here taken, and instead of a mere 'honorary preeminence' the bishop of Constantinople acquires a vast jurisdiction, the independent authority of three exarchs being annulled in order to make him a patriarch. Previously, he had προεδρία: now he gains προστασία. As we have seen, a series of aggrandisements in fact had prepared for this aggrandisement in law; and various metropolitans of Asia Minor ex-expressed their contentment at seeing it effected. 'It is, indeed, more than probable that the self-assertion of Rome excited the jealousy of her rival of the East, and' thus 'Eastern bishops secretly felt that the cause of Constantinople was theirs' (Gore's Leo the Great, p. 120): but the gratification of Constantinopolitan ambition was not the less, in a canonical sense, a novelty, and the attempt to enfold it in the authority of the Council of 381 was rather astute than candid. The true plea, whatever might be its value, was that the Council had to deal with a *fait accompli*, which it was wise at once to legalise and to regulate; that 'the boundaries of the respective exarchates ... were ecclesiastical arrangements made with a view to the general good and peace of the Church, and liable to vary with the dispensations to which the Church was providentially subjected,' so that 'by confirming the ἐκ πολλοῦ κρατῆσαν ἔθος' in regard to the ordination of certain metropolitans (see Ep. of Council to Leo, Leon. Epist. 98. 4) 'they were acting in the spirit, while violating the letter, of the ever-famous rule of Nicæa, τὰ ἀρχαῖα ἔθη κρατείτω' (cp. Newman, Transl. of Fleury, iii. 407). It is observable that Aristenus and Symeon Logothetes reckon this decree as a 29th canon (Justellus, ii. 694, 720).

The title of 'archbishop,' here given as a title of honour to the bishop of Constantinople, is assigned in the documents of the Council to Leo (Mansi, vi. 1011, 1029; vii. 8 etc.), to Anatolius (ib. vii. 8, 60, 452), to the bishop of Alexandria (ib. vii. 56), to the bishop of Jerusalem (ib. vi. 681), and to the bishops of the greater sees (see below, c. 29). It appears first in the list of Meletian bishops embodied in Athanasius' Apol. c. Arian. c. 71, where it most probably means the bishop of Alexandria. Epiphanius gives it both to him and to Meletius as bishop of Lycopolis (Hær. 69. 1, 3); Marcellinus and Faustinus, to Damasus of Rome (Sirmond. Op. i. 149). In the records of the Council of Ephesus it is given both to Celestine and Cyril (Mansi, iv. 1124, 1145); in those of the Council of Constantinople, in 448, to Flavian of Constantinople (ib. vi. 652); in those of the 'Latrocinium' of Ephesus, to Dioscorus and Flavian (ib. vi. 615, 645). Theodosius II. applies it to the exarch of Cæsarea in Cappadocia (Mansi, vi. 599). Thus, as Le Quien says, it was 'in the fourth and fifth centuries' a title peculiar to the occupants of the principal sees, and was long retained by the bishop of Ephesus, but at last (and at least as early as the time of Photius) 'was cheapened among the Greeks' (Or. Christ. i. 669, comp. ii. 167) into a mere 'title of honour given to some prelates ... but not implying ... the possession of any metropolitical rights' (Neale's Essays on Liturgiology, p. 301. He adds that even the title of metropolitan is now, 'in most cases' within the Eastern Church, merely honorary). It should be added that Justinian uses 'archbishop' in its old sense, as practically equivalent to patriarch; as when he orders that the bishop of Justiniana Prima 'non solum metropolitanus, sed etiam archiepiscopus fiat' (Novel. 11).

When on the following day, Nov. 1, the Council assembled in full numbers (Mansi, vii. 425), the Roman delegate Paschasinus said to the commissioners, 'If your Grandeur orders us to speak, we have something to lay before you.' 'Say what you wish,' was the brief answer. Paschasinus, after a few general remarks on the evils of dissension, proceeded thus, 'Yesterday, after your Excellences had gone out, and our Humility had followed you, certain things are said to have been done which we consider to be contrary to the canons and to discipline. We request that your Splendour will order the minutes to be read, that all our brethren may see whether what was done was just or unjust.' This speech having been interpreted into Greek, the commissioners ordered, 'that if any proceedings had taken place after their departure, the minutes of them should be read.' Aetius interposed in order to explain the circumstances under which, after due notice given and license obtained, the Council had come to a resolution, 'not clandestinely nor stealthily, but according to due canonical order.' Veronicianus the imperial secretary then read the resolution with a list of 192 signatures, including those of the bishops of Antioch, Jerusalem, and Heraclea, but not of Thalassius of Cæsarea, although he afterwards assented (Mansi, vii. 455). The see of Ephesus had been declared vacant. The number contrasts remarkably with the 350 signatures (not reckoning the delegates and proxies) attached, a week before, to the doctrinal 'definition.' Lucentius' suggestion, that 'the holy bishops must have been surprised or coerced into signing it,' was repelled with the cry of 'No one was forced!' He then took up a more telling objection: In 'this resolution they ignore "the 318," and appeal to "the 150," whose canons are not among the canons of Councils,' meaning that they were not in the collection of canons then received (see Baller. de Ant. Collect. i. 2. 3). 'If they have had this advantage since "the 150" met, what do they want now? If they have not had it, why do they want it?' Aetius, instead of meeting this dilemma, asked whether the delegates had any instructions on that point. Boniface, the presbyter delegate, replied by reading a passage in which Leo had exhorted them to guard 'the ordinances of the fathers, and the dignity of his own person,' against possible 'usurpations on the part of those who might rely on the splendour of their cities' (e. g. of Constantinople).

The commissioners then directed both parties to produce the canons on which they relied. Accordingly Paschasinus gave out 'the 6th canon of the 318 holy fathers.' Let it be remembered that he was the representative of Rome; that Rome had been proved, in the case of Apiarius, to have quoted as 'Nicene' a previous canon which was not in the authentic Nicene text, and appears as one of the canons of Sardica: that, in consequence, it was specially incumbent on all who spoke in her name to be scrupulous in ascertaining the actual words of 'the 318' before appealing to their authority: and we shall then appreciate the assurance of this Roman delegate in quoting the 6th Nicene canon thus: 'Quod ecclesia Romana semper habuit primatum: teneat igitur et Ægyptus,' etc. (see on Nic. 6). (It is but fair, indeed, to Paschasinus, to remember that he was only following in the wake of Leo himself, who, six years previously, had caused Valentinian III. to assert in a too famous rescript, reckoned as Leo's Epist. 11, that the primacy of the Apostolic see had been established not only by the 'merit of St. Peter' and 'the dignity of the City,' but by 'the authority of a holy Synod,' alluding to Nic. 6). When Paschasinus had concluded, Aetius handed a 'codex' to one of the secretaries, who read from it the authentic Greek text of the canon in question. The 'Ballerini' attempt to exclude this 'iterata Nicæni sexti canonis recitatio' as a Greek student's gloss; partly because that canon would not help the pretensions of Constantinople, but 'multo magis' because it is not found in an ancient version 'quæ pura conservatur in codice ... capituli Parisiensis' (de Ant. Collect. Can. i. 6. 8). Nothing but an intelligible bias could account for a suggestion so futile. If we place ourselves, for a moment, in the position of the ecclesiastics of Constantinople when they heard Paschasinus read his 'version,' which the Ballerini gently describe as 'differing a little' from the Greek text, we shall see that it was simply impossible for them not to quote that text, as it was preserved in their archives, and had been correctly translated by Philo and Evarestus, in their version beginning 'Antiqui mores obtineant.' No comment on the difference between it and the Roman 'version' is recorded to have been made: and, in truth, none was necessary. Simply to confront the two, and pass on to the next point, was to confute Paschasinus at once most respectfully and most expressively. Aetius proceeded to cite, as an authority in favour of his own church, a 'synodicon of the second synod.' The phrase has been thought to betoken a later period: but at Constantinople, as we know, the Council of 381 had all been treated as œcumenical (Theod. v. 9), and in that sense might reasonably be ranked next to the 'first' œcumenical synod, although it was long ignored in some other churches (cp. Ballerini, de Ant. Collect. ii. 1. 6). This 'synodicon' consisted of three canons of Constantinople massed together as one constitution.

The commissioners then asked those 'Asian' and Pontic prelates who had signed the new canon (here called a 'Tome,' although that term was usually applied to a dogmatic formulary, see Const. 5), whether they had done so of their own free-will, or under constraint. They all came forward, and Diogenes the metropolitan of Cyzicus said, 'As before God, I signed it of my own will.' Six other 'Asian' metropolitans, and three from Pontus, with three suffragans, made similar declarations, (see above on can. 9). One of them described the archbishop of New Rome as πατέρα ἐξαίρετον. Four referred to the canon of 381 as authoritative. Eusebius of Dorylæum, an 'Asian' bishop, went so far as to say that he had read 'this canon' to 'the holy pope of Rome in presence of clerics of Constantinople, and that he had accepted it.' But the speaker, a man of very impulsive temperament (Mansi, vi. 716), may here be credited with a misapprehension. The rest of the bishops appealed to (among whom was Theodoret) declared that they had signed voluntarily. It appears however, from the acts of the eleventh session, that the Asian episcopate was by no means willing to allow their exarch to be consecrated at Constantinople. Several of them had actually fallen on their knees, protesting that in that event the lives of their children would be forfeited to the indignation of their people: when the commissioners asked the Council where the bishop of Ephesus ought to be ordained, the answer was given by acclamation, 'In the province:' Diogenes had sarcastically remarked that 'in Constantinople they ordained salad-sellers:' and Leontius of Magnesia (who did not sign the new canon) averred that from St. Timothy downwards all bishops of Ephesus save one (Bassian) had been ordained at Ephesus. On the other hand, the clergy of Constantinople asserted that some had been ordained at Constantinople: and, in spite of the Council's demand that the canons should hold good, they insisted that Constantinople should retain its privilege, and that the new bishop of Ephesus should be ordained by their archbishop (Mansi, vii. 2923). The Council however, on the next day, ruled that the consecration should take place 'according to the canons' (ib. 300).

The commissioners next appealed to those bishops who had not signed the canon. Eusebius, metropolitan of Ancyra, professed to speak for himself without compromising the general body; and described his own conduct, when asked to consecrate a metropolitan for Gangra, as a proof that he was not tenacious of that privilege (see above, on c. 9). Having thus far ascertained the absence of coercion, the commissioners proceeded to consider the new canon on its own merits, and finally approved it with some significant modifications: (1) they emphasized the maintenance of the first or chief rank for the see of 'the elder Rome;' (2) securing a free election of 'Asian,' Pontic, and Thracian metropolitans by the clergy and laymen of property and rank (compare Bingham, iv. 2. 18) in their own cities, together with the comprovincial bishops; (3) providing that the archbishop of Constantinople *might*, if he thought fit, (and thereby suggesting that he should,) allow a metropolitan to be 'ordained' in his own province; (4) distinctly excluding him from any control over the 'ordination' of ordinary bishops, which was to be performed 'by all or by the majority of the comprovincial bishops, the ratification (τὸ κῦρος) resting with the metropolitan according to the canons (Nic. 4), and the archbishop of Constantinople taking no part whatever in such ordinations' (which restriction must be applied to the language of the emperor Basiliscus, 'the right of ordaining for which provinces belonged to the see of the imperial city,' Evagr. iii. 7). They then called upon 'the holy and œcumenical synod' to express its mind. Forthwith cries of assent arose: 'This is a just resolution,' 'This we all say,' 'This is a just judgment,' 'Let what has been determined (τὰ τυπωθέντα) hold good,' 'We pray you, dismiss us,' 'We all stand by this decision.' When the noise subsided, Lucentius made himself heard: 'The apostolic see cannot be humiliated in our presence: we therefore request your Excellences that, whatever was done yesterday, in our absence, in prejudice of canons, may be rescinded: or else let our dissent be recorded, that we may know what report to make to the successor of the apostle, the Pope of the universal Church, so that he may express his judgment on the wrong done to his own see, or in the subversion of the canons.' The commissioners met this high-toned protest with cold gravity: 'Our "interlocutory" sentence has been ratified by the Council.' (The word διαλαλία occurs repeatedly in the acts of the Council. It is applied to an individual vote, Mansi, vii. 181, 300; at the end of the second session the commissioners use τὰ διαλαληθέντα for their order adjourning the decision on Leo's Tome, ib. vi. 973; and in the twelfth session they use ἡμῶν διαλαλησάντων as to expressions of their own mind coupled with requests for a decision on the part of the Council, ib. 296; διαλαλία being thus used for a provisional and non-decisive judgment.) The matter, however, was not thus easily settled. The synodal letter to Leo assumes, not without a touch of diplomatic insincerity, that, as having presided by deputy, he will sanction the resolution against which his delegates had protested (Leon. Epist. 98. 4). Marcian wrote to him in the same sense (Epist. 100. 3). Anatolius also wrote blaming the delegates, and describing the resolution as a synodal act duly performed, and as giving less to the see of Constantinople than in fact it had enjoyed for 'sixty or seventy years,' i.e. by restricting its action to the consecration of metropolitans (Epist. 101. 4, 5). Neither emperor nor patriarch understood the man whom they were attempting to wheedle. In a letter to Marcian he uttered an apophthegm which did not always govern his own policy, 'Propria perdit qui indebita concupiscit' (Epist. 104. 3): to Pulcheria, declaring the aggression on 'the primacies of so many metropolitans' to be wholly inconsistent with the sacred Nicene decrees (Epist. 105. 2): to Anatolius himself, taking up the cause of Alexandria and Antioch, proclaiming the immutability of Nicene arrangements with a rigid absoluteness which might well prove embarrassing to his own pretensions, and assuming, in default of evidence, that the assent given to what he so much disliked was compulsory and therefore null (Epist. 106).

These three letters were all dated on one day, May 22, 452. Marcian did not reply until the 15th of the following February, and he then intimated his dissatisfaction at not having received Leo's assent to the acts of the late synod (Epist. 110). Leo sent an evasive reply, intimating that he suspected Anatolius of an inclination towards Eutychianism; and here, remarkably enough, he takes occasion to panegyrize, as 'a man of Catholic faith' and irreproachable conduct, that very Aetius who had promoted the obnoxious innovation, but had since then been virtually 'degraded under a show of promotion;' Anatolius having ordained him presbyter for the cemetery outside the city, in order to secure the archidiaconate for an 'Eutychian' named Andrew (Epist. 111. 2). Leo 'showed his hand' more plainly in a letter to the bishops who had attended the Council, accepting their conclusions on the question of faith, but setting aside the new canon as adopted under pressure and incompatible with Nicene law (Epist. 114). To Marcian he again wrote, in terms almost obsequious: 'Since we must by all means obey the most religious will of your Piety, I have willingly given my assent to the synodical constitutions, which have given me satisfaction in regard to the confirmation of the Catholic faith,' etc. (Epist. 115, 2). But the breach between himself and Anatolius became a serious difficulty. Marcian, it appears, endeavoured to mediate: Leo replied, in effect, 'Anatolius has not replied to my letters; let him satisfy the canons, and assure me that he has given up his culpable ambition, and then we will be friends again' (Epist. 128; March 9, 454). Forthwith Anatolius, by Marcian's advice, wrote to Leo in a somewhat abject strain.

'It was not my fault: from my youth up I have loved repose and quiet, and have kept myself humble: it was the clergy of Constantinople who wished to have that decree enacted, and the Eastern bishops who agreed in enacting it: and even thus the entire ratification of the act was reserved for your authority' (Epist. 132. 4). As far as words could go, 'the submission is complete: and as such Leo accepts it' (Gore, Leo the Great, p. 124). But he does so with a grave admonition: 'You would have made fuller amends for your fault if you had not thrown the responsibility for it upon your clergy. However, I am glad that you now express regret for it. This avowal of yours, and the attestation of our Christian monarch, suffice to restore our friendly relations. Let the craving for an unlawful jurisdiction, which has caused the dissension, be put aside, once for all; be content with the boundaries traced by the provident decrees of the fathers,' etc. (Epist. 135. 3).

So ended this famous correspondence; and Leo might persuade himself that he had annihilated the obnoxious canon: but it soon appeared that the smooth words of Anatolius were not to be taken as committing the Eastern church and empire. 'As a matter of fact, the canon did take effect' (Gore, l. c.). For a time, indeed, there was some opposition. Not only did the Monophysites of Egypt, headed by Timothy 'the Weasel,' take hold of the canon as an argument against the authority of the Council, but the orthodox of Egypt, under St. Proterius and his successors, for a long time disowned it (Le Quien, i. 48); and, as we have seen, it was ignored in the paraphrase of Joseph the Egyptian. That Antioch naturally disliked it would appear from its omission in the collection of canons made by John Scholasticus while yet an Antiochene presbyter (Justellus, ii. 502); but it is more remarkable to find Theodore the Reader of Constantinople saying, about A.D. 518, that at Chalcedon twenty-seven canons were published (Hist. i. 4). The church of Ephesus, illustrious from its manifold Apostolic associations, is said to have been induced by resentment against the 28th canon to accept from Timothy the Weasel a 'restoration of its patriarchal' or exarchal independence (cp. Evagrius, iii. 6): and although for the time compelled to submit to Acacius of Constantinople, it did not finally yield until the reign of Justinian. Its bishop regained the title of exarch in the new sense of delegate of the patriarch (Le Quien, i. 668). The readier submission of Cæsarea was rewarded by the title of 'Protothronus.' (See Neale, Introd. East. Ch. i. 31.) On the whole, a hundred years after the Council, Liberatus of Carthage could not only write of the protest of the Roman delegates at Chalcedon, 'A judicibus et episcopis omnibus illa contradictio suscepta non est,' but could add, 'Et licet sedes apostolica nunc usque contradicat, quod a synodo firmatum est imperatoris patrocinio permanet quoque modo' (Breviarium, c. 13. Galland. Bibl. Patr. xii. 144). The see of Constantinople retained its precedency and its patriarchal jurisdiction: and the 28th canon is the acknowledged law of the East.

Canon XXIX.

This is not a canon, but a mere extract from the acts of the fourth session, containing, indeed, a general resolution suggested by a particular case and clothed with 'perpetual' validity, but also exhibiting portions of the debate, as will appear by comparing it with Mansi, vii. 96. It is absent from the Latin collections, and is not included by John Scholasticus or Photius in their enumeration of Chalcedonian canons: but Aristenus and Symeon Logothetes, in their abridgments, reckon it as can. 30, can. 28 being broken up into two (Justellus, ii. 694, 720).

The case of Photius of Tyre has come before us in can. 12. It appeared that after his revolted suffragan Eustathius had extracted from him, by threats of deposition, a written submission to a decree of the Home Synod of Constantinople declaring Eustathius to have jurisdiction over six Phœnician sees, Photius, regarding this submission as invalid because compulsory, ignored it by performing a consecration, as he himself told the Council, 'when the comprovincials were present with me, according to the ancient order' (ἀκολουθίαν), and thereafter received from Constantinople a document professing to excommunicate him, —which in fact proceeded from the Home Synod. 'I remained excommunicate for 122 days: and again I ordained two bishops; and he (Eustathius) deposed them, and made them presbyters' (Mansi, vii. 92). After the bishops present had clearly expressed their mind on the iniquitousness of condemning a man unheard, as to which the bishop of Nicomedia cited, as he said, 'the words of a Roman' (Acts xxv. 16), Photius said, 'I ask nothing more of you as just judges, than that the canons may stand, and that those who were legitimately ordained by me, and were afterwards expelled and made presbyters, may be restored, and that I may have my churches.' The Council declared that this request was reasonable. The commissioners caused the 4th Nicene canon to be read. It was then decided that Photius should remain the sole metropolitan of Phœnicia Prima. Then, asked the commissioners, what of the bishops who were ordained by him, but removed by Eustathius and ordered to become presbyters? The Council answered, 'We think it right that they should be bishops; let the ordination performed by Father Photius take effect.' 'We all ask this,' said a Thracian bishop. 'It is for the Synod,' said the commissioners, 'to come to a final resolution and decision (τυποῦν) on this subject.'

It was then that the Roman delegates expressed their mind in the first paragraph of this so-called canon (Mansi, vii. 96). 'To bring a bishop into the rank (βαθμόν, see c. 2, etc.) of a presbyter is sacrilege. If any just cause removes bishops from the episcopal functions, they ought not even to hold the place of a presbyter: but if they have been removed from their dignity without having anything proved against them, they shall return to the episcopal dignity.' The point of the remark about 'sacrilege' is this,—that the sacred functions of the presbyterate would be profaned by entrusting them to a person who had been justly deposed from the episcopate. The maxim is not inconsistent with Nic. 8, which does not deal with the case of a bishop deposed for crime, but only provides that an ex-Novatian bishop on joining the Church shall have the place of a presbyter or of a chorepiscopus found for him, simply in order to guard the principle that there could not be two bishops of one city.

Anatolius followed the delegates in the same sense. He had indeed lent his authority to the ambitious schemes of Eustathius; he had attempted to defend the action of his Home Synod, on the ground that Photius had 'acted irregularly:' but, on finding that the stream of opinion was against him, he yielded to it, and was content to give a somewhat weak paraphrase of the terse speech of Paschasinus. Then, according to the 'acts,' Maximus of Antioch, Juvenal of Jerusalem, Thalassius of Cæsarea in Cappadocia, Eusebius of Ancyra, successively expressed their assent. Julian of Cos, who had long resided in the East, and whom Leo had desired to act in conjunction with Paschasinus and Lucentius (Epist. 92), so that he is ranked among the representatives of 'the Apostolic see,' spoke at somewhat greater length. 'It is irregular and irreligious that bishops who have been canonically ordained, and have willingly received their ordination, should again hold the presbyteral dignity, contrary to all canonical order. If they are justly accused, as having been detected in some crimes, the holy Council will inquire into the real state of the case; and, when the truth is brought to light, they will be deprived of the episcopal office. For the lower degree cannot be allowed to succeed to the greater dignity.' Eunomius of Nicomedia said briefly, 'He who is not worthy to be a bishop is not worthy to be a presbyter;' a proposition which must be read in the light of the context. Then came a general acclamation from the bishops, echoing the sentiments of the fathers and 'archbishops,' i.e. of the eminent prelates who had already spoken: 'archbishop' being here, as elsewhere, a title of honour (see on c. 28). The commissioners then pronounced that 'what had seemed good to the holy Synod should be maintained in full force for all time' (Mansi, vii. 96).

CANON XXX.

This resolution is even less deserving of the name of a 'canon' than the one which we have just considered. It is simply a vote relating to the temporary position of certain individuals who were placed in a difficulty by a previous decision of the Council. Yet Aristenus and Symeon reckon it as canon 31.

We must go back to that memorable fourth session (October 17), in which the 'Tome' of Leo was accepted by the bishops, not simply because it came from the see of Rome, but because they had 'ascertained,' or 'perceived,' or 'found on examination,' that it agreed with the Creed, or with the Creed and the teaching of Cyril of Alexandria (Mansi, vii. 12 ff.); certain prelates also declaring that the difficulties which they had found in it had been removed by explanation (ib. vii. 32). After this the commissioners announced (ib. vii. 49), that on the day before, October 16, i.e. three days after the deposition of Dioscorus of Alexandria, thirteen Egyptian bishops had presented a memorial to the Emperor, and that, by his order, they were now to be admitted to a hearing. They entered accordingly, and were requested by the Council to sit down. The commissioners asked them, 'Have you presented a petition?' They answered in terms singularly obsequious: 'Yes, by your feet!' (ναὶ τῶν ποδῶν ὑμῶν). 'And you have signed it?' 'Yes, we acknowledge our signatures, the letter (τὰ γράμματα) is ours.' It was then read, to this effect: 'We hold by the faith handed down from St. Mark, and taught by Peter bishop and martyr, by Athanasius, Theophilus, Cyril, and by the 318 at Nicæa: we condemn all heresies, including Apollinarianism.' Not unnaturally, the Council asked, 'Why have they not anathematized the doctrine of Eutyches? Let them sign Leo's letter,' by way of proving their orthodoxy on the matter now in hand. Hieracas, their spokesman, attempted to give satisfaction by saying, 'Whosoever, whether Eutyches or any one else, thinks otherwise than as we have set forth in our petition, let him be anathema. But as for the letter of archbishop Leo, you know that we must wait for the judgment of our own archbishop: the Nicene Council ordered that all Egypt should follow the archbishop of Alexandria and do nothing without him.' He was interpreting the 6th Nicene canon by the Egyptian tradition of entire obedience to the see of St. Mark (see above, p. 17), a tradition which led Synesius of Ptolemais to say, at the commencement of a letter to his patriarch Theophilus, 'It is at once my pleasure and my sacred duty to esteem as a law whatever that throne shall ordain' (Epist. 67). But the bishops did not allow for this tradition. 'They lie,' cried the fiery zealot Eusebius of Dorylæum. 'Let them prove what they assert,' said the gentler bishop of Sardis. Other prelates exclaimed, 'He who will not sign Leo's letter is a heretic.' 'Anathema to Dioscorus and his friends!' 'Do they, or do they not, accept Leo's letter as the Council accepts it?' The chief delegate of the Roman see was shocked to find 'aged bishops dependent for their belief on the judgment of another.' 'How,' asked Diogenes of Cyzicus, 'can they ordain another bishop when they do not know what they themselves believe?' The poor Egyptians, harassed by 'the pelting of this pitiless storm,' said anathema to Eutyches 'and all who relied on him.' But this was deemed an evasion: 'Let them sign Leo's letter.' No, they could not sign it 'without the consent of their archbishop.' Angry voices arose, bidding them choose between signature and excommunication, or denouncing them as bent on rebellion against the Synod. They asserted the contrary, pleading that they could not speak for the many prelates of their 'diocese,'—or rather that these very colleagues would rise up against them if they returned home after transgressing the 'ancient customs' (comp. Nic. 6) of the church of Egypt, with which, they added, Anatolius himself was well acquainted.

Their lives would not be safe: it were better for them to die at Chalcedon than by the hands of indignant fellow countrymen. As if in extreme bodily terror, they flung themselves on the pavement of the church: 'Have pity on our old age,—spare a few men who are in your power,—let us wait here until you have elected our archbishop, and then punish us if we do not obey him.' Unmoved by these piteous entreaties, the bishops kept on shouting, 'These men are heretics,—let them sign the condemnation of Dioscorus!' It was by the presiding State officers, seventeen in number, that this great assembly of Christian pastors was at last recalled to the obligations of humanity and equity; and the first paragraph of this 'canon' is the decision pronounced, not by 'the most pious bishops,' but by 'the most magnificent and illustrious magistrates, and the eminent senate' (Mansi, vii. 60). 'Whereas the most pious bishops of Egypt have deferred for the present their signature of the letter of the most holy archbishop Leo, not in opposition to the Catholic faith, but on the plea that it is a custom in the Egyptian "diocese" to do nothing contrary to the will and direction of the archbishop, and they ask to be excused' (ἐνδοθῆναι, 'concedi sibi dilationem,' Hervetus) 'until the ordination of the future bishop of the great city of the Alexandrians; it has appeared to us reasonable and humane (φιλάνθρωπον, cp. Nic. 5) that they be so excused, remaining in possession of their own (episcopal) status (σχήματος, cp. Nic. 8), within the imperial city, until the archbishop of Alexandria shall be ordained.' Paschasinus suggested a guarantee, but in words which betrayed his hard temper and his dislike of the concession. 'If you command that some indulgence ("aliquid humanitatis") be shown to them, let them find security that they will not leave the city until Alexandria shall receive a bishop.' The commissioners accepted the proposal with a modification: 'Let them find security if they can, but if they cannot, they shall be trusted on their solemn oath (ἐξωμοσία).'

This scene deserves to be remembered, for the warning that it gives to ecclesiastics. Had Socrates lived to describe it, he would have found in it a fresh illustration of that tendency of controversy to develope violence and unfairness, or of hierarchical power to produce imperiousness, on which he dwells with an emphasis which makes his book such a healthy one for clerical readers (see Introduction to Soc. Eccl. Hist. Oxford, 1878, p. xxi). The Council could insist with all plainness on the duty of hearing before condemning (see on c. 29): yet on this occasion, bishop after bishop gave vent to a harsh unfeeling absolutism, the only excuse for which consists in the fact that the outrages of the 'Latrocinium' were fresh in their minds, and that three of the Egyptian supplicants, whom they were so eager to terrify or to crush, had actually supported Dioscorus on the tragical 8th of August, 449 (compare Mansi, vi. 612, vii. 52). It was not in human nature to forget this: but the result is a blot on the history of the Council of Chalcedon.

ADDITIONS.

Page 3. On 'canonici' see also Dict. of Chr. Antiq. I. 281.

Page 5. On the moral preparation of catechumens, a reference to Clement of Alexandria ap. Euseb. iii. 23 was here omitted: Ἔτρεφε, συνεῖχεν, ἔθαλπε, τὸ τελευταῖον ἐφώτισε.

Page 16. On 'offering the gifts' in St. Clement of Rome's Epistle, c. 44, see W. H. Simcox, The Beginnings of the Christian Church, p. 217, —a volume which appeared while these sheets were passing through the press.

Page 32. On coadjutors see too Euseb. vi. 11.

Page 38. On the offering of bread and wine by the people, see also Cosin, Works, v. 321 (notes written before the revision of the Prayer Book in 1661).

Page 52. An instance of the long vitality of the use of παροικία for diocese occurs in Thomas Gascoigne's Liber Veritatum, a curious work of 1433–1457, edited by Mr. J. Thorold Rogers: 'Episcopus ... superintendens curae tocius suae parochiae seu diocesis suae' (p. 41).

Page 96. See Le Quien, i. 66. Papal legates, indeed, signed the 21st canon of the Council of Constantinople in 869, which ranked Constantinople between Rome and Alexandria: Mansi, xvi. 174.

Page 112. On the relation of Nestorianism to Pelagianism, see also Wordsworth's newly published Bampton Lectures, p. 65, and Bp. Mylne in Church Quarterly Review, i. 134.

Page 140. For another case of fanatical violence on the part of monks, see St. Chrysostom, Epist. 14, on the furious demonstration of monks at Caesarea in Cappadocia against himself during his exile in 404.

Page 145. On the way in which Christianity dealt with slavery, see also Wordsworth's Bamp. Lect. p. 298.

ERRATA.

Page 22, line 6 from bottom, *after* 'dignity' *insert* '.

Page 51, line 5, *for* archbishopric *read* bishopric.

Page 68, line 6, *for* baptizer *read* baptized.

Page 85, line 12, *for* Liberus *read* Liberius.

Page 128, l. 16, *for* Pelasium *read* Pelusium.

INDEX.

A.

'Αδιαφόρως, 42, 141.
Aetius, part taken by at Chalcedon, 192.
'Ακοινώνητος, 12, 53.
Alexandrian see, powers of the, 17, 208.
Ambrose, St., sudden promotion of, to episcopate, 7.
'Αναβαπτίζεσθαι, 66.
Anathema against heresies, at Council of Constantinople, 82.
Anatolius, correspondence of, with Leo, 202.
Anomœanism, 83.
Antiochene see, powers of the, 21, 90.
'Αντισυνάγω, 103.
Apiarius, case of, 121.
'Απολελυμένως, 146.
Apollinarianism, 87.
Appeals, provisions as to, 156.
'Archbishop,' title of, 195.

B.

Baptism, question of heretics', 67.
Βαθμός, 109, 114.
Bishops, mode of appointing, 10.
— consecration of, 11, 187.
— translation of, restricted, 48.
— not to interfere with each other's clergy, 53.
— faults of, provided against, 14.
— accusers of, 102, 182.
— secularised tone of, 131.
— arbitrative jurisdiction of, 152.
— personal property of, 183.
— function of, towards Church property, 135, 189.
— authority of, over monasteries, 141.

C.

Candidates for orders, scrutiny of character of, 33.
Canons, Nicene, only twenty, 77.
— general code of, how formed, 123.
Catechetical system, the, 4, 47, 106.
'Cathari,' the, 24.
Celestius, 112.
Charisius, case of, 115.
Chorepiscopi, 29.
Clergy, offences of the, how tried, 153.
Commendatory letters, 162.
Communicatory letters, 163.
Communion, mode of receiving the, 75.
— of the dying, 44.
Constantinople, growth of power of see of, 94, 157, 192.
Creed, Nicene, only to be used, 116.
— development of Nicene, 80.
'Custom,' Nicene regard for, 17.
Cyprus, case of church of, 118.
Cyril of Alexandria, at Ephesus, 110.

D.

Deaconesses, 69, 171.
Deacons, duties of, 63.
— presumption of, restrained, 57.
Desertion of clerical or monastic life, 150.
Digamy, 27.
Διοίκησις, sense of, 88.
Δῶρον, 15.

E.

Ecclesiastical boundaries conformed to civil, 88, 176.

Egyptian bishops, pressure put upon, 207.
Ἔκδικος, 129.
Ἐξετάζεσθαι, 1.
Ephesian Council, why summoned, and how opened, 110.
Ἐφόδιον, 43.
Epiphanius, creed published by, 80.
Episcopate, unity of the, 32.
Ἐπιστόλια, 162.
Ἑτέραν πίστιν, sense of, 116.
Eucharist, doctrine of the, 62.
Eunomians, 106.
Exarchs, 88, 104, 156.
Excommunication, 12.
Exemption, clerical claim of, 154.
Exorcism, 107.

F.

Finances of the Church, 135.
'Formatæ,' 163.

G.

Gregory of Nazianzus, deceived by Maximus, 97.

H.

'Hearers,' lower class of catechumens, 5.
'Hearers,' lowest class of penitents, 37.
'Home Synod,' the, 159.
Hospices, 161.

I.

Ibas, case of, 177.
Interest, taking of, disapproved, 56.
'Invalidity and irregularity,' 54.

J.

Jerusalem, see of, 22.
John of Antioch, 111, 119.
Jurisdiction, limits of ecclesiastical and civil, 154.

K.

Κανών, 2.
Καθαιρεῖσθαι, 69.
Κλῆρος, 2.
'Kneelers,' the, 37.
Kneeling in prayer, when forbidden, 73.
Κῦρος, 12.

L.

'Lapsi,' the, 24, 35.
Λειτουργία, 133.
Lent, 15.
Liberty of churches, guaranteed by a decree, 121.

M.

Macedonianism, 84.
Marcellianism, 86.
Marriage, not to be contracted with heretics, 171.
'Martyries,' 147.
Maximus, 97.
Metropolis, titular erection of a, 165.
Metropolitan, office of, 12, 186.
Migration of clergy forbidden, 48.
Μικροψυχία, 13.
Military life, not in itself prohibited, 29.
Monasteries, secularisation of, 185.
Monasticism, abuses of, 139, 184.
Money-making, unclerical, 132.
Montanists, 108.
'Mourners,' the, 36.

N.

Nestorianism, 115.
Nestorius, at Ephesus, 110.
Novatianism, 24, 105.

O.

Oblation, the Eucharistic, 15, 47, 60.
Οἰκονομεῖν, 101.
Οἰκόνομος, 189.
Orders, the minor, 127.
Ordination, by laying on of hands, 10.
— cancelling of, 55.
— premature, forbidden, 6.
Ὅρος, 48.

P.

Παροικία, 51, 174.
Paschasinus, at Chalcedon, 193.
'Patriarch,' name of, 90.
Paul of Samosata, 8, 65.
Pelagianism, 112.
Penitential system, the, 36.
'Pentecost,' sense of, 72.
Photinianism, 87.

Photius, case of, against Eustathius, 165, 204.
Πίστις, 79, 116.
Pluralities, 181.
Poor, the Church's care of the, 134.
'Pragmatic,' a, 164.
Πρεσβεῖα, 21, 93.
Προσμονάριος, 129.
Προσφέρω, 61.
Προσφορά, 38.
Πτωχεῖον, 150.

Q.

Quartodecimans, 105.

R.

Readers, order of, 167.
Roman see, jurisdiction of the, 18.
— primacy of the, 20, 93.

S.

Sabbatians, 105.
Sabellianism, 85, 106.
Σχῆμα, 28, 42.
Schism of Antioch, 95.
Secular functions, forbidden to clergy, 131.
Secularity, growth of among clergy, 48.
Self-mutilation, 1.
Simony, 127.
Singers, order of, 170.
Slavery, how dealt with by the Church, 144.

Στρατεία, 148.
Συνείσακτοι, 8.
Συνιστάμενοι, 38, 75.
Συνωμοσία, 178.
Synods, provincial, regular holding of, 14, 180.

T.

'Title,' necessary for ordination, 146.
'Tome of the Westerns,' 99.
Trade, how far unlawful for clergy, 137.
Τύπος, 175.

Υ.

Υἱοπατορία, 106.
Ὑπηρέτης, 63.
Ὑπόληψις, 162.

V.

Virgins, dedication of, 173.

Φ.

Φιλανθρωπία, 14.
Φρατρία, 178.

Χ.

Χειροθεσία, 26, 71, 148.
Χειροτονία, 10, 127.

Ψ.

Ψῆφος, 14.

THE END.

SELECT LIST
OF
STANDARD THEOLOGICAL WORKS
PRINTED AT
𝕿𝖍𝖊 𝕮𝖑𝖆𝖗𝖊𝖓𝖉𝖔𝖓 𝕻𝖗𝖊𝖘𝖘, 𝕺𝖝𝖋𝖔𝖗𝖉.

THE HOLY SCRIPTURES, ETC.	page 1
FATHERS OF THE CHURCH, ETC.	,, 4
ECCLESIASTICAL HISTORY, ETC.	,, 5
ENGLISH THEOLOGY	,, 6
LITURGIOLOGY	,, 8

1. THE HOLY SCRIPTURES, ETC.

HEBREW, etc. *Notes on the Hebrew Text of the Book of Genesis.* By G. J. Spurrell, M.A. Crown 8vo. 10s. 6d.

—— *Notes, Critical and Philological, on the Hebrew Text of I, II Samuel.* By S. R. Driver, D.D. 8vo. *In the Press.*

—— *Treatise on the use of the Tenses in Hebrew.* By S. R. Driver, D.D. Second Edition. Extra fcap. 8vo. 7s. 6d.

—— *The Psalms in Hebrew* without points. Stiff covers, 2s.

—— *A Commentary on the Book of Proverbs.* Attributed to Abraham Ibn Ezra. Edited from a MS. in the Bodleian Library by S. R. Driver, D.D. Crown 8vo. paper covers, 3s. 6d.

—— *The Book of Tobit.* A Chaldee Text, from a unique MS. in the Bodleian Library; with other Rabbinical Texts, English Translations, and the Itala. Edited by Ad. Neubauer, M.A. Crown 8vo. 6s.

HEBREW, etc. *Hebrew Accentuation of Psalms, Proverbs, and Job.* By William Wickes, D.D. 8vo. 5s.

—— *Hebrew Prose Accentuation.* By the same Author. 8vo. 10s. 6d.

—— *Horae Hebraicae et Talmudicae,* a J. Lightfoot. A new edition, by R. Gandell, M.A. 4 vols. 8vo. 1l. 1s.

—— *The Book of Hebrew Roots,* by Abu 'l-Walîd Marwân ibn Janâh, otherwise called Rabbî Yônâh. Now first edited, with an appendix, by Ad. Neubauer. 4to. 2l. 7s. 6d.

GREEK. OLD TESTAMENT. *Vetus Testamentum ex Versione Septuaginta Interpretum secundum exemplar Vaticanum Romae editum.* Accedit potior varietas Codicis Alexandrini. Tomi III. 18mo. 18s.

Oxford: Clarendon Press. London: HENRY FROWDE, Amen Corner, E.C.

HOLY SCRIPTURES.

GREEK. *A Concordance to the Greek Versions and Apocryphal Books of the Old Testament.* By Edwin Hatch, M.A., D.D., assisted by other Scholars. *In the Press.*

—— *Essays in Biblical Greek.* By Edwin Hatch, M.A., D.D., Reader in Ecclesiastical History, Oxford, and sometime Grinfield Lecturer on the LXX. 8vo. 10s. 6d.

—— *Origenis Hexaplorum quae supersunt; sive, Veterum Interpretum Graecorum in totum Vetus Testamentum Fragmenta.* Edidit Fridericus Field, A.M. 2 vols. 4to. 5l. 5s.

—— NEW TESTAMENT. *Novum Testamentum Graece.* Antiquissimorum Codicum Textus in ordine parallelo dispositi. Accedit collatio Codicis Sinaitici. Edidit E. H. Hansell, S.T.B. Tomi III. 8vo. 24s.

—— *Novum Testamentum Graece.* Accedunt parallela S. Scripturae loca, etc. Edidit Carolus Lloyd, S.T.P.R. 18mo. 3s.
On writing paper, with wide margin, 10s. 6d.

—— *Appendices ad Novum Testamentum Stephanicum*, jam inde a Millii temporibus Oxoniensium manibus tritum; curante Gulmo. Sanday, A.M., S.T.P., LL.D. 1. Collatio textus Westcottio-Hortiani (jure permisso) cum textu Stephanico anni MDL. II. Delectus lectionum notatu dignissimarum. III. Lectiones quaedam ex codicibus versionum Memphiticae Armeniacae Aethiopicae fusius illustratae. 18mo. *Just ready.*

—— *Novum Testamentum Graece juxta Exemplar Millianum.* 18mo. 2s. 6d. On writing paper, with wide margin, 9s.

GREEK. *The Greek Testament,* with the Readings adopted by the Revisers of the Authorised Version:—
(1) Pica type, with Marginal References. Demy 8vo. 10s. 6d.
(2) Long Primer type. Fcap. 8vo. 4s. 6d.
(3) The same, on writing paper, with wide margin, 15s.

—— *The Parallel New Testament, Greek and English;* being the Authorised Version, 1611; the Revised Version, 1881; and the Greek Text followed in the Revised Version. 8vo. 12s. 6d.

—— *Outlines of Textual Criticism applied to the New Testament.* By C. E. Hammond, M.A. Extra fcap. 8vo. 3s. 6d.

—— *A Greek Testament Primer.* An Easy Grammar and Reading Book for the use of Students beginning Greek. By E. Miller, M.A. Extra fcap. 8vo. 3s. 6d.

LATIN. *Libri Psalmorum Versio antiqua Latina, cum Paraphrasi Anglo-Saxonica.* Edidit B. Thorpe, F.A.S. 8vo. 10s. 6d.

—— *Old-Latin Biblical Texts:* No. I. The Gospel according to St. Matthew, from the St. Germain MS. (g₁). Edited with Introduction and Appendices by John Wordsworth, D.D. Small 4to., stiff covers, 6s.

—— *Old-Latin Biblical Texts:* No. II. Portions of the Gospels according to St. Mark and St. Matthew, from the Bobbio MS. (k), etc. Edited by John Wordsworth, D.D., W. Sanday, M.A., D.D., and H. J. White, M.A. Small 4to., stiff covers, 21s.

HOLY SCRIPTURES.

LATIN. *Old-Latin Biblical Texts*: No. III. The Four Gospels, from the Munich MS. (q), now numbered Lat. 6224 in the Royal Library at Munich. With a Fragment from St. John in the Hof-Bibliothek at Vienna (Cod. Lat. 502). Edited, with the aid of Tischendorf's transcript (under the direction of the Bishop of Salisbury), by H. J. White, M.A. Small 4to. stiff covers, 12s. 6d.

Nouum Testamentum Domini Nostri Iesu Christi Latine, secundum Editionem S. Hieronymi. Ad Codicum Manuscriptorum fidem reconsuit Iohannes Wordsworth, S.T.P., Episcopus Sarisburiensis. In operis societatem adsumto Henrico Iuliano White, A.M., Societatis S. Andreae, Collegii Theologici Sarisburiensis Vice-Principali. *Partis prioris fasciculus primus. Euangelium secundum Matthevm.* 4to., papers covers, 12s. 6d.

OLD-FRENCH. *Libri Psalmorum Versio antiqua Gallica e Cod. ms. in Bibl. Bodleiana adservato, una cum Versione Metrica aliisque Monumentis pervetustis.* Nunc primum descripsit et edidit Franciscus Michel, Phil. Doc. 8vo. 10s. 6d.

ENGLISH. *The Holy Bible in the Earliest English Versions*, made from the Latin Vulgate by John Wycliffe and his followers: edited by Forshall and Madden. 4 vols. Royal 4to. 3l. 3s.

Also reprinted from the above, with Introduction and Glossary by W. W. Skeat, Litt. D.

The Books of Job, Psalms, Proverbs, Ecclesiastes, and the Song of Solomon. Extra fcap. 8vo. 3s. 6d.

The New Testament. Extra fcap. 8vo. 6s.

ENGLISH. *The Holy Bible, Revised Version* *.

Cheap Editions for School Use.

Revised Bible. Pearl 16mo., cloth boards, 1s. 6d.

Revised New Testament. Nonpareil 32mo., 6d.; Brevier 16mo., 1s.; Long Primer 8vo., 1s. 6d.

* The Revised Version is the joint property of the Universities of Oxford and Cambridge.

—— *The Oxford Bible for Teachers*, containing supplementary *Helps to the Study of the Bible*, including summaries of the several Books, with copious explanatory notes; and Tables illustrative of Scripture History and the characteristics of Bible Lands, with a complete Index of Subjects, a Concordance, a Dictionary of Proper Names, and a series of Maps. Prices in various sizes and bindings, from 3s. to 2l. 5s.

—— *Helps to the Study of the Bible*, taken from the *Oxford Bible for Teachers*. Crown 8vo. 3s. 6d.

—— *The Psalter, or Psalms of David, and certain Canticles*, with a Translation and Exposition in English, by Richard Rolle of Hampole. Edited by H. R. Bramley, M.A. With an Introduction and Glossary. Demy 8vo. 1l. 1s.

—— *Studia Biblica.* Essays in Biblical Archæology and Criticism, and kindred subjects. By Members of the University of Oxford. Vol. I. 8vo. 10s. 6d.

London: HENRY FROWDE, Amen Corner, E.C.

ENGLISH. *The Book of Wisdom:* the Greek Text, the Latin Vulgate, and the Authorised English Version; with an Introduction, Critical Apparatus, and a Commentary. By W. J. Deane, M.A. 4to. 12s. 6d.

GOTHIC. *The Gospel of St. Mark in Gothic*, according to the translation made by Wulfila in the Fourth Century. Edited, with a Grammatical Introduction and Glossarial Index, by W. W. Skeat, Litt. D. Extra fcap. 8vo. 4s.

2. FATHERS OF THE CHURCH, ETC.

St. Athanasius: *Orations against the Arians.* With an account of his Life by William Bright, D.D. Crown 8vo. 9s.

—— *Historical Writings, according to the Benedictine Text.* With an Introduction by W. Bright, D.D. Crown 8vo. 10s. 6d.

St. Augustine: *Select Anti-Pelagian Treatises, and the Acts of the Second Council of Orange.* With an Introduction by William Bright, D.D. Crown 8vo. 9s.

Canons *of the First Four General Councils of Nicaea, Constantinople, Ephesus, and Chalcedon.* Crown 8vo. 2s. 6d.

—— *Notes on the above.* By William Bright, D.D. Crown 8vo. 5s. 6d.

Catenae *Graecorum Patrum in Novum Testamentum.* Edidit J. A. Cramer, S.T.P. Tomi VIII. 8vo. 2l. 4s.

Clementis Alexandrini *Opera, ex recensione Guil. Dindorfii.* Tomi IV. 8vo. 3l.

Cyrilli *Archiepiscopi Alexandrini in XII Prophetas.* Edidit P. E. Pusey, A.M. Tomi II. 8vo. 2l. 2s.

Cyrilli *in D. Joannis Evangelium.* Accedunt Fragmenta Varia necnon Tractatus ad Tiberium Diaconum Duo. Edidit post Aubertum P. E. Pusey, A.M. Tomi III. 8vo. 2l. 5s.

—— *Commentarii in Lucae Evangelium quae supersunt Syriace.* E mss. apud Mus. Britan. edidit R. Payne Smith, A.M. 4to. 1l. 2s.

—— *The same*, translated by R. Payne Smith, M.A. 2 vols. 8vo. 14s.

Ephraemi Syri, *Rabulae Episcopi Edesseni, Balaei, aliorumque Opera Selecta.* E Codd. Syriacis mss. in Museo Britannico et Bibliotheca Bodleiana asservatis primus edidit J. J. Overbeck. 8vo. 1l. 1s.

Eusebii Pamphili *Evangelicae Praeparationis Libri XV.* Ad Codd. mss. recensuit T. Gaisford, S.T.P. Tomi IV. 8vo. 1l. 10s.

—— *Evangelicae Demonstrationis Libri X.* Recensuit T. Gaisford, S.T.P. Tomi II. 8vo. 15s.

—— *contra Hieroclem et Marcellum Libri.* Recensuit T. Gaisford, S.T.P. 8vo. 7s.

Eusebius' *Ecclesiastical History*, according to the text of Burton, with an Introduction by W. Bright, D.D. Crown 8vo. 8s. 6d.

Evagrii *Historia Ecclesiastica*, ex recensione H. Valesii. 8vo. 4s.

Irenaeus : *The Third Book of* St. Irenaeus, Bishop of Lyons, against Heresies. With short Notes and a Glossary by H. Deane, B.D. Crown 8vo. 5s. 6d.

Origenis *Philosophumena ;* sive omnium Haeresium Refutatio. E Codice Parisino nunc primum edidit Emmanuel Miller. 8vo. 10s.

Patrum Apostolicorum, *S. Clementis Romani, S. Ignatii, S. Polycarpi, quae supersunt.* Edidit Guil. Jacobson, S.T.P.R. Tomi II. *Fourth Edition.* 8vo. 1l. 1s.

Reliquiae Sacrae *secundi tertiique saeculi.* Recensuit M. J. Routh, S.T.P. Tomi V. *Second Edition.* 8vo. 1l. 5s.

Scriptorum *Ecclesiasticorum Opuscula.* Recensuit M. J. Routh, S.T.P. Tomi II. 8vo. 10s.

Socratis *Scholastici Historia Ecclesiastica.* Gr. et Lat. Edidit R. Hussey, S.T.B. Tomi III. 8vo. 15s.

Socrates' *Ecclesiastical History,* according to the Text of Hussey, with an Introduction by William Bright, D.D. Crown 8vo. 7s. 6d.

Sozomeni *Historia Ecclesiastica.* Edidit R. Hussey, S.T.B. Tomi III. 8vo. 15s.

Theodoreti *Ecclesiasticae Historiae Libri V.* Recensuit T. Gaisford, S.T.P. 8vo. 7s. 6d.

3. ECCLESIASTICAL HISTORY, ETC.

Baedae *Historia Ecclesiastica.* Edited, with English Notes, by G. H. Moberly, M.A. Crown 8vo. 10s. 6d.

Bigg. *The Christian Platonists of Alexandria;* being the Bampton Lectures for 1886. By Charles Bigg, D.D. 8vo. 10s. 6d.

Bingham's *Antiquities of the Christian Church,* and other Works. 10 vols. 8vo. 3l. 3s.

Bright. *Chapters of Early English Church History.* By W. Bright, D.D. *Second Edition.* 8vo. 12s.

Burnet's *History of the Reformation of the Church of England.* A new Edition. Carefully revised, and the Records collated with the originals, by N. Pocock, M.A. 7 vols. 8vo. 1l. 10s.

Cardwell's *Documentary Annals of the Reformed Church of England;* being a Collection of Injunctions, Declarations, Orders, Articles of Inquiry, etc. from 1546 to 1716. 2 vols. 8vo. 18s.

Councils *and Ecclesiastical Documents relating to Great Britain and Ireland.* Edited, after Spelman and Wilkins, by A. W. Haddan, B.D., and W. Stubbs, D.D. Vols. I and III. Medium 8vo. each 1l. 1s.

    Vol. II, Part I. Medium 8vo. 10s. 6d.

    Vol. II, Part II. *Church of Ireland; Memorials of St. Patrick.* Stiff covers, 3s. 6d.

Fuller's *Church History of Britain.* Edited by J. S. Brewer, M.A. 6 vols. 8vo. 1*l*. 19*s*.

Gibson's *Synodus Anglicana.* Edited by E. Cardwell, D.D. 8vo. 6*s*.

Hamilton's (*Archbishop John*) *Catechism*, 1552. Edited, with Introduction and Glossary, by Thomas Graves Law, Librarian of the Signet Library, Edinburgh. With a Preface by the Right Hon. W. E. Gladstone. Demy 8vo. 12*s*. 6*d*.

Hussey. *Rise of the Papal Power, traced in three Lectures.* By Robert Hussey, B.D. *Second Edition.* Fcap. 8vo. 4*s*. 6*d*.

John, *Bishop of Ephesus. The Third Part of his Ecclesiastical History.* [In Syriac.] Now first edited by William Cureton, M.A. 4to. 1*l*. 12*s*.

—— *The same,* translated by R. Payne Smith, M.A. 8vo. 10*s*.

Le Neve's *Fasti Ecclesiae Anglicanae.* Corrected and continued from 1715 to 1853 by T. Duffus Hardy. 3 vols. 8vo. 1*l*. 1*s*.

Noelli (A.) *Catechismus sive prima institutio disciplinaque Pietatis Christianae Latine explicata.* Editio nova cura Guil. Jacobson, A.M. 8vo. 5*s*. 6*d*.

Records of the Reformation. *The Divorce,* 1527–1533. Mostly now for the first time printed from MSS. in the British Museum and other Libraries. Collected and arranged by N. Pocock, M.A. 2 vols. 8vo. 1*l*. 16*s*.

Reformatio *Legum Ecclesiasticarum.* The Reformation of Ecclesiastical Laws, as attempted in the reigns of Henry VIII, Edward VI, and Elizabeth. Edited by E. Cardwell, D.D. 8vo. 6*s*. 6*d*.

Shirley. *Some Account of the Church in the Apostolic Age.* By W. W. Shirley, D.D. *Second Edition.* Fcap. 8vo. 3*s*. 6*d*.

Stillingfleet's *Origines Britannicae,* with Lloyd's Historical Account of Church Government. Edited by T. P. Pantin, M.A. 2 vols. 8vo. 10*s*.

Stubbs. *Registrum Sacrum Anglicanum.* An attempt to exhibit the course of Episcopal Succession in England. By W. Stubbs, D.D. Small 4to. 8*s*. 6*d*.

---

4. ENGLISH THEOLOGY.

Bradley. *Lectures on the Book of Job.* By George Granville Bradley, D.D., Dean of Westminster. Crown 8vo. 7*s*. 6*d*.

—— *Lectures on Ecclesiastes.* By G. G. Bradley, D.D., Dean of Westminster. Crown 8vo. 4*s*. 6*d*.

Bull's *Works, with Nelson's Life.* Edited by E. Burton, D.D. 8 vols. 8vo. 2*l*. 9*s*.

Burnet's *Exposition of the XXXIX Articles.* 8vo. 7*s*.

Butler's *Works.* 2 vols. 8vo. 11*s*.

Comber's *Companion to the Temple;* or a Help to Devotion in the use of the Common Prayer. 7 vols. 8vo. 1*l.* 11*s.* 6*d.*

Cranmer's *Works.* Collected and arranged by H. Jenkyns, M.A., Fellow of Oriel College. 4 vols. 8vo. 1*l.* 10*s.*

Enchiridion Theologicum *Anti-Romanum.*
- Vol. I. Jeremy Taylor's Dissuasive from Popery, and Treatise on the Real Presence. 8vo. 8*s.*
- Vol. II. Barrow on the Supremacy of the Pope, with his Discourse on the Unity of the Church. 8vo. 7*s.* 6*d.*
- Vol. III. Tracts selected from Wake, Patrick, Stillingfleet, Clagett, and others. 8vo. 11*s.*

Greswell's *Harmonia Evangelica.* Fifth Edition. 8vo. 9*s.* 6*d.*

Hall's *Works.* Edited by P. Wynter, D.D. 10 vols. 8vo. 3*l.* 3*s.*

Heurtley. *Harmonia Symbolica:* Creeds of the Western Church. By C. Heurtley, D.D. 8vo. 6*s.* 6*d.*

Homilies *appointed to be read in Churches.* Edited by J. Griffiths, M.A. 8vo. 7*s.* 6*d.*

Hooker's *Works,* with his Life by Walton, arranged by John Keble, M.A. *Seventh Edition.* Revised by R. W. Church, M.A., Dean of St. Paul's, and F. Paget, D.D. 3 vols. medium 8vo. 1*l.* 16*s.*

—— *the Text* as arranged by J. Keble, M.A. 2 vols. 8vo. 11*s.*

Jackson's (Dr. Thomas) *Works.* 12 vols. 8vo. 3*l.* 6*s.*

Jewel's *Works.* Edited by R. W. Jelf, D.D. 8 vols. 8vo. 1*l.* 10*s.*

Martineau. *A Study of Religion: its Sources and Contents.* By James Martineau, D.D. 2 vols. 8vo. 1*l.* 4*s.*

Patrick's *Theological Works.* 9 vols. 8vo. 1*l.* 1*s.*

Pearson's *Exposition of the Creed.* Revised and corrected by E. Burton, D.D. *Sixth Edition.* 8vo. 10*s.* 6*d.*

—— *Minor Theological Works.* Edited with a Memoir, by Edward Churton, M.A. 2 vols. 8vo. 10*s.*

Sanderson's *Works.* Edited by W. Jacobson, D.D. 6 vols. 8vo. 1*l.* 10*s.*

Stillingfleet's *Origines Sacrae.* 2 vols. 8vo. 9*s.*

—— *Rational Account of the Grounds of Protestant Religion;* being a vindication of Archbishop Laud's Relation of a Conference, etc. 2 vols. 8vo. 10*s.*

Wall's *History of Infant Baptism.* Edited by H. Cotton, D.C.L. 2 vols. 8vo. 1*l.* 1*s.*

Waterland's *Works,* with Life, by Bp. Van Mildert. *A new Edition,* with copious Indexes. 6 vols. 8vo. 2*l.* 11*s.*

—— *Review of the Doctrine of the Eucharist,* with a Preface by the late Bishop of London. Crown 8vo. 6*s.* 6*d.*

Wheatly's *Illustration of the Book of Common Prayer.* 8vo. 5s.

Wyclif. *A Catalogue of the Original Works of John Wyclif.* By W. W. Shirley, D.D. 8vo. 3s. 6d.

Wyclif. *Select English Works.* By T. Arnold, M.A. 3 vols. 8vo. 1l. 1s.

—— *Trialogus.* With the Supplement now first edited. By Gotthard Lechler. 8vo. 7s.

5. LITURGIOLOGY.

Cardwell's *Two Books of Common Prayer,* set forth by authority in the Reign of King Edward VI, compared with each other. *Third Edition.* 8vo. 7s.

—— *History of Conferences on the Book of Common Prayer from 1551 to 1690. Third Edition.* 8vo. 7s. 6d.

Hammond. *Liturgies, Eastern and Western.* Edited, with Introduction, Notes, and a Liturgical Glossary, by C. E. Hammond, M.A. Crown 8vo. 10s. 6d.

An Appendix to the above, crown 8vo. paper covers, 1s. 6d.

Leofric Missal, *The,* as used in the Cathedral of Exeter during the Episcopate of its first Bishop, A.D. 1050–1072; together with some Account of the Red Book of Derby, the Missal of Robert of Jumièges, and a few other early MS. Service Books of the English Church. Edited, with Introduction and Notes, by F. E. Warren, B.D., F.S.A. 4to. half morocco, 1l. 15s.

Maskell. *Ancient Liturgy of the Church of England,* according to the uses of Sarum, York, Hereford, and Bangor, and the Roman Liturgy arranged in parallel columns, with preface and notes. By W. Maskell, M.A. *Third Edition.* 8vo. 15s.

—— *Monumenta Ritualia Ecclesiae Anglicanae.* The occasional Offices of the Church of England according to the old use of Salisbury, the Prymer in English, and other prayers and forms, with dissertations and notes. *Second Edition.* 3 vols. 8vo. 2l. 10s.

Warren. *The Liturgy and Ritual of the Celtic Church.* By F. E. Warren, B.D. 8vo. 14s.

Oxford
AT THE CLARENDON PRESS
LONDON: HENRY FROWDE
OXFORD UNIVERSITY PRESS WAREHOUSE, AMEN CORNER, E.C.

www.ingramcontent.com/pod-product-compliance
Lightning Source LLC
Chambersburg PA
CBHW021819230426
43669CB00008B/807